I0224449

loved. saved. healed

louise wilkinson

Ark House Press
arkhousepress.com

© 2024 Louise Wilkinson

All rights reserved. Apart from any fair dealing for the purpose of study, research, criticism, or review, as permitted under the Copyright Act, no part may be reproduced by any process without written permission.

All scripture is taken from the New Living Translation Bible

Some names and identifying details have been changed to protect the privacy of individuals.

Cataloguing in Publication Data:
Title: Loved. Saved. Healed.
ISBN: 978-0-6459938-4-4 (pbk)
Subjects: FAM001010   FAMILY & RELATIONSHIPS / Abuse / Child Abuse;
REL012170   RELIGION / Christian Living / Personal Memoirs; REL050000
RELIGION / Christian Ministry / Counseling & Recovery;

Design by initiateagency.com

To Jesus – thank you for giving your life so that I could have mine.

For my husband, my soulmate. Thank you for taking a chance on me.
For my children, thank you. You have made me a better person.

Contents

Part One

BEFORE

Please note that my story may trigger some survivors

Chapter 1

1969

My parents met at a bible youth camp when they were both young and it was love at first sight. Mum used to tell me they were not allowed to walk on the path together, so my dad would walk on one side, and my mum on the other. My mum Clara was incredibly beautiful with dark hair and blue eyes. She had this elegance that you could not help but notice, but back then she was very shy. My dad Oliver was handsome with light blue eyes and a crew cut. He liked cars and was on an electrical apprenticeship. Mum said that when her dad saw him pull up in front of their house in his Ford Prefect, he instantly disliked him. My grandad did not think my dad was good enough for his little girl, but my dad was witty and charming, and a bit of a clown, and I think in the end he won both her parents over. Mum would tell me that on Friday afternoons all the girls would go to the salon and get their hair set in curlers for their dates, and my dad would come and pick her up and they would go to the cinema or a party. She was only 15 when she met dad, and he was 18. My grandad had a heart attack just after my dad came on the scene. It all happened very quickly and unfortunately the ambulance went to the wrong address, so Grandad passed away that night in their home. Mum never spoke much about it, just that she had loved her dad very much. So, my nanna was widowed, and my mum ended up leaving school and getting a job as a bookkeeper to support them. A few years later mum married my dad, and they lived in Wellington.

My dad was the eldest out of three boys and he had one sister, who was a few years older than him. His mum, my grandma was a tiny little woman, she had a cold kind of demeanor, never liking any physical affection. My grandpa was a Major in the NZ army, he was a larger-than-life character, but he was strict. My dad was conceived in 1945 while Grandpa was on leave from fighting in WWII. Grandpa was an incredibly skilled Engineer and would often go behind enemy lines to retrieve weapons so he could repair them. He received quite a few commendations from the British army, and even carried out a secret mission for the US army at one point. Grandpa even had an alias and a fake passport. My grandma and grandpa already had one daughter when dad was conceived, and Grandma ended up living in a tiny flat with her parents while Grandpa was in the war. Grandma ran her home with military precision, serving the same meals on each day of the week, and she rarely showed any type of affection to her children or us. She was a faithful and loyal army wife, a nurse for many years before she married. She was also an organist at their church and served in the church faithfully for most of her life. Grandma was a librarian and I credit my early love of books to her.

My parents were married in September of 1969, and they lived in a small flat in Wellington. At some point my parents moved to the Wairapa so my dad could work as an electrician. It also meant they could be closer to my nanna who lived there too. The house had three bedrooms and a beautiful garden with fruit trees, and my mum saw my nanna regularly and they were close. My sister Dana arrived in 1972 and was an adorably chubby baby with beautiful blue eyes and a gorgeous smile. I love the early photos of my mum and sister, my mum's hair in curlers and my sister so smiley and cute looking. Dana was christened in the family gown when she was about six months old. Mum never talked about what it was like having a baby so young, and what it was like having to give up her job to be a stay-at-home mum. Dad went to work every day and she did all the chores and the cooking. That was the norm back then and you did not question it, most women just did what they were expected to do and fulfilled their roles as loving wives and mothers. I wonder if mum had any struggles and, if she did, how did she cope with them? I remember looking back on my baby book and thinking how funny the old child rearing practices were. Everything was so strict and on schedule: "Feed baby, wind baby, put baby to sleep, put baby on porch, bring baby in." It was so clinical and cold and nothing about developing a relationship with your baby, just focusing on the physical growth of your baby. It was about making sure your baby 'thrived' and not about your emotional connection with your newborn or your mental health. Mental health for new mums was not a concept you talked about in the 1970's.

When my sister was twenty months old my mum fell pregnant with me. My sister was a highly active toddler and mum said it was very tiring being pregnant and still having to do all the stuff around the home. Mum struggled with morning sickness, and it was a tough time for her. Mum said when she was around 36 weeks, she got sick with a bug and had bad diarrhea. She called her mum and told her she thought the baby was coming and she went to hospital. I do not think my labour was particularly long and I was born on the 21st of August 1974. I was a tiny baby, weighing around 6lb 6 oz. At some point when I was still in hospital I was put in the nursery, and one day a nurse left a window open, and a south westerly blew in. I got sick and my core temperature dropped, and I was put in an incubator for a few days. That and the story about my labour are the only things I know about my birth. Mum would have had to come home to an energetic toddler and had to care for me. I was a difficult baby in the first few weeks, and certainly did not thrive like I was meant to. I was a fussy baby and caused mum a lot of stress. Mum said when I was six months old, things were better, and I started to put on weight. I was christened in the Methodist church too, in the family gown of course. I was told that I was really upset during the whole thing and ended up pooping on my auntie's lap at some point. My sister was jealous of me and bit my hand quite badly one day, but the jealousy did not last long though and we became best friends.

I have talked about my mum a lot, that's because writing about my dad is quite difficult for me. He was highly energetic and was the centre of attention at family gatherings and parties. He was the clown and always cracking jokes. Unfortunately, my dad's sense of humour was often crude, having spent so long in a workshop. I can remember when I was christened, do not ask me how I remember, I just do. All I can say is that I do remember being that small and how it felt to be in my cot waving my arms and legs around. I remember being able to make noises and babble and look around at all the things around me. I also remember the exact day that my dad chose to sexually abuse me. It feels surreal writing about this and sharing my story, I know what I remember, and this feels like the right time to get it all out. To lay it out on the table, this is not so I can be a victim, those days are long gone. It is not so I can paint my father to be evil, that is not it either. I hope he knows that he made a mistake and regrets it. It is not so I can get money, fame, or attention, I am sharing my story so that I can connect with other survivors and hopefully bring some light into their darkness. I am sharing my story so that other survivors can make some sense of what happened to them and so I can help them in some way; so, I can bring hope and healing and so I can share my testimony of what Jesus Christ has done for me.

So, I grew up with this happening to me, I guess you could say I was groomed. I remember dad changing my nappy and he would tickle me down there. I would just lie there, as babies do, totally trusting in this man who was meant to be protecting me, not violating me. I did not know the difference between right or wrong, I was just an infant. I have memories of this been done to me and it being gentle, and I would just sort of float away really, like I was not even there. Again, you may feel disbelief at what I am saying, that there is no way I could remember that at such an early age. All I know is I *do* remember. How long this went on for I am not sure, all I know is that it is extremely hard for me to write about this. I remember the floaty feeling changed into something not nice one day, like pain and fear. We were in the bathroom, and I remember the floaty feeling and then something different like pressure, and then more pressure and a lot of pain. I remember crying and then I heard his voice and then nothing, absolutely nothing. I floated away and then I was gone. I am not sure how to describe it any other way. All I know is that I was born on 21 August 1974 as Louise, but something happened in that bathroom, something happened to baby Louise. I was her; I remember being her, and then I was not her. I was gone and someone else was in my head and my body. I know that it must have been some sort of extreme disassociation, the pain and trauma of my father penetrating me with his fingers that caused my brain to completely shut down, switch off, and fly away. I became a different person, a different me. That first baby was still in me somewhere though. She would come back to me some 32 years later to remember that incident in the bathroom, to shed some light on all the memories of what seemed like another life.

There I was, an abused baby, and I do not believe there were too many physical signs. My father was very gentle, nothing was done in a hurry as to draw attention to the situation. Some people see sexual abuse as rough and violent, that the perpetrator wants to inflict harm or injury. That might be the case for some, but my father was the complete opposite, mostly it was soft and gentle. This became my life, and I continued growing and developing, if not a little slower than other babies. If it was the abuse or the incident in the nursery that made me develop my milestones a little late, I do not know. I have had memories of being in intense pain however and trying to roll over to relieve some of the agony. I remember being on the floor as mum was giving me tummy time and being so sore that I was just rolling and rolling and ended up under the dining room table. I have had memories of trying to tell my mum I was in pain, but it just coming out like 'ain.'

I have this early memory of dad doing that to me, even some 48 years later it is hard to process. And I do not remember much after about 10 months of age. In fact, I do not remember anything before I started school but a few flashes. One of me nearly drowning in someone's pool and someone's hands coming under the water wearing rubber gloves to pull me out, and one of me falling down the back steps and cutting my head open. I do remember going to school on my first day of year one. I walked with my sister and no parents, as was quite common back then. We would walk with the other kids from our street, and it was not close by either. I remember playing with my next-door neighbor Bridget who had a cat and a lamb, playing in our cubby house with our dolls, and caring for our rabbits. I remember all of this like I am watching a movie about someone else's life, like there are pictures of all these events but it is hard to attach emotions to them. I remember textures like the scratchy 1970's couch we had and mum's bright green carpet in her bedroom, and how I was obsessed with my dad, like my life revolved around him and everything that he did. He would come home in his work van, and I would fly out the back door and run to meet him, so enthusiastically that one day I jumped off the back porch and broke my collar bone. I am unsure to how or when things progressed with my dad and me. It all just seemed to lead on from the previous thing and I would find myself drifting away again, to be replaced by someone else, a more mature version of me who could cope with what was happening to her. Like the old me was always there but somehow, she was in the background. I kept on living though, and going to school and playing with my sister, she was my other favourite person. I just did what other kids did, except I was being sexually abused.

My little brother was born in December 1978. His name was Dylan, and he was blonde and perfect. He was the most beautiful thing I had ever seen, and I was instantly smitten with him. Mum was tired all the time, so my sister and I helped in any way we could. I would stand by the pram and watch him sleep and even at such an early age, I wanted him to be my baby, which was such a strange concept for a child my age to have. My relationship with my dad was still the main focal point of my life and I started to feel different when we were alone together. I remember starting to see my mum in a different light too, I am not sure when it happened, but there was a feeling of 'us' and 'her.' I felt like I belonged to my dad, and she was becoming an outsider. My mum was a good mum, but she was not really that affectionate towards us, or emotionally connected. She showed her love by doing things for us, like making us an outfit or baking us a cake. I honestly believe she did not know what was going on in that house.

My father's parents were still living in Wellington, and they thought it was a good idea for my sister and I to visit them on the train. So, on the school holidays dad would drive us to the station and mum would give us a packet of Sparkles lollies and tell us when we had finished them, we would arrive. I would get anxious and worried being on the train, but my sister would always try and distract me and look after me. Finally, we would arrive, and Grandpa would be waiting with his Princess car. He would hug us and say he had arrived in his Princess car to pick up his princesses. He would always have lollies in his car which he would share with us. I loved their house; it was huge with a giant staircase and a brass gong on the wall. There was plastic on my grandma's couch, and we were not allowed to sit on it. The kitchen was quirky with knick knacks hanging on hooks and Grandpa's tin of nuts and sultanas on top of the fridge. My grandma was such a funny little woman, standing not even 5 feet tall. She was very clever but not affectionate at all, and she would always say, "good things come in small packages like poison and diamonds." We all got hugs from Grandpa, and we would sit on his knee, and he would sing songs and bounce us around, we loved it. Grandma had the most amazing garden with so many flowers and trees and bird baths, you could get lost in it. She would work in the garden and make her own lemon squash and quince jelly. There was a love swing near the back door, and Dana and I would sit on that thing for hours. Grandpa had a huge workshop with a deep pit in the ground for working on cars. Their house was strict, no TV or elbows on the table but we loved it there. Grandpa would rescue old bikes and fix them up for us, and my favourite was a little blue scooter, and I rode that thing all over the place. I would fly along on it feeling so free and full of joy at being away from my dad. I think at those times I realised somehow that what he was doing was not right and being away from him meant I could be myself.

We would go with Grandpa to church, and he would do the gardens and Grandma would arrange the flowers and play the organ. Grandma would take us to the local library which was always such a privilege. I would read 'Miffy,' and Grandma would get the books out for us to take home. One library trip I was wearing sandals and I walked through some glass, which cut my ankle open badly. My poor sister had to run all the way back to their house to get my grandpa. I had five stitches that day and I have still got the scar. I remember at the end of our stay I would see dad's car pull into the driveway and I would feel drawn to him but at the same time I did not want to go home. Despite the strict rules and plain food, I could have happily lived with my grandparents forever. I felt like I could be a kid at their house, that adult things were adult things, and they did not involve me.

When I was about six years old dad got another job in Wellington and we sold our house. I do not think mum really wanted to go and leave my nanna; she loved being near her mum as they were so close. My nanna was such a lovely lady and whenever she saw us, she would give us a five-dollar note from her purse. When we went to her house, we would have Schweppes lemonade in real crystal glasses, and she would give my brother a bucket of pegs to play with. There were no swings or scooters at Nanna's house though, so we were sent into her backyard to play. I think it broke mum's heart to leave my nanna, but she was a faithful wife and followed what her husband wanted.

So, we moved to a brand-new house in Wellington, and it was a split-level home with a few stairs which we thought were cool. It was built on a huge section and mum said she had big plans for the garden. There was a double garage under the house which dad said he would turn into the workshop. We were sad there was no cubby house, but dad promised us he would build one. Dana and I started at the local school which was also brand new. I remember being super anxious on the first day, as it was a lot to deal with, moving house and then having to start at a new school. I just wanted to stay at home with mum and Dylan. We were foundation students at the school, and we had a tree planting day and an opening ceremony. I still remember us students going onto the front steps of the school to have our photo taken, and the school had an open plan design which was unusual. There was a communal space in the middle and all the classes were off to the side, and my class had a carpeted area called the kiva, it was like a mini amphitheatre and I loved it. One of the teachers was super mean and used to hit the kids with a huge ruler. We were terrified of her, but weirdly she would lead us in group singing everyday which we all loved. Music was a huge part of the curriculum, and the principal had a guitar, to which we would all sing along.

We did not have much play equipment, so the parents built a huge adventure playground for us kids. When I think back now, I am horrified to think that we played on it. It was so high up with a huge slide and no side rails on it, and it was so dangerous, but it had a rope swing, and a fireman's pole, and of course it was a huge hit. These were the days of no safety equipment and teachers smoking in the playground, that was the 1980's for you.

I was very anxious to start school, but I made friends quickly. Mum and dad worked hard on the new house, laying a concrete driveway, and planting many trees. Mum planted a huge veggie garden and after school we would pull up the carrots, wash them under the tap, and eat them. We got a new rabbit named Hoppy, and Dana and I would put him in our prams and cradles and cover him with blankets. We also got a cat named Miss Kitty and boy did I love that cat. She ended up having kittens and we got to watch them being born, so that was exciting. On weekends we would go down to the creek and play or ride around on our bikes all over the place. Mum and dad never knew where we were, there was no parental supervision in those days, not even on play equipment. We had no parents following us around, we were left to our own devices, and we loved it. At some point mum enrolled me in a drama class after school and I discovered that I really loved acting. I remember our first production was The Pied Piper and I got to wear a red wig.

Dad built us a go kart and we would take turns riding it down our street which had a very steep hill, and when I say steep, I mean steep; not just a little hill, but a huge winding road that was more like a mountain than a hill. We would come barreling down that hill at the speed of light and somehow screech to a stop at the bottom of the cul de sac, which was funny as the go kart had no brakes. On Guy Fawkes night we would have a massive street party where we would share all our fireworks. The parents would get drunk, and the kids would end up letting the fireworks off. I remember the bottle rockets shooting off into space and the 'screaming meemies' which whizzed around everywhere while making a screeching noise, it was so much fun. When I think back now, I am amazed we survived the 1980's, as we were left on our own so much, it is hard to think what that was like for us. Considering the level of helicopter parenting that is around nowadays, it is a surprise we did not get more injured. To be honest we worked out how to deal with a lot of stuff on our own, and it taught us to be resilient. Life was so much simpler than it is now, we did not have a whole bunch of toys; we had a couple of knock off barbie dolls, some cheap shoe – skates and our bikes, we had home birthday parties with fairy bread and jelly and kids were kids. We were not following the news on social media, and we were left to play and explore and work things out for ourselves. Sure, we had tough times with bullies or crappy home lives, but we were not stressed about what was happening in the world, and we got a break from the mean kids on the weekends. Life was simple and we liked it like that.

When I look back on my childhood, it feels like I was living two lives. The life I had with my friends was incredible and we did everything together. The life I had at home, however, was a different story, and the relationship I had with my dad was taking over everything and was starting to smother me. During the day I was at school and was a regular girl who was happy and was learning all that I should have been. When I was with my friends, I could be myself and feel genuinely happy. Towards the evening though everything would change, and I would feel this dread well up inside me, threatening to choke me. I would feel anxious and sweaty and completely overwhelmed with emotions. I would feel fearful and sometimes after dinner I would start to disassociate myself from reality. The abuse was part of my life now, like eating and breathing, it just was. I had never known a life without anything else, but things were progressing, and I was being sucked into an adult role that I neither wanted nor could cope with emotionally or physically. Every night dad would come into my room, sometimes it was before I fell asleep and other times, he would wake me up. It got so bad that I developed insomnia, lying in bed every night, paralaysed with fear and dreaded anticipation that he would come. I was in a horrifying catch 22; if he came to me, I would feel loved and special, but gosh, it was awful. But if he did not come in, I would feel rejected and unloved. By the time I was eight years old he was forcing himself on me every night of the week, and because he had 'trained' my body, I could not help but respond to him. I would wait until it had finished and then I would clutch my teddy bears and sob myself to sleep. I would cry silently, the tears soaking into my soft toys, and eventually I would fall into an exhausted sleep, and when I woke up, I would be so sore and would feel so ashamed and dirty. I was constantly in pain, and I also had recurrent thrush and UTI's. On those nights that he did not come for some reason, I would be equally devastated, feeling abandoned and rejected. But it did give my body some time to recover. Dana and I shared a room, and even though I should remember, I do not know if she knew what was going on between my dad and me. This is also the time that my mother also learned of the abuse, as it was a small house, and all the bedrooms were next to each other. Strange that Dana never said a thing about it, or I said to her, we just learned to accept that this was the way it was in our family, no one questioned it. What my father did was law, and no one was brave enough to ask what was going on. I did not even know what sex was, I certainly did not know that this is what he was doing to me every single night of the week. I had no idea; my dad was the centre of my universe, and it was only normal for me. I felt like he controlled all aspects of my life. I relied on him for survival, like Stockholm syndrome, he was my abuser, but he was also my life force. I was connected to him emotionally, mentally, and physically and he was my entire world.

Unfortunately, the relationship with my mum was distant. She was a classic 1970's housewife and mum, the husband works and makes all the decisions, and she cleans and looks after the kids. Mum was never overly demonstrative with us, she only showed us affection when we were injured or sick, and I got sick all the time. I had throat infections every few months, and mum was good at looking after me though, she would wrap me up in the feather quilt and put me on the couch and bring me Disprin and soup. But mum did not play with us, only showed us she loved us by coming to school events and baking us treats. All my attention and affection came from my dad. He would play games with us and tickle us, and he converted part of the garage into a playroom for Dana and me.

We would go on holiday every term, camping in a tent or staying in my grandparents' caravan. One year we took the caravan to a caravan park, and a huge storm came in, and the caravan filled with water and the wind was so strong I thought we would get blown off the cliff. Dad went outside to try and find where the water was coming in and I was terrified he was not coming back. The abuse did not stop on those trips though, and as I had short hair, my dad would often sneak me into the men's showers, announcing to me that "no one will notice because you look like a boy." Camping in the tent was fun though and I have good memories of finding random kids to spend all our time with.

Things continued, and I became older and interested in boys. In fact, at around ten years old I became obsessed with them, and I had a boyfriend Shane, who was sweet and cute, and we spent all our lunchtimes together.

A popular game we played was 'kiss - catch' and Shane was my first kiss. I felt like we had an actual relationship, and he was a welcome distraction from my dad. The shining lights in my childhood were my auntie's. Mum had two sisters, Anna, and Faith, and they were kind and loving and even though their children were mostly grown up, they still had time for us. My favourite aunt was my dad's sister, Francine. Dana and I would go to her place in the school holidays, and her house was big and built into the side of a cliff. Auntie Francine would play the piano and we would do ginormous puzzles with her that nearly covered the entire lounge room floor. We would also go there at Christmas and have huge luncheons that went on for hours. Francine was a schoolteacher and would always have the patience to answer my never-ending questions. I remember when Dylan started school and I would keep an eye on him. He was so cute in his little home-made red overalls, and as I watched him play, I would feel such love for him.

At this point things with my dad just seemed like a hassle now, like I was tied to something I did not want to be a part of anymore. I wanted my freedom and being with boys seemed to be an effective way to go about it. I fantasised about running away with Shane and being able to escape my dad eventually. My friendship group also became particularly important to me, and we spent every weekend at each other's houses. Sleepovers were a fantastic way to get a break from my dad. I did not care that most of my friends' families were quite dysfunctional, some of my friends would get hit, or screamed at by their parents, or neglected, but it did not bother me. My girlfriends and I would watch music videos and make up dances together, it was great fun. One day when I was eleven years old, my dad came home and announced that we would be moving to the UK.

"We're moving to London," he said grinning at us.

Dana and I were devastated, and as she was over two years older than me, of course her peer group was equally important to her. I had no concept of Britain except the Royal family, but dad had been given the opportunity to start a business with a colleague and had decided to go for it. I was gutted about leaving my friends and Shane, and I begged my dad to let us stay but he would not budge. Of course, my mum just went along with it, but I could tell she was not happy about leaving everything behind.

Chapter 2

london

In June of 1985 we rented our house out and first flew to the USA. We had a 3-day stopover in LA, and it was all a blur really, as we went to the hotel and then visited Disneyland. I still remember how sunny LA was, and everyone was super friendly. The food portions were also enormous, and we ended up sharing two plates between us. When we landed at Heathrow, dad's business partner met us there, but he was unfriendly to us kids. When we saw the house that we were provided with we were happy, but so surprised as it was a three-story brick house that was only about 12 feet wide! It was what I know now to be a terrace home, and it was amazing and fully furnished, so we spent the first few hours running around like headless chickens, checking everything out. My mum cried though and said she wanted to go back home, and it all felt like a weird dream to be honest. The house had a kitchen and 2 dining rooms on the first floor and a small toilet. The garden was the size of a postage stamp, and we were shocked as we were so used to having such a huge backyard. The second floor had a lounge room and a room for Dana and me; it had 2 pine beds with matching side tables and lamps, and we instantly fell in love with it.

There was wood paneling around the walls and lovely soft duvets on the beds. The third floor contained Dylan's and my parents' bedrooms and an ensuite bathroom which we had never really seen before. The next few weeks went so fast, and because it was July, we would not be starting school until September (another weird thing), so we had lots of time to look around London. It was so busy on the roads that my mum refused to drive, but I did not blame her, as the traffic was crazy compared to Wellington. We spent our days visiting various places, so that was exciting. We walked around the Thames and checked out Harrods which mum liked. Dylan also loved Harrods as it had a huge Lego section. We discovered that Dylan was very skilled at putting Lego together, and even I would play with him as it was so much fun. My favourite thing to do was when we would go to a pub for dinner, and us kids could play out in the back garden.

I waited for my dad to come and see me at night, but weirdly, it did not happen. I felt both relieved and rejected, but I was too distracted to think any more about it. As September approached, I felt so anxious, as I was really missing my friends and the thought of starting school just felt awful. I could not believe that I had to start high school, I was too young! Even worse was the uniform, it was formal with a skirt, shirt, tie, and blazer, and I cried when I saw it. I was twelve years old by then and just a terrified little kid, I had no concept of what it would be like and how I was meant to cope with it all. The day arrived and when mum went to leave, I broke down and cried.

"Please don't leave me," I sobbed and cried as she hugged me and then left.

I was terrified as the school was huge and I was expected to go to different classrooms of course. I felt like an alien, and the other kids could not understand my accent and picked on me. They had no concept of where NZ was, and they acted like they did not even know that my country existed. They thought I was Australian which was funny, as I had no idea about Australia at all. Eventually I made a few friends, and we would spend time together on the weekends going ice skating. My brother started primary school and it was quite difficult for him at first, but eventually he made some friends.

I joined St John's ambulance cadets and that was great fun, we did lots of first aid training and would help injured kids at the ice rink. It was freezing cold even to my NZ standards, and we had to walk to school in the snow. My nanna came for a visit which was lovely, and mum was overjoyed as she missed her a lot. My sister had settled into the school well, had lots of friends and an impressive social life. Sometimes I would tag along too, and her friends never seemed to mind. It was so much fun for both my sister and me to be part of the UK scene in the 1980's, the fashion and music for that time were iconic and we felt extremely happy with our new lives.

I kept waiting for my dad to come to see me at night but to my surprise he stayed away, and at night I would cry sometimes and worry my parents were going to get a divorce because of me. I am not sure if it was the change in environment, but I felt safe, content, and happy. It was not long before I forgot all about Shane and developed a new crush. His name was Anthony, and he was a friend of my sisters. He was super cute, and I spent most lunchtimes giggling about him with my girlfriends. We ended up going to France for Christmas and saw snow for the first time. Stupidly my dad also took us camping in Wales toward the end of winter, which was silly, as we nearly froze to death, but it was fun visiting all the castles. Summer came and it was lovely as we went to the pool with our mates, and I started hanging out at my girlfriend's place on the weekend. I watched my first horror movie, A Nightmare on Elm Street and stayed up all night. One friend had a dog that simply hated me. It was a huge German shepherd and as soon as I stepped in her house that thing would smell me and come flying down the stairs, snarling, and snapping at me. Her mum would take us to the pool, but she was a chain smoker, so in winter we would be dying in the back seat with all the windows up and breathing in all the smoke. I had a diary and every day I wrote in it about how much I liked Anthony, and wondered how I could get him to like me too. In 1986 Dad dropped a bombshell on us.

"We're going back home," he told us.

Dana and I were devastated, and our friends could not believe it when we told them. We had a big party in a hall, and I ended up playing spin the bottle and got to kiss Anthony, so I was happy about that. But it was hard on me and especially for my sister who had formed such close friendships while living in the UK. Dana and I had made a new life for us, and it was gut wrenching to leave it all behind. Upon arriving back in NZ, I started back at my previous school, and it felt weird seeing all my old friends. I felt more grown up somehow and my classmates could not believe my "posh accent." I was upset to learn that Shane had moved away shortly after we had left to live in the UK, but I managed to fit back into year six and soon felt at home. Anthony started to write me letters and I replied with gusto. His letters were funny, articulate and filled with quirky characters. I would lie on my bed and read those letters for hours, laughing at his funny jokes, they sure got me through some very dark times.

It was not long before my dad turned his attention back to me, and I was shocked I guess, having become accustomed to being left alone. I was older now too and I was not happy at all. I had been so alive in the UK; I had felt a freedom I had never felt before and now it was over. I silently grieved, feeling smothered and controlled once again. I tried to manage it the best I could, but for the first time in my life, I began to feel depressed. That summer I started my period and man was it bad! I am not sure if it was because of what my dad was doing, but I bled so much even my mum was shocked. I hemorrhaged every month, and it was so heavy that I had to have a plastic sheet on my bed. If we travelled anywhere in the car I would have to sit on a towel as I would bleed all over the back seat. It was weird, I was this stick thin little child with no boobs or any sign of puberty, yet I had the period of a grown woman.

Life at school was good, and I had started babysitting for my teacher Mrs. Dean who was my favourite person on earth. I would take her key at three o'clock and walk her kid home from school and watch him until she got back. I would feel very grown up and would make him a snack and myself a coffee. I had also started babysitting for my mum's friends, and one family had three kids under the age of 6, including a 3-month-old, and boy was that a challenge. I remember one night being at this family's house and the baby was so red in the face and cried for hours. I carried him around, but he screamed for so long that I got scared and ended up calling my mum to ask her what to do.

"Just keep trying to burp him," she told me.

I thought that she was going to offer to come over and help me, but she didn't so I struggled through it until his parents came home. I realise now looking back, that the baby might have had colic that night, but being a child myself, I had no idea what to do. Back in the 1980's it was completely normal for a 12-year-old to look after a newborn for hours at a time!

My friends were once again the main focal point of my life, and we spent every weekend together. I desperately missed Shane, although I was not short on admirers. Anthony kept up the letter writing, and I was always so happy when I came home from school and would see one of his letters on my bed. I loved the weekends, as it was a chance to get away from my dad. I was keeping this awful secret from everyone; I was leading a double life really and there was no way my mum did not know. Things had progressed even further; he was coming into my room every single night and the abuse was becoming more physical and more intense. I would not usually get to sleep until around 1am or later, and it was so exhausting that I could barely concentrate at school. I was in pain all the time, and my poor little brother must have heard us at night because he started to have bad nightmares, where he would say there were "monsters in his cupboard." I tried to cope the best I could, but I was so sad deep inside and longed to be free of my dad. I started to resent him and the relationship with my mum was really fractured. I resented her so much for staying with him, and I would pick fights with mum and scream the house down; I was just so stressed. She would get angry and threaten to send me away to 'health camp.' So, I would retreat to my room, listen to my Walkman, and read Anthony's letters repeatedly. I loved my teacher Mrs. Dean and fantasied about telling her the truth, but knew it was not safe, as she was friends with mum. There was no one to turn to and I felt like I was the other woman in my parents' marriage, and I guess in a sick kind of way I was. My dad had complete control over my entire life, including the thoughts I had and decisions I made.

The abuse continued, and then just before I turned thirteen, my dad got the idea to turn our old playroom in the garage into a bedroom for me. I was excited having always shared with Dana. The thought of having my own space was something I had always wanted, but I did not realise the full extent of his plans, or that mum had put her foot down about the two of us and ordered me out of the house. We began to choose wallpaper, paint and within a few weeks my new room was ready, but I never really settled in that room to be honest. I was so excited at first but being so far away from everyone else felt lonely and being away from Dana made me anxious. The constant threat of my dad visiting also put me on edge, so I barely slept. I did enjoy it during the day and spent hours decorating it. I would pretend it was my mini apartment and that I was living alone and sometimes that made it better. I put up curtains and spent weekends tidying and organizing it. It never occurred to me that dad had more of a sinister motive for moving me out of the house. It was a few months later that I realised the truth.

It was normal for my dad to come to my room every night, but sometimes he did not come, so, the next morning he would lure me into the shower, and I would be expected to perform oral sex on him before he went to work. That also became the norm, and I never questioned what was going on as all my life, I had known no difference and I never argued or said no. It had been happening to me since I was a baby, and it was the only thing that I knew. I know it sounds horrible, but it just felt normal for me to be having a full sexual relationship with my own father. My body learnt to adapt to the pain and the constant burning feeling l got when I went to the toilet. Sometimes the itching nearly drove me mad, and I had thrush a lot of the time and would scratch myself so badly I would bleed. One night I got so desperate that I put toothpaste on my vagina, hoping it would cure the itch, but it burned so bad I cried and told mum. She took one look at me down there and gave me some cream. My body never felt like mine and I spent years disassociating and, on the ceiling, but the before work oral sex thing just seemed to tip me over the edge. I was older, going through puberty and it was as if I woke up one morning and suddenly realised that what was going on was wrong, like I suddenly had a revelation or something. It was like my developing body just said, 'this is not right.' A lightbulb went off in my brain and I suddenly knew I had to speak up, so I went to my mum, and I told her I wanted out. I mean she was my mum and surely, she cared about my feelings and what was happening to me.

"I've had enough mum," I said to her one day, as she sat on my bed, not looking at me.

"Mum, I don't want dad to do that to me anymore," I said but she barely replied to me. We both sat for a few moments and then she got up and left the room. I felt so relieved, and stupidly I thought that she was on my side, that once I had told her that it would just stop. How wrong I was.

Chapter 3

those men

Mum must have had some sort of conversation with my dad, but I never thought for one minute that he would react the way he did. It was a weekend night, a Saturday, and my mum was frantically cleaning the house, and it was a little strange even for my mum who was a cleaning freak. It was late when my dad came in and saw me, I was on the couch watching tv and he told me to go to the garage. As I made my way down the stairs, I began to have a bad feeling. When I saw the group of men gathered down there my mind did not click to what was about to happen, they were drinking beer and there was music playing, so I thought that dad was having a party. My dad pulled me down the stairs and he was talking a lot and squeezing me around the waist, his eyes were glittering somehow, and he kept looking at me funny. As I walked towards them, I could feel myself drifting away and someone else coming to the front, taking over. This was common, it often happened when my dad ramped things up with me physically, every time he introduced something new which was often, I would feel another part of me take over. A stronger part would come forward, a tougher part who could cope with the trauma of what was expected of me. Funnily enough,

I always felt protected when that happened, that a part of me knew I could not cope with it, and I needed help. I felt safe knowing the real me was tucked away somewhere, safe from harm. I stared at these men and the slow realisation of what was going on suddenly dawned on me. I turned to look at my dad, but he seemed high somehow and maybe not entirely present either.

"Daddy I can't do this," I whispered to him, and he smiled coldly at me.

"Well," he whispered back to me. "You shouldn't have told your mum you didn't want me anymore."

I opened my mouth to say something, but he shoved me forward. Tears formed in my eyes as one of the men stepped towards me and took my hand. I looked back at my dad, but he was not there really, I could see him physically, but his eyes were dead. They broke me that night, those men, they used me and abused me until there was nothing left. I do not know if my mum knew what was happening, but I pretended she had left; it was easier than remembering she was upstairs. I lost count of how many there were, seven or eight, and some wanted oral sex, some wanted more.

"I'm sorry," I kept saying as I pleaded with my dad that I had made a mistake, but he did not listen, he just sat and watched those men do whatever they wanted to me. The pain was so intense that I just drifted in and out of consciousness the whole night. I would wake up in some other position with those men doing things to me, and I would feel so many hands on me that I would drift away again. At some point I woke up covered in goodness knows what to find myself being pushed onto my stomach roughly and a voice saying, "are we going to double dip this bitch or what?" After that I do not remember anything else and I woke up in my room the next day, curled on my side in so much pain I could barely breathe, let alone move. I was covered in bruises and crept upstairs for a shower and hid myself in there until the water went cold. Afterwards I stared at myself in the mirror, not sure of who I was seeing, looking back at me. I certainly did not feel real, I felt like the nice part of me had gone. Just like when I was first touched by my dad, a part of me had disappeared and another Louise had taken over. I did not feel connected to my body at all, I felt like just a head and the rest of me was invisible. I could not look either of my parents in the eye, I avoided my dad and strangely he did not come near me for at least a week or two. Perhaps he felt some shame or regret at his actions, but he never said a thing to me. Slowly my physical body recovered, but I felt broken inside and deeply depressed. I knew it had been all my fault, if only I had not told my mum what I did then it would not have happened. I did not realise that he had planned it for months, and that it was not my fault at all. Instead, I felt angry, but not at my dad or those men, but at myself.

My dad did not come into my room much anymore, instead, it was the shower every morning before school and work, but I did not care though; it was something from him and it meant he still loved me. We never talked about that night; it was like this unspoken thing between us. A few months later though he came into my bedroom, and it started up again, but this time it was different though. Usually, he was gentle and loving but now he was cold to me and rough. I was gutted inside, I had grown up my whole life receiving what I thought was love from him, and now it was just a horrible, detached thing that felt so wrong. He seemed angry and distant and took pleasure in hurting me. I felt worthless, ashamed, and extremely depressed. One weekend I came home and found my mum frantically cleaning and I knew it was going to happen again. When my dad called me down the stairs, I felt detached from my body, like I was looking down at myself from the ceiling. As I approached him my physical body reacted instantly and I wanted to pee, poop, and run away, all at once. I felt myself drifting away even before I hit the bottom step, and I do not remember anything after that, I must have been far away during the whole thing. I do remember waking up wishing I were dead, wishing they had killed me. Same as last time, my dad avoided me afterwards, but I was glad. For the first time in my life, I hated him. After that night I made sure I was never home on the weekends, always staying at my friends' houses.

In 1988 I started at our local secondary college, and it was hard for me because I was out of my comfort zone, and everything terrified me. Fortunately, I made a new friend, Jane, who was as anxious and awkward as me and we became close. College was hard to navigate, and I was bullied by some popular boys which made me even more anxious. Jane's friendship meant a lot to me, and I was always at her house after school and at weekends.

Later in the year, we were sitting around the dinner table and my dad casually announced that we were moving yet again.

He said, "where do you want to go? Sydney or Perth?"

I had never even heard of those places and had no idea where they were. My mum was terribly upset and so were we. I had started high school, and it was hard enough trying to fit in and feel normal. I was convinced mum would stand up to him this time, but she didn't and before I knew it, we were moving to Perth.

Chapter 4

perth

My parents put our house on the market, and we started packing. Dana and I were upset as we did not want to leave our friends again, and we cried together as we packed. The day before we had a huge family gathering and said goodbye to everyone, my mum had put on a brave face, but I knew she was devastated to leave my nanna once again. The day arrived and my friends came to the airport. As we went down the little corridor towards the plane, I suddenly turned back and ran back towards my friends crying my eyes out and it was Dana who came back for me, and we slowly boarded the plane. We arrived on 28th May 1988, and as we stepped off the plane we were greeted with sunshine and what seemed like a desert before us. The land was flat and there was sand everywhere, and it all looked so foreign to us. I could not believe what I was seeing, and I felt more depressed than ever. Unlike when we arrived in the UK, there was no one to meet us, which was odd. Somehow, we made it to the crummy motel that had been booked for us, and that night my dad found takeaway food, but when he got back, we did not like the look of it. We had only ever had Maccas burgers, and these were different, filled with salad and mayonnaise. We all cried, and dad got angry and yelled at us. The first few days were a blur, as we were jet lagged and emotional, our environment such a contrast to NZ. It was so flat! I felt depressed and none of the excitement we had felt in the UK. My dad bought a huge Ford Fairlane which he could not stop boasting about.

"I'm not driving that enormous car," my mum said, and I did not blame her.

The car salesperson lived in the northern suburbs, so we started to look for houses in that area. One house had four bedrooms and two bathrooms and seemed huge compared to our old place in Wellington. Whatever sadness my mum felt seemed to disappear once she saw the house, as it had 2 living areas, a formal dining room, 2 bathrooms and a pool. We moved in and spent the first few months without much furniture, and then my mum discovered Ikea and she bought a couch and some chairs. We wanted to swim in the pool, but the water was completely freezing, and we lasted about five minutes. Mum was so happy in the house, so that was nice to see, and eventually our furniture arrived, and it was like Christmas as we hurriedly unpacked our boxes. I was happy that I finally had my own room and I got to decorate it. Life felt strange in the new house though, we were all so far apart from each other, unlike Wellington where we seemed to live on top of one another. As summer approached the heat was overwhelming. We bought fans for our rooms, but those first few summers were hard to adjust to. NZ was cold all year round compared to Perth and thank goodness we had the pool; it was a real lifesaver.

Since arriving in Perth, I had been waiting for my dad to see me, and every night I waited and waited but weirdly he never came. At first, I was overjoyed as I finally had control over my body and boy did it feel good. My parents were also strangely overly affectionate with one another, which was odd too. Perhaps they felt released from the horrors of the past also, but after a few weeks in the new house, I became depressed again, as part of me still waited every night for him to come and he never did. Eventually my waiting went from weeks to months, and then it finally dawned on me that it was over. Things had ended, and I felt abandoned and very unloved. The result was this feeling of depression that settled over me like a blanket and I began to resent both my parents and spent most of my time locked away in my room listening to music. I did not know who I was anymore as the abuse had shaped me and defined me, so who was I without it?

Dana and I started high school, I went into year eight and my sister into year eleven, and it was particularly hard for both of us to form friendships. I was paired up with a group of girls who pretended to like me, but they were not really that welcoming. I was miserable and spent lunch time feeling so overwhelmed and anxious, I felt out of place and so depressed. I was picked on for my accent and the bullying was relentless. It seemed like I was never going to make any real friends, and then one day I was in the gym playing badminton and I met Veronica. She started to chat to me about how her budgie had died, and we just hit it off. Suddenly I made a connection with someone, and we quickly became good friends. Veronica introduced me to a couple of other girls and at last I felt accepted. One of the girls, Connie, lived across the road from me and I finally felt a sliver of hope. The friendship group became important to me, and we spent every weekend together. My parents seemed to have discovered each other again, and they were so lovey dovey with each other it made me sick, so any time I could get away from them was good. My friends and I would have sleepovers and talk endlessly about make-up and boys. We went into the city to the movies, sometimes we could find huge office buildings and play in the lifts. Other times boys would come, and we would run around the city like little kids having fun. I felt accepted and loved and could feel my depression lifting.

One guy I met through Veronica was Charlie and he was a Christian and went to a private school. On the weekends I would stay at Connie's and around one o'clock in the morning we would sneak out her bedroom window and go and hang out at parks. We never drank or smoked, just walked around talking, and sometimes Charlie would bring a mate and we would sit in the playground. Sometimes we would stay at my place, and one night our friend Shelley got stuck on my fence while we were sneaking out and Connie and I spent about twenty minutes trying to get her down. Another night we were out and when we walked back to Charlie's place, we realised his parents were awake and we quickly ran home, breathless with excitement and fear. We were convinced our ruse was up, but surprisingly they never told our parents. When I was fifteen, I started dating boys, and one was a Latino kid named Rafael who was a graffiti artist and liked to spray paint my name around various places. One time I was mortified when some guys from school went surfing down at Trigg beach and came back to tell me there was a huge 'piece' on the wall down there with my name on it. Rafael was a sweetheart and even though he lived in a poorer suburb to me, he was kind. At some point I joined army cadets and spent weekends on camps out in the middle of the bush. I got to fire rifles and go abseiling; it was great fun. One time I went abseiling on a weekend in a quarry, and when I went down backwards, I forgot to take a step back and flipped upside down and went careening down the cliff. When the brake was applied, I smashed into the side of the rocks, and I was upside down for a good fifteen minutes before an army Seargent came down to me.

"What's your name?" he asked me.

"Wilkinson," I stammered.

"No, your first name," he said gently as I took a wobbly breath in.

"Louise."

"Okay Louise we're going to get you untangled and down from here."

I felt so silly afterwards and had a huge bruise on my butt cheek where I had hit the rock. Dana joined cadets as well, and we would go out to

Bindoon in the blistering heat and do field exercises and obstacle courses. Somehow, I ended up with the rank of Lance Corporal, which was fun, as I got to boss all the boys around. It was funny though as I had no idea how to navigate at all, and every camp I would get our section hopelessly lost in the bush. It seemed no matter how many lessons I sat through about navigation, I still had no clue. Back then cadets were just an excuse for kids to dress up in uniform and date each other, and I gave sassy young boys plenty of punishments for flirting with me and saying inappropriate things. I would make them run around the parade ground on a Wednesday night with their rifles held above their heads. When I think back now to all the risky things we did, I cannot believe more kids did not get hurt, but boy it was fun. One weekend we went on a trip to Rottnest Island with cadets, but it was more of a social event. I have no idea where the adults were on that trip, but us teenagers got up to all sorts of stuff. We were drinking and running around the island like little kids in a candy shop. I ended up with a guy I did not even particularly like, and he kept pressuring me to have sex with him. I was only 15 at the time and kept saying no but we ended up mucking around together on the side of a hill, before we caught up with my sister and everyone else. On the way home on the ferry someone thought it would be a good idea to share a watermelon around, but the weather was bad, and the waves were rough. At one point some of us were throwing up over the side of the boat, and the birds were flying in and eating the watermelon.

One weekend I thought it would be a clever idea to sign up for a small - arms shoot in Bindoon. When I arrived, I realised to my dismay, that I was the only female. We did a lot of weapons training and I got to fire some sort of machine gun, an F1 I think and gosh that was scary. First, I held it on my shoulder and when I fired it, I shot backwards and fired a round of bullets into a canopy of trees above me.

"F***, that has some kick to it eh Wilkinson?" a corporal said to me, but I was shaking all over and just managed some sort of wobbly smile.

"You need to hold it at your hip," the corporal said to me.

I took a deep breath and lifted it on to my hip but still it gave me a good kick backwards. After that I decided I had enough of firing weapons, and I ended up doing most of the cooking for the men. There seemed to be a lot of drinking going on that weekend but fortunately I decided not to have any alcohol. On the second night I was going to bed and suddenly one of the NCO's came into my dorm and sat on the end of the bed and started talking to me.

"You know you're really pretty," he said to me.

I froze, not sure where the conversation was headed, and I was polite but inside I was terrified he was going to try something. He chatted to me for a few minutes.

"Well, it's probably not very appropriate for me to be in your room, is it," he said and off he went.

As soon as he left, I let out a huge sigh as I had not realised I had been holding my breath the whole time. I slept with one eye open that night.

We went to Bindoon for a camp one weekend and on the first night we were fast asleep when the officers raided us in a simulated attack. There was lots of yelling, screaming and the firing of blanks and I had to scramble around madly trying to gather my troops and find them a good place to hide. My adrenaline was so high afterwards that I could not get back to sleep. The second night it started raining, and all our tents and gear got completely saturated. Being a corporal, I was expected to give my dry gear to my recruits, and at about 3am I was curled up on my pack in the rain, shivering uncontrollably and nearly hallucinating from lack of sleep. But come Sunday morning, the sun was shining, and we all gathered around for a barbecue breakfast like nothing had ever happened. That was cadets back then, crazy, unpredictable, and not very safe.

Dana did very well in cadets and obtained the rank of RSM. She had a sword for ceremonies, and seemed to much better with rank than I was. I ended up leaving cadets due to bullying, as I grew tired of having the responsibility and even after obtaining the rank of Sargeant, it still was not enough to make me stay. It had all become a bit too serious for me, and I was tired of the endless camps in the heat, eating crappy ration pack food and peeing in a hole in the ground. I was also sick of the other Sargeant's being so arrogant and controlling over us, they did not respect me, and I felt like I'd had enough of being made fun of.

My brother Dylan had started playing cricket in our local club, and he turned out to be quite a fast bowler. I spent many weekends with mum and dad at the cricket ground watching him. I felt happy that he had found something that he really enjoyed, and it was a way for my parents to meet new people too.

When I was sixteen, I met a guy at a party, Jack, who was twenty-two years old. We started dating and he was a lovely guy and never pushed me into anything sexual. We would hang out on weekends and get drunk and listen to music. I cannot believe my parents let me do that sort of thing, and they did not really care what I got up to on the weekends. Dana and I did not have any sort of curfew either, they would tell us to come home when we thought it was 'sensible.' Dana was dating an older guy, Sam, who had a car, so we would go driving to the beach and hang out. I liked Jack, but he was very clingy emotionally, and I felt smothered a lot of the time. I ended up breaking it off with him as he was getting too attached to me and I was so young, I just wanted to have some fun. He took it badly which I felt guilty for. To make matters worse Jack worked at our local shops so I would bump into him often, which was so awkward. He was a sweet guy and never treated me badly, I just did not want anything serious.

When I was seventeen years old, I started dating a guy I knew from cadets, Scott. He was cute and witty, and we got along well. He had very controlling parents and ended up moving into a friend's place who had been my Sargeant at cadets. Scott changed after leaving his parents' house, he became abusive and started being possessive and controlling of me. He would get angry for no reason, and it started to scare me. One day we were making out in his room, and he forced me to have sex. I did not want to, and said no a few times, but he insisted, so I went along with it. He was the first boy I had let have sex with me and I felt so horrible afterwards. As I went home on the bus that day, I expected to feel something special, but all I felt was shame and humiliation. A few weeks later he ended it with me saying that the only reason he had gone out with me in the first place was because he liked my sister. Dana laughed so hard when I told her.

"As if I would date him Lou, he's like three years younger than me!" she said to me.

I was mortified to say the least, as he also said the guys at cadets had dared him to 'take my cherry," so of course that just led me to feel even worse. He really messed me up and it took months for me to recover.

Once again, I had joined a drama club, but this one was bigger, and we did proper productions with lighting and sound crews. We did a play where I was selected to star as an army recruit whose father was an abusive drunk. I had to dye my hair black for the part and had an impressive monologue that left most of the audience in tears. I absolutely loved acting because it was a way to escape my painful past and forget about what had happened to me as a child. Mum ended up joining the group too and one play had a dinner party scene. To the Director's horror, mum cooked up some lamb chops, mashed potato and peas and proceeded to put them onto plates on the stage. The Director got so angry and kept yelling, "you are meant to mime the eating," but mum would not hear of it, and we all went backstage and laughed our heads off.

Once we moved to Perth, my dad stopped coming to me and somehow my brain just decided to let all those memories go. I know it sounds weird, but I cannot describe it any other way; it was like a veil came down on all that horrid stuff and it simply disappeared. All the memories of my abuse simply slipped away, and I did not have to live with it any longer. I cannot say the exact time that it happened, but as I got older, I had no active memories of the abuse at all. Those first few months of living in Perth had been a dark time for me as I had felt worthless and abandoned by my father. I had been homesick for NZ but also grieved the loss of the relationship with my dad; he had abused me for over thirteen years and then suddenly there was nothing. That feeling of loss really screwed me up. I think when I realised it was finally over my brain decided to give me another chance at having a normal life. And so, I was living it, and it was a good life with my friends and school and a newfound sense of freedom. I had a part time job at the local YMCA office, taking kids enrolments and fees. It was a decent job, and it gave me some money to spend on the weekends. In year 10 we had a school dinner dance and I wanted to bring a date, but I could not think of anyone to ask. The boys in my year were so immature so I set out on a mission to find someone to take me. There was a cute guy at the YMCA who taught a karate class, and I spent weeks trying to get up the courage to ask him. I would see him every week and we would chat and have a laugh together. One day around three weeks before the dance, I saw him after all the kids had left his class.

"I'm having a dinner dance at school; I was wondering if you want to go with me?" I blurted out, feeling my face go red.

"Ah I have a girlfriend," he replied, and I ran off feeling completely mortified.

From then on, I would hide in the bathroom any time he came into the office. I had to come up with a new plan as I was determined to show up to the dance with a date.

We had some new neighbours from New Zealand who had moved in next to us, and they had a son, Stephan, who was tall and very handsome. I had spoken to him a few times before and he was funny, shy and a little bit dorky, but I figured I had nothing to lose by inviting him. I had already made a fool of myself with the karate guy, so I decided to go for it. To my surprise he said yes, and I was over the moon with excitement. Mum was very excited about the dance too and we went shopping together for a new dress for me. The day arrived and Stephan came to our house to pick me up. I had to laugh when I saw that he was wearing a nice shirt and pants with sneakers, but I did not care as he was cute, and I was keen to go and show him off to my friends. The dance was great fun, and Stephan and I had a few slow dances. Towards the end of the evening, one of my friends took a liking to Stephan and kept trying to lure him away from me. They ended up dancing together and I felt jealous as I really liked Stephan but did not know how to tell him. On the drive home I felt upset and did not talk to him much. When he got out of the car at my place, I thought he was going to kiss me, but he did not so I said goodbye and walked away. We did not see much of each other after that night, but I still thought he was cute and fun to be around.

Even though I had been badly bullied in the first two years of high school, it ended up being mostly a positive experience for me. My favourite subjects in years 11 and 12 were history, drama, and photography. We had a dark room where we would develop our photos and it was such fun to muck around in there. We did a few drama productions and our own version of Romeo and Juliet which we filmed in the school grounds. The history teacher was one of my favourites and during lessons he would sell us cans of coke and mars bars for a dollar from his mini fridge. We also went on a couple of camps for Drama and History, it was such fun. Our year 12 drama teacher was amazing, with such an incredible energy and heart for young actors like us. We went to his house a couple of times to practice plays and hang out. Instead of doing sport in upper school, some of my friends and I joined a YMCA Leadership training course which ran at the same time as PE. We did all sorts of training that related to leadership, like communication skills, marketing, and how to set up and run activities and programs in community. I learned so many things in those two years, and as I hated doing school sports, it suited me well.

My 18th birthday arrived, and my parents agreed to let me have a party, it was a big event, and all my friends came. I can still remember my parents' faces when some boys walked in carrying cartons of beer on their shoulders. It was such a great party and my parents had bought me a nice ring and my mum had ordered a special cake for me. High school was over, and even though I had enjoyed the last two years, to be honest I could not wait to leave. I was ready for something else. I graduated high school in November 1992, but I was devastated to discover I had not passed my TEE. I had wanted to study teaching but had not scored enough points to get into university and I was gutted. I had really wanted to do an early childhood degree, but now that was out of the question. I was doing quite a bit of volunteer work with the YMCA so that was good, and it made me feel better about stuffing up my chances of getting into university. I went to camps with young kids as a youth leader and I loved it. I ended up enrolling in a night course at Tafe studying childcare, and as I had always done a lot of babysitting, it was natural I would gravitate towards that career.

After my 18th birthday I saw my neighbour Stephan outside the front of his house one day, and we started talking. He made me laugh a couple of times and I realised that I still had feelings for him. Stephan had grown taller, was even more handsome than before and I felt something click with him that day. He was now 6 feet 7 and had such a gorgeous smile and when he asked me out, I said yes, so we started dating, and he was so much fun to be around. I felt the hurt and betrayal of Scott slipping away, as Stephan was funny, gentle, and treated me like a princess. Dana had met her boyfriend Richard the year before, so we started hanging out together. We went to watch bands and to pubs for dinner and we all had such a fun time. Stephan had never slept with a girl before, so it was fine with me to take things slow. His parents were odd to say the least, and they had horribly loud arguments that the whole street could hear. His dad was very abusive towards his mum, which was so hard for Stephan to watch.

About six months into our relationship, Stephan got a bad cold which he could not seem to shake. He had blood tests done after collapsing at work one day and the results were shocking; he had non - Hodgkins Lymphoma. I was devastated as he was such a young, strong guy, and I just could not believe he had cancer. Stephan started his first round of chemo straight away and it was a rough ride for him, all his hair fell out and he lost around twelve kilograms. The whole thing was so awful for all of us, and I tried to support Stephan the best I could, but I was young and had no idea how to navigate through such an illness. Stephan was sick all the time and became angry and frustrated at how weak he was becoming. His parents were suffocating him, and by the time he started radiotherapy, his health had gone downhill. He would come home after treatment with ferocious headaches that sent him to his bed where he would writhe around for hours in intense pain, and it was horrific to watch. I was convinced the doctors were not giving Stephan the right treatment, as it did not make any sense to blast him with the chemo and radio when all it did was make him so bloody ill. He was a fit, young man and now he was wasting away so much that I barely recognised him.

Our relationship had collapsed at that point, as his parents made no secret of how much they did not want me at the house and wanted us to break up. I had started a full-time job in a childcare centre, so I did not see much of him during the week. It was a hard transition for me to work long hours every day too as I would wake up at 6.30am and catch two buses and a train to get to work. I would finish at 5pm and catch the two buses and train back and I would not be home until 6.30pm some days. For the first few weeks I would collapse into bed after getting home, but I loved the job, the kids were so cute, and I finally felt like I had found a purpose. My boss Hillary was horrid though, she was an old school midwife and was not nice to the children at all. She would yell at all of us and when she was on the warpath, we would put our heads down and hope we were not her next target. Hillary would come barreling out of the nursery with a baby under each arm and would head to what she called the 'presidential suite.' It was a room with two cots at the front of the centre, and she would put the babies who were not 'behaving' in that little room and leave them to cry. Apart from her, I made some good friends, and I loved the families. I was around so many children and exposed to so many new germs, that I got a couple of colds in the first few weeks, the kids were always so snotty. After a few months, I had saved up enough money to buy a car. Grandpa and Grandma had sent me some money towards it, so one weekend my dad took me to buy a green Ford Escort. I fell in love with that car and could not believe it was mine. I washed it every weekend and bought a stereo and speakers for it. Stephan's parents did not want him to get any more unwell than he already was, and because I was working around kids, they told me to stay away from him. I had a job I really enjoyed but I was losing the only person I had ever really loved. Eventually Stephan broke it off with me.

"I don't want you to love me anymore," he said to me one day and I felt my heart break at his words.

I spent most of my weekends crying in my room, and I would listen to Led Zeppelin and Counting Crows and cry and cry and cry. Being in such proximity to Stephan every day was exceedingly difficult, as I would come home from work and instantly look for his car. I would go out with Dana and Richard to watch bands and drink, but my heart was never in it, all I thought about was Stephan.

I threw myself into my job and tried to move on the best I could. I went out with Veronica and Connie to clubs, and we would stay out until 3am dancing. I did not drink much, so I would always be the driver.

My sister Dana had graduated from university by then with a teaching degree. She had to do a country posting and I was gutted that she would be leaving home. I was so proud of her, and I went to stay with her a few times and helped set up her new classroom.

A few months later while I was at a club, I met a guy named Patrick who was cute and friendly, and we were drinking and dancing together.

"Hey," he said in my ear. "I really like you."

I drove him home, and he expected me to come in that night, but I was not ready, so we agreed to be friends. We saw each other a couple more times before we started dating. Patrick had been born in Zimbabwe and his family had moved to Australia when Patrick was young, and they were lovely people. I spent most weekends over at their place and eating was an important thing. I fell in love with their food and Patrick's grandma was always trying to 'fatten me up.' I became close with them, and it felt so nice to be a part of such a loving family. Patrick drove a fast Commodore and one night he asked if I wanted to become part of the '200 club'. He let me drive on the freeway and with his coaxing I pushed the speed limit past 200km hour, and it was such an adrenaline rush! We had sex a lot, but it was fun, and he never pressured me. I was happy but at times I would become demanding and emotional, as Patrick was not the type of guy to show emotions and I would pick fights with him over nothing and fly into a rage. Sometimes I would drive off in his car at 2am but nothing fazed him, he was so laid back and that made me worse. I am not sure why I would behave like that; it was like I would be calm and relaxed one minute, and then something would set me off and I would yell and scream. Most of the time Patrick would fall asleep during my ranting, which made me even angrier.

"Just relax Lou," he would say when I woke him up.

Most weekends we would spend time together at Patrick's house and watch the footy and surfing on tv. He loved to drink beer and surf and I would sit on the beach sometimes and watch him.

After 12 months at my job, I decided I wanted to study to become qualified in early childhood, so I enrolled in Tafe in an Associate Diploma of Social Science (Childcare). I got a job at the weekends at our local pizza shop to pay for my fees and I absolutely loved studying. Doing a diploma full-time was a lot to deal with but I met some new people, and I really enjoyed it. The diploma was competency based which meant no specific grades, you either passed the units or you did not. There was a lot of pressure on us to do well. The course had practical components, and we found ourselves in a childcare centre in the first few months of studying. It was hard to work full-time and keep up the workload of full-time study as well. I met some great girls at Tafe, and we started hanging out together, it was great fun going for lunch in the cafeteria and studying in the library. I was learning so many new things, for instance, during a lesson on social development we watched a video on the stolen generation. I watched in horror as they explained what had happened to all the indigenous tribes once Australia was colonized. I remember sitting there and listening to the accounts from relatives and feeling so in shock that I had been living in this beautiful country for years yet had no knowledge at all about what had occurred. I turned to face my friends and asked,

"Did you guys know about this?"

They mostly just shrugged. "Yeah, kind of," they said.

I spent the next few days reading about it in the library, but the shock was huge as I tried to understand why I had not learnt about it in high school.

My 21ˢᵗ birthday came, and I had another party, my parents did not have a lot of money, so Patrick brought most of the alcohol. It was a big party, and Stephan ended up coming over and I could not believe how well he looked. I overheard him telling Veronica that he wished that we had never broken up. That night I went to bed but all I could think about was Stephan.

At some point Patrick decided he would join the police force, so I helped him with the application. I ended up writing an essay for him and helped him in any way that I could. I was happy for him when he made it in, and we went out for dinner with his family to celebrate. I was pleased for Patrick, but I was starting to feel that I was not entirely happy with him, as we would sit at his place with his mates on the weekend and I would get so bored.

"Let's go on a picnic," I would say to him, but he would laugh and turn back to watching the footy.

"A picnic? Nah, I'm good," he would reply.

I wanted him to be romantic, spontaneous and he was just not into it. Weirdly he did not even like kissing, and that bothered me too. About eight months later I realised deep down that I was still in love with Stephan, and

I broke it off with Patrick. We just did not click together like Stephan, and I did. I felt bad for breaking his heart, as he had been so kind and loving to me, but I had to be true to myself. Telling Patrick was not easy, and he would call me and become upset.

"Can you come over Lou?" He would beg me, but I had made my mind up.

Patrick could not understand what was going on and I did not either, but I knew I was not in love with him and could not see a future for us.

Chapter 5

stephan

I was still working in the pizza shop, and I would do deliveries for customers in the owner's little car. Friday nights were crazy at the shop, and I briefly dated one of the other drivers, Irwin. He was sweet and we spent time together a after work or on the weekend. Things ended with him and a few weeks later I called Stephan on the phone.

"Are you still with Patrick?" he asked me.

"No, we broke up," I replied. There was a long pause.

"So, do you want to go out for dinner?"

Of course, I agreed, and we got back together pretty much straight away, and we were more in love than ever. Stephan moved out into a shared house, so we spent every minute together that we could. He was well and we would have such fun together, he totally understood me and could make me laugh and laugh. Even doing boring everyday things together felt so much fun with him. I felt deliriously happy, and we made plans to move in together once I had finished my studies. Once I graduated, we found a town house in Balcatta, it was a little 3-bedroom place, and it was amazing.

I got a full-time job in a childcare centre in Joondalup, and I loved coming home to Stephan, and we would cook together and listen to music.

Shortly after that my mum found a lump in her breast, and she had a biopsy, and it came back as a malignant tumor. We were all so shocked I think, as she had never had any problems with her health at all. Mum ended up in hospital and had the lump removed and her lymph nodes scraped out. She started radiotherapy and Richard, who was into natural medicines, told her to use cabbage leaves afterwards. I made up a cabbage poultice and I was shocked to feel the heat coming off that cabbage! It really helped reduce the severity of the side effects. After a year or so mum got better, and I had to hand it to her, she was so positive and refused to believe that she was going to die. She had also become much more present emotionally and would tell us she loved us all the time. Mum started to have vitamin C therapy too which really helped with her energy levels.

Stephan loved to have a smoke of marijuana and eventually I decided to try it. I did not like it at first, but it slowly grew on me, and we started to smoke together most weekends. We would talk about marriage and go for drives to look at blocks of land. I was so happy with him and could not imagine life without him as he was my soulmate and we belonged together.

Dana got married to Richard in January 1997, it was a beautiful wedding, and I was a bridesmaid. Stephan came to the wedding in a gorgeous suit with a top hat, as his hair had yet to grow back. It made him even taller but gosh he was handsome. The wedding was amazing, and my sister had done such a terrific job of organising everything.

Around two months later Stephan discovered a lump in his groin, and I felt my world falling apart again as we both realised the cancer had returned. Stephan remained so positive throughout his next treatments, but I knew deep down that he was going to die.

"What are we going to do?" I sobbed in his arms.

"I'll be fine Lou," he replied, and that was the end of the conversation.

He would brush off my concerns and say that he had no intention of leaving me. Stephan had chemo for about three months and then he told his parents and doctor he could not do it anymore.

"How can you do this," they yelled at him. "It's so irresponsible."

His parents were angry, and I felt like they blamed me for Stephan refusing to have any more treatment. At that stage Stephan's entire right leg was ulcerated, and he used the weed as pain relief. He was covered in tumours but that did not stop me from loving him, he was my gorgeous man, and I did all that I could to help him. Stephan quit his job and became a house husband, which he quite enjoyed. I would work all day, and he spent his days pottering around our home and garden. I bought him a tiny little kitten named Candy, and he would walk around the house with her on his shoulder.

Things at work were bad as I was being bullied terribly by an older lady named Nicole, who had instantly disliked me from the very beginning and made my life hell at the centre. Management did not seem to care what Nicole did to me and the stress of that and Stephan dying was just too much to cope with. I watched him get more unwell with each passing day, my big strapping man was disintegrating before my very eyes, and it was heartbreaking to watch. The life we had built together was slowly slipping away and I felt powerless to stop it. Stephan remained so positive though, and he refused to believe he was not going to recover.

One night a girlfriend from Tafe, Raquel, invited me out and I decided to go. I had not been out except for work, in months, and Stephan encouraged me to have some fun. We went to a pub, took a pill, and started drinking. It was not long before we met two guys and started chatting to them, one was tall and handsome, like my type, the other was skinny and arty, who was more Raquel's type. We kept drinking as the night went on and somehow, I ended up driving us back to their place. When we got there, we all smoked weed and kept drinking and went for a swim in their pool. Raquel went upstairs with the arty dude and left me alone with the other one. We chatted for a few hours and kept drinking and swimming, and at some point, I started making out with this guy, and Raquel came down the stairs and saw me. Even though she knew about Stephan and how much I loved him, she never said a word to me to stop, she just went back upstirs and had sex with the arty guy. In the end I slept with this other guy. Even though I loved Stephan so dearly, I wanted to block out how hard it was to watch him die a horribly slow and painful death, and being with this guy did exactly that.

Around five o'clock in the morning and full of shame and regret I drove home. I had a quick shower, slipped into bed, and tried not to wake Stephan up as I wanted to pretend that I had been home already for hours. Stephan never suspected anything, and I did not tell him. I could not believe that I had cheated on this beautiful man, and as the days went on, it became harder and harder to keep my infidelity a secret. I felt like I was living in a nightmare, I went through the motions at work and cared for Stephan, but I was dying inside. I did not even know why I had cheated on him; he was the love of my life. I just could not wrap my head around what I had done, I did not want to be with anyone else, so how could I have betrayed him? I could feel that the lie was starting to consume me, so finally, after driving home from dinner one night, I suddenly had the urge to come clean.

"Stop the car!" I yelled at him, and he gave me a surprised look but pulled over.

"What's going on Lou," he asked me.

At that moment, the truth came spilling out, and he stared at me in shocked silence as I told him what I had done. Stephan just looked at me and I could tell that I had broken his heart.

"What do you mean you had sex with some guy? What are you talking about?"

He was completely bewildered, but I kept on crying and shaking my head, as he turned in his seat to look at me.

"Well," he said as I sniffed and wiped my face with my hand.

"I'm so sorry," I sobbed. "I didn't know what I was doing," but Stephan snorted at me.

"You didn't know what you were doing? What a load of bulls*** Lou," he yelled at me.

He put the car in gear, and we drove home in silence. Stephan was upset and angry of course, but more than that he was in complete disbelief. The next day we talked, and Stephan was still very confused.

"Why Lou? Why did you do it," he asked me, but I did not have an answer for him.

I saw the pain on his face, and I wanted to crawl away somewhere and die. We tried going to counselling together, and the counsellor explained to Stephan that I had been under immense pressure and stress from working and caring for him. The counsellor said that my acting out was a way of coping, and that deep down I did not want to admit that my boyfriend was potentially dying in our home, and that is why I had taken drugs and slept with a stranger.

"It's a load of bulls***," Stephan shook his finger at me.

"It's the truth," I sobbed in the counsellor's office. "I just can't handle the fact that you might die."

But no matter what the counsellor or I said, Stephan would not accept any type of explanation, and a few days later he packed a bag and left me. I was utterly devastated and felt like my entire world had fallen apart. My fairytale life had come crashing down around me and there was nothing I could do to stop it. Stephan moved in with his dad and refused to see me, so I went to work like a robot and at night I drank and smoked myself to sleep. After a week or so, Stephan's dad came around and cleaned out the house of his furniture; he took the dining room table, couch, and our bed. He left me with nothing, so I slept on the floor on my old single mattress. I cried an ocean of tears, and every day I called Stephan, but he refused to speak to me. I knew deep down that it was over, and I had no one to blame but myself. I had destroyed the only good thing I had ever had, and the only person I had ever loved. I walked around in a daze, not really feeling anything but gut-wrenching sadness and nothing seemed to matter anymore. When Stephan did answer the phone, I begged him to take me back, but he said no every time, and I felt him slip further and further away from me. He was also becoming increasingly unwell, and when I did see him briefly at his house one day, I was shocked at how skinny and sick he looked. A week or two later Stephan was back in hospital, and I tried not to think about how he might die, but I was in such denial. I was also really struggling, especially financially. I had no idea how to balance my money or pay bills, as Stephan had taken care of those things. I felt lost, hopeless, and completely alone.

Chapter 6

the memories

One weekend I went to a friend's place after work. Paula was an older lady and would sell me weed, and we had struck up a friendship and I would go over to her house on the weekends and smoke with her and talk. That night we were talking about a little girl in our centre who would behave in an odd way at rest time.

"Have you noticed how she does that weird humping thing?" Paula asked me.

"Yeah, I've noticed that too. It looks like she is trying to self soothe herself by masturbating on her bed," I answered as my friend looked at me.

"Is that normal?" she asked me, and I shook my head.

"No, not really," I answered. "It could indicate something not right is happening at home as she is so young."

"What are you saying?" Paula asked me. "You mean she could be being sexually abused?"

I stared at my friend, and I tried opening my mouth to reply, but nothing came out. Suddenly I felt like I was being sucked into a big black hole. I could not see or hear anything, but I felt like I was spinning into a big vortex, and I had no control over it. I no longer knew who I was, or where I was, I just felt the spinning getting faster and faster. It was like there was this void and I was trapped inside, it was something dark and horrible and I felt terrified. I could hear Paula's voice, but she was far away and then after a few minutes, my vision cleared, and I was back. Then I just started hyperventilating and screaming and Paula was staring at me and did not know what to do.

"Are you ok Lou? Lou! Are you all right?" Paula kept asking me, but all I could do was breathe fast, panic and scream.

In the end she looked like she was going to slap me to snap me out of it, and I stopped. When I stopped yelling there was this voice in my head saying, "your dad abused you." I started to shake uncontrollably, and I was crying and holding out my hands to my friend, but Paula started to get angry at me, she thought I was having a bad reaction to the weed.

"You have to go home," she yelled at me. "You're having some sort of attack, and you can't stay here," but that made me cry even more.

"Please let me stay," I begged her with tears pouring down my face.

In the end I went to her spare room and just lay on the bed breathing heavily. My dad, abuse me? My dad? I could not believe what I was thinking or hearing in my head, and I was in complete shock. I felt this rushing in my head like a wind getting louder and louder, and with it came this sickly feeling and a revelation, my father had sexually abused me, and I had forgotten everything. I lay in the dark all night, feeling such disbelief and just sobbing and sobbing. The next morning, I went home and called my friend Raquel, I had to tell her what was going on. I drove to her house, and we sat chatting over a couple of beers. She had met my dad a few times and was just as shocked as me. We smoked some weed and I tried to get my thoughts together.

"What do you need me to do?" she asked me.

"I don't know," I replied. "Give me a hug and tell me that you believe me."

She reached over and pulled me close to her as I took a few deep breaths and tried to calm my heart which was beating so fast.

"I believe you," she told me, and I felt a bit better, but I still thought I was going crazy.

I was also starting to feel pain in different areas of my body, especially in my pelvis and groin, and I thought it was period pain but it was not due so that was weird. I went to work that day feeling like a zombie as I was in complete shock over what I had remembered. How on earth could this be true? I was so panicky at night, and I was having awful nightmares of being smothered and would wake up gasping for air. I would crawl into the shower and stay in there for hours on the weekends, just sobbing and holding myself. The pain in my pelvis was getting worse and worse and when I looked at a book from the library about repressed memories, I realised I was having body memories. The more I read, the more I understood repressed memories and how these were presented after so many years of being hidden away. I was in such shock that at times I would just start to shake all over, and my body would feel not real, like it was miles away.

I saw Stephan and I told him about my dad, but he just sat there looking at me in disbelief.

"Are you sure?" he kept asking me.

"Yes, I'm sure," I said. "Either that or I'm going crazy."

I had coffee with Veronica and told her what was going on. She sat with me while I cried and cried, then we discussed her moving in with me. So, Veronica came to live with me, and it helped a lot. The worst part was I could barely speak to my mum or dad. I could manage a quick conversation with mum on the phone but every time she mentioned dad, I would have a panic attack. I ended up telling her that I had remembered some stuff from my childhood, and she went very quiet on the phone. One day

I was so upset that I decided to call my dad to confront him, and when he got on the phone, I spoke angrily to him.

"You better make yourself alone," I snarled.

"What do you mean by that?" he asked me.

"What did you do to me?" I sobbed and sobbed but he tried to blow me off.

"I am your father Louise and I love you," he said sternly, but I hung up and burst into tears.

Veronica tried to support me the best she could but even she did not know what to do with me. Money was tight so we decided that we would advertise for a flat mate, so we put an ad in the paper and a few people applied. We ended up choosing a guy called Ben who seemed nice, he had a decent job and we thought he was the best choice. Having people in the house with me was great and really lifted my mood.

One weekend Veronica and I decided to go on a road trip with one of her guy mates, Marty. His family lived in a country town, so we were going to stay with them and attend a festival in a neighbouring town. I said that I would drive my car, which probably was not the smartest move, as the radiator leaked, and I was always filling it up with water. My old Escort liked to overheat regularly too, but late one afternoon we packed up all our stuff and off we went. We were all so excited, talking non-stop and singing along to cassette tapes and me stopping every hour or two along the way to smoke of course. Marty was sweet and witty and kept us in stitches with his funny stories. I was the main driver and once it got dark, Veronica and Marty fell asleep in the back seat. At one point, my car started to overheat and make a very loud noise, but it was so dark and late at night, that I was too afraid to stop. I just kept on driving and even turned my radio up to drown out the noise. I thought to myself, 'if I keep on driving until we get there it will be ok.' So, I did, my car making this awful banging noise and me just ignoring it and driving along with my two friends sleeping in the back. I kept on singing and driving and I knew that if I stopped the car, we would be stranded in the dark in the middle of nowhere. By then, the temperature gauge needle was stuck in the red, but I followed the map book and then woke Marty up when we were getting close to his town. I drove up his street and into the driveway, where my car promptly stalled and died. I could not believe that we had somehow made it, but I was hysterical as my car was dead, and even when I tried to start it, nothing happened. Marty's mum was understandably upset with us arriving so late at night, and me being in such a tizzy about my car did not help the situation. Since she owned a bakery in the town, she made us work there for a day or two, so we helped with serving and cleaning. We ended up at the festival where Veronica had organised for us to do some work and stay with a family that she knew. Veronica, Marty, and I went to a bush dance which was filled with country people wearing flannel, and I felt very out of place. I wanted to party, and smoke weed but had to restrain myself. I decided to have a drink and just join in the line dancing, and it ended up being a lot of fun. I was worried about my car situation though, as we were stuck in this country town with no way of getting home. The next day Marty's mum drove us to the bus station, which was so kind of her, and we all caught the bus back to Perth. I had called my sister Dana and Richard to ask them if they would lend me some money so I could get my car towed home. Thankfully, they agreed, and I was so relieved and grateful, as it was quite a lot of money. A few days later my car arrived on a big truck, and I asked my brother Dylan to come and have a look at it.

"I dunno about this sis," he said as he opened the bonnet. "From what you told me it sounds like the head gasket has blown."

"What does that mean?" I asked him anxiously, as he took the cap off my radiator and shook his head.

"Bloody hell sis, it's bone dry," Dylan said, as I looked at him and shrugged my shoulders.

He made a grunting sound, grabbed his tools, and took the radiator out, putting it in my carport.

"I'll get you a second hand one sis, but I won't know if the head is cooked until I put it in. The oil doesn't look too bad so you might be lucky."

The next day Dylan came over with the used radiator and put it into my car. He filled it up with water from the tap and looked at me, with his eyebrows raised.

"Hold your breath Lou," he said, as he turned the key.

The car spluttered and died, and I felt my heart sink. Dylan shook his head and tried it again and after a minute or two, it roared into life and Dylan let out a whoop as he gunned the accelerator. He let it run for a while and then jumped out and unscrewed the radiator and stuck his finger into the water. Dylan shrugged his shoulders and then checked the oil and wiped the dipstick on a rag. He shook his head again and looked at me.

"Bloody hell!" he exclaimed, and my eyebrows shot up. "The oil is perfect; I can't believe it Lou."

I let out a little squeal and rushed to hug him.

"Does this mean that it's ok?" I asked, and he shrugged, putting his tools away.

"Yeah, I think so, but s*** you got lucky sis. These old Escorts are bloody tough. Any other car would be f***ed."

I hugged him again and jumped up and down with excitement.

After the trip I found out that Stephan was back in hospital and he let me see him a few times, but it felt awkward and not nice. He was cold to me, and after I left, I would feel so much worse, but I kept persisting hoping that one day he might change his mind about us. One night I went to a party with Ben and ended up meeting one of his friends named Pete.

Even though I was still in love with Stephan, I needed a distraction, and we ended up dating. I was looking for anything to take my mind off Stephan leaving me, I knew deep down that he was dying as he was not having any treatment but was getting weaker every day. Worse, his parents were going to the hospital and having these huge fights in front of him, and the few times he did let me stay and talk to him; he would say how much he resented them both. I could not imagine how Stephan felt and my heart broke for him. One night I was feeling so distraught about Stephan that I went over to mum and dad's house, desperate for some comfort. I knelt at my dad's feet, sobbing, and sobbing but he only looked up from his book briefly, before saying to me,

"I am not sure what you want me to do."

I stood up shakily on my feet and left their house, feeling completely alone.

I drank heavily, and Pete and I spent most of our weekends together getting stoned and having sex. I knew I was in a bad way mentally, but I did not know how to deal with Stephan dying any other way. I was still having memories, but I tried to stay distracted with the weed and sex. I had decided to not see either of my parents at that stage, and even though mum called me often, I kept telling her I was too busy to see her. I would visit Stephan in hospital but sometimes he would get angry.

"Go away Lou," he would say to me. "I don't want you to see me."

It broke my heart when he would order me out, but I would do what he asked and leave the hospital, and then sob all the way home. Stephan was so sick, and they monitored him constantly; he was weak, so thin and barely eating and it was awful to see him like that. A few months later I was at work when I got a call from Stephan's dad. I stepped into the hallway with the cordless phone for some privacy.

"I'm sorry Louise," I heard him say. "But Stephan passed away this afternoon."

I remember so clearly just crying out and dropping to the floor, it was like someone had reached into my chest and pulled out my heart. I felt like the entire world was spinning around and around and I could not see or hear anything, then I heard this awful noise like a howling and realised it was me. I stood up slowly, shuffled to the office and called Dana on the phone.

"He's gone," I managed to blurt out, and she knew instantly what I meant.

I left work in a complete daze and drove home where I went to my room to smoke. I lit my bong with shaking fingers as it hit me that I would never see my beloved Stephan again. I waited for Dana to finish work and then I drove to her house, where I lay on the couch sobbing and sobbing. I could not believe that he was gone, I had not even been there to say goodbye, and now it was over and there was nothing more I could do. I do not remember how long I stayed at my sister's, but when I went home Veronica met me and just held on to me while I cried. I felt like a piece of me had been taken away and there was this giant void inside me. The next few days were a blur, as I took some time off work and just wandered around the house crying uncontrollably. I went to see Stephan's dad to ask him if I could speak at the funeral, and he agreed so I went home and started to write a speech. I sat in my room and listened to Stephan's favourite band, which was Led Zeppelin, and I cried as I wrote about our life together. Inside I felt like I was dying too, if only I had not cheated on him that night, I would have still been with him up until the end. I hated myself so much for betraying him and now it was over, he was gone, and I was all alone. Dylan came to see me, and we would smoke and drink and chat about Stephan, and my brother's support meant the world to me. Dana also came to see me often and we would hug each other and cry together. Dana and Richard's support helped me so much in those first few days, and Richard was devastated to have lost his friend too.

The day of Stephan's funeral arrived, and I wore a new dress that I thought Stephan would have liked. All my family were there with me, and I remember looking into his open casket and he was wearing a purple shirt he had bought when we lived together. As I looked down at him, I could hear his voice saying, "look at all this fuss, I didn't want all of this and they're all ball bags." I started to laugh quietly as that had been Stephan's favourite expression, to call someone a 'ball bag.' When I began to speak, this renewed strength came from somewhere and I took a deep breath and was able to keep going. After I spoke his dad got up and started going on about how close they were (they were not), and to my shock mentioned an old girlfriend from NZ. I could not believe it! I felt hollow and, on the ceiling, as I had been the only woman in Stephan's life, and his parents could not even acknowledge it. Afterwards his friends and I went to one of their houses and we sat around playing music and smoking and talking about his life and what he had meant to all of us. I do not think any of us could comprehend that he was gone, he was such a larger-than-life character, always laughing, joking, and lending a hand to anyone who needed it. I attended the wake where his mum just sat and cried the whole time, and his poor younger brother looked lost. His dad's new girlfriend let me go into his room, and I grabbed a jacket that I had bought him when we were together. To my dismay she had washed it, and I was gutted as I wanted to have something with Stephan's scent on it. I took it home anyway but felt upset as it did not smell like him. Our home was so empty without him, and I sat and cuddled Candy and cried an ocean of tears. Even though Veronica was there, and Ben came and went, it was not the same. I was struggling financially too, as Stephan had paid all the bills, and I had no idea how to budget. I paid the rent and bought weed and that was all that mattered to me.

We would hang out on Friday nights, Veronica, and Ben and me, drinking beer and cooking tea, so at least that made me feel more human again. I still saw Pete on the weekends too, having sex with him messed me up now I was having memories, but I did it anyway. At least I was making a choice to do it and I felt like I had some control over my body which was empowering. But I still had lots of memories and I spent hours in bed, or in the shower just reliving every devastating moment of my abuse. At times I was in such excruciating pain that I just crawled around everywhere not even being able to stand up properly. I was smoking so much weed so I could get a few hours of sleep. The nightmares never ceased, and I often woke up screaming. I had not seen my dad since the funeral, and my mum was unwell with cancer, but I no longer cared. The physical pain from the memories was so bad that I thought I might die. I could not believe what was happening to me and I spent all my time crying and smoking. I was really struggling at work and felt my patience with the kids getting thin. I had been pulled up by management for raising my voice at the toddlers, and one day two of the management committee team members called me into the office and told me I had to choose between resigning and them firing me. I sat and looked at them.

"Do you know what's been happening with Nic?" I asked them.

One of the committee members looked up from the file on her lap.

"Is that your boyfriend that died?" she asked me, and I shook my head.

"No," I answered. "That's Nicole who works here that has been bullying me for over two years now."

Tears came to my eyes, and I tried to swallow them down.

"That's not the issue," she informed me. "We don't think you are suited for the job anymore."

I felt myself becoming angry and tried to blink the tears away.

"But that's not fair," I said. "Nic has always bullied me, and no one has done anything about it!"

Tears started to fall down my cheeks and I wiped them away. It did not seem to matter to them what I had been through, and although I tried to plead my case, they would not listen.

"Fine," I said angrily. "I resign then."

I went home crying feeling lower than ever. After a week I decided to apply to do relief work at a childcare centre and the first day felt good. I could show up and do my job and then go home, it was great. No more putting up with management and horrible coworkers. Finally, I felt some normality return.

My 24th birthday came around and Raquel and I threw a huge party. I thought it would make me feel better, and it was a good party and Raquel made a huge cake laced with marijuana, but as the drugs and booze wore off, I felt awful again. Around 6 months later I received a letter from the owners of the town house saying they were selling the property. I was hysterical and did not want to move, as I would have to leave the only home that Stephan and I had shared, and it made me feel more depressed than ever. After talking to Veronica and Ben, we decided to go our separate ways, so I applied for a cute apartment in Bassendean which was close to the centre I had been getting relief work at. It was such a nice apartment with yellow walls and a new kitchen. The week I had to move, I came down with a bad case of glandular fever, and I was so sick I could not get out of bed. My family came to help me move as I lay in bed sobbing the whole time. It was like my brain had just shut down and refused to acknowledge what was happening. My dad was there, and it was the first time I had seen him in a year, and it made me want to vomit. My mum stayed with me the first night in my new place, as I was too sick to look after myself and mum begged me to quit the weed. I agreed, knowing it was a lie, as it was the only thing I had left of Stephan, and I was not going to give it up. A few days later I was better and went back to work, and a colleague suggested I try some grief counselling and I agreed as I was tired of being so depressed all the time. It had been well over a year since Stephan had passed and I felt trapped and stuck in my grief, like I could not accept that he was gone. It still felt like a bad dream, and I kept expecting him to come home to me.

By that stage I had taken a new job as coordinator of a small centre in Carlisle. I tried hard in that job, working weekends and after hours to improve the centre. The owner was from Melbourne and was ruthless. She demanded I help her pass accreditation and even though I did try, we did not pass, and she fired me. It was not my fault at all, I had told her that we needed to buy more equipment such as new bikes, that we did not have enough per child, but she did not listen. Man, I worked hard on that centre and was there after work every night of the week trying to make it good enough to pass.

I ended up back doing relief work, and after the grief counselling the counsellor suggested I have some therapy for survivors of incest. I started group therapy on Saturdays, and I met some amazing women, and we became close. Tania and Ingrid were so much fun, and we spent the weekends together connecting and drinking. I started a new job as an Inclusion Support Worker, and I loved it. I would go to different childcare centre's and help integrate children with special needs, and it was an excellent job, and the pay was good. I finally felt appreciated and that I was really helping. One day I was driving to work, and I saw my dad driving in the opposite direction and it sent me into a meltdown. I ended up in my manager's office crying uncontrollably, and after she heard how long I had been unwell for, she took me to a GP who prescribed me anti-depressants. They did help, and I felt like I was not so depressed. I had had a couple of boyfriends since moving into the flat, but I always felt like I was cheating on Stephan and spent most of the time on the ceiling. Most Friday nights Tania would come over and we would eat take away together and spend hours on my tiny balcony drinking and talking, and her friendship was a lifeline for me. Every week mum would show up with a box of groceries, and I would chat to her, hug her, and tell her I was fine.

"When are you going to see dad?" she would ask me.

"Soon," I would reply.

The flat was always messy, so she would wash my dishes and tell me to eat more fruit and vegetables. I lived mostly on hot chips, tuna, rice, and coffee. I did not see my dad at all, and I knew it was hurting my mum, but the flashbacks were still occurring most days, and I just could not do it. My little brother was about 20 years old then, and he would come to my flat off his face on speed and stay with me. He would stay up all night drinking coffee and sitting on the balcony, and sometimes he would take my car in the middle of the night and drive to some seedy block of flats up the road to score drugs. I would have to walk over there and scour the urine smelling hallways until I found him. I was not into speed, just marijuana and the odd ecstasy tablet. Mum was always calling me looking for Dylan and she would break down and cry and tell me how he was stealing from them to fund his habit. A few times guys showed up at the house threatening my parents because Dylan owed them money. I did not know what to do with my brother, or how to make him stop breaking mum's heart.

Chapter 7

addicted

I was still doing group therapy, and we did anger therapy and learned about our inner child. It was hard, but I felt like I was starting to understand the abuse a bit more and how much it had affected me. I met an older lady named Anita and she seemed nice enough, but her abuse had been a lot worse than mine. Anita had two kids and we started hanging out together. One day she came over to the flat by herself and brought some speed with her in a little bag. At first, I was dead against it, but she showed me how to sprinkle it on the weed before smoking it, something she called a 'snow cone,' so I decided to try it. I got a hit from that, and it hooked me instantly. Now I could see why my brother was so attached to it, as the adrenaline rush it gave me was amazing, and soon I forgot all about Stephan and the abuse as it blocked out my pain and made me feel invincible. Most weekends she would now come over and we would smoke and chat until 3am. Some weekends I would go out with Raquel, and we would pop a pill and go out to clubs and concerts and drink all night. We went to the Big Day Out, and I was so high that when I climbed a fence to have a pee, I promptly cut my leg open from my ankle to my thigh but did not even feel it until a stranger told me to find the medical tent. I was partying hard and did not want to stop and could not go anywhere without my weed and pipe. I had been dating a guy in my building for a few months, Matt, and he was kind and we liked hanging out together. I also slept with Raquel some weekends too and I was infatuated with her. I was spending most of my money on drugs and alcohol and was now behind in my rent. Budgeting was still difficult for me and now I was into the harder drugs, I had less money for food and bills.

My 25th birthday was coming up and Raquel had planned a massive surprise to celebrate. She had been dating a guy for a while, but I did not like him much. He was a bit sleazy to my liking, but she was really into him, so I was happy for her. On the night of my birthday Raquel and Ewan picked me up, and we ended up in a hotel and took a lot of speed. I had never been that high before and when I was in the bar drinking, I could feel the blood pumping in my veins. I lost count of the drinks I had consumed, and that was the thing with speed, you could have ten or twelve drinks and not feel drunk at all. Matt ended up at the same bar as us and I was dancing with him, he had taken one look at me and knew instantly how high I was. I kept jumping up and down and hugging him and drinking, all the while feeling so intensely focused on the conversation and my surroundings. I was so switched on that I was almost counting the seconds as they went by. Matt came up into the room with us, but Raquel and Ewan were not friendly to him at all.

"Hey, do you want to go back downstairs and get a beer?" Matt asked me and I grabbed his hand.

"No, let's stay up here," I said.

"Come on, let's go back to the bar," Matt said as he put his arm around me, and I could feel Raquel glaring at us.

"No, let's stay here," I replied.

In the end Raquel got s***ty and told him to leave, but I barely noticed as Ewan was mixing another drink with more speed in it. That night was the worst, as I would like to say I knew what they had both planned, but I was so high and really had no clue. We went to bed together and it just went on and on and on. I was not able to give consent that night even if I had tried to. I could not say no, but I did not say yes either. The next morning, we drove back to Raquel's and smoked some weed, and I was coming down hard.

"So next weekend let's do it again, but we'll take E's instead," Ewan casually announced.

Something in me snapped so I left and drove home, and I sat in the corner of my apartment not moving for hours, just rocking back and forth, and staring at the wall. I felt like I was in a permanent flashback and could not get out of it. I stopped eating and showering and just lay on my bed. The assault played out in my head repeatedly, why hadn't I gone with Matt? If only I had gone with him, it would never have happened. For the first time in my life, I felt suicidal. Anita came around to see me and I blurted out what had happened. She was so angry at Raquel and said she could not believe she had done that to me. My brother showed up and took one look at me and I cried as he held me. The next day I was getting into the shower, and I forgot to put the cold water on, and I stepped into the boiling water. I felt this rush of adrenaline as the water hit my skin and for a moment, the pain disappeared. The next day I did it again but on purpose and behold my journey with self-harm began. It became a way of coping for me, as I was like a pressure cooker and the burning was the steam being let out. It was a release and it felt good. Raquel kept calling me, but I ignored her calls, so she would leave me messages on my answering machine.

"Hi Louise, I can't believe you're ignoring me! It was my birthday yesterday and you didn't even call me."

I would play the messages and delete them straight away; I would rather have died than see her. Matt came over a few times, but I could barely look at him. Anita and Dylan stayed with me as much as they could as I had completely stopped functioning. I took leave from my job and Anita would sit with me while I cried.

"Raquel called mum and dad sis," Dylan said one day while he was visiting me.

"What did she say?" I asked him as Dylan narrowed his eyes.

"I spoke to her, and she asked me what was wrong with you and why didn't you call her back. And I said, gee, why don't you tell me Raquel!"

I smiled at my brother and hugged him for standing up for me.

I had always been able to smoke myself to sleep, but since the assault I just could not switch my brain off. A few days later I finally took a valium that Anita had left me and fell into a deep sleep, and when I woke up about ten hours later there was a note on my bed from Anita.

"Dear Louise," it read. "I don't know how to tell you this, but I have strong feelings for you, and I want you to come and live with me and the kids. I want you to know you will be safe with me."

I sat there and cried and cried, as I knew I needed help, that I could not do it on my own anymore. I had a shower and a coffee, and I called Anita.

"Yes, I'll come and live with you," I said.

I felt like I had been drowning for a long time, and she was throwing me a lifeline. A couple of days later I called the owner of the flat and told him I was unwell and needed to end my lease early. Thankfully, he agreed, and the next day Anita showed up with an old friend and they proceeded to move all my stuff, not an easy task being up two flights of stairs. The guy was a terrible sleaze and kept hinting about how we were going to pay him. I could not stop crying the whole time and was not able to help much, so I wandered around putting my belongings into boxes. My dream of living this independent life was being stripped away from me, and I felt worthless, fragile and could not seem to make any decisions. I tried the best I could, and even after Anita started yelling at me to help more, I was not able to.

"God you're pathetic Louise," she shouted at me, but that just made me cry even harder.

I should have run when she started on me, but instead, I just went along with the move and before I knew it, I was in her house and my beloved flat was gone. I had loved that apartment and I had failed; I was in a huge hole and did not know how to climb out. Nothing felt real. I still mourned Stephan and did not feel right at Anita's, but it was too late now, I was stuck in a deep well of grief and I had moved in with someone I barely knew.

I started my life with Anita and her kids, and she was older than me and seemed to have it all together. Anita was a tomboy really, but I thought she was cool and sophisticated. She was an excellent listener and knew exactly what I had been through with my dad, as she had been abused by her dad and her older brother. Anita knew what it was like to be a survivor and I looked up to her. She had experienced trauma, and my past seemed like a picnic compared to hers. And then there were the drugs, and it did not take me long to move on to using needles, the snow cones no longer giving me a buzz or the oblivion I craved. Anita always said it was cleaner to use needles and more economical, so I listened to her and did what she said. She would shoot me up, and we would spend our days looking after her kids. I became completely hooked on speed, I loved the needle, and it was all I ever thought about. I wanted that adrenaline rush that took my breath away and made me forget. Forget about Stephan and the abuse, forget about how my life had gone to s***.

I took on a parenting role to her daughter and son that I was not ready for. Her kids were beautiful, and I got along with them great, but it did not take long for Anita to start abusing me. We would get in massive fights, usually after we had attempted to be intimate with one another, and she would attack me and scream the house down. Anita also abused her kids mentally and it was heartbreaking to watch. I felt trapped and helpless, and I was desperately unhappy but did not know how to leave. I stopped seeing my friends, and my mum and sister could not understand how I had gotten myself into this lesbian relationship. We were so dysfunctional, Anita and me, the only good times were when I was with the kids. I would take them to the park and felt like I could not just leave them. Somehow, I kept on working, and by then I had a new job as a driver for a childcare resource unit, and sometimes I would drive the van to our dealer's house to escape from Anita. Every time I saw mum, she would break down and cry.

"What are you doing Louise?" she would ask me tearily, but I had no answer for her.

Anita and I never had any money, we lived mostly on pasta, two-minute noodles and hot chips. I barely ate, my diet consisted of diet coke and iced coffee. I was down to 47 kg and my eczema was so bad that I was just shedding skin all over the house. The fights with Anita were at an all-time high as everything I did would make her angry, until one day I began to fight back. Anita was a lot bigger and heavier than me, but it turned out I was a ferocious fighter. We would go at it until one of us would back down and then we would be crying our eyes out together. Afterwards we would go and score drugs and be best friends again. It was a horrible cycle that never ended, and I barely knew who I was anymore. One night we were watching TV, and I made a comment that set her off, and before I knew it, Anita was up on the bed kicking the crap out of me. Then she pulled me onto the floor and started dragging me around the room by my hair. Something snapped in me that night, and I grabbed my bag and jumped out the window. I ran to a phone box and called Connie, and her boyfriend came to pick me up and took me back to their place. I knew I may have cracked a couple of ribs, because I could barely breathe without being in pain, so I stayed with them for a few days. Then I went back home to mum and dad, and mum took one look at me and burst into tears.

"You are skin and bone," she sobbed as she hugged me.

My dad was all over me, but I was too tired to even care. The next day I called the police and asked them to do a stand-by so I could get my stuff from Anita's. I was terrified of her and there was no way I was going to go there alone. The police said they could do it in a few days' time and I felt so relieved. The day arrived and my brother drove us there and pulled up in his Ute next to Anita's house. We sat there quietly waiting for the cops to come and I was feeling so sad as I missed the kids terribly, but I knew I could not go back. Anita opened the door, and she was wearing only a t shirt and no pants. She started yelling at us and the kids were crying and calling out to me. When the police arrived, I started to get my things from the house, and the kids were crying so much and asking me to come back, that I could barely look at their sweet faces.

"I can't take it anymore," I told them. "I'm so sorry."

We loaded all my stuff into the Ute, and after the cops had left, I was going down the path when Anita yelled something out at me, and I flew into a rage and went running back towards the house. She had locked the fly screen, but I was so angry I began to kick at the door madly. I ended up kicking it off the hinges and Dylan stopped me.

"You'll have to pay for a new door," Anita screamed at me.

I was glad to be away from her, but as we drove away, I felt overwhelmed with emotion; here I was, a 26-year-old with no real belongings, no car, and living with my parents once again. I was a drug addict and a skinny, beaten-up, emotional wreck, with no real direction in life. The first few weeks at home all I did was work and sleep. Mum kept trying to make me eat and fussed over me like a baby, and I was so anxious, depressed, and tried hard to avoid my dad. He was so happy to see me that he kept this stupid grin on his face, but oh how I hated him. He would cook barbecues and we would sit around playing happy families. I was feeling better physically since I had let the speed go, and Dylan and I would sit together after work and chat and laugh while we both smoked weed. Mum and dad were not happy about us having drugs in the house, but we would sneak out to the garage and smoke together after work.

Veronica and I chatted every week, and she would listen while I cried and sobbed about my life.

"I want you to come over for a holiday," Veronica said one day, as she was living in South Australia.

"I'll pay for your ticket," she suggested.

"Okay," I said. "I'll come for a visit."

I booked a week off work and flew to Adelaide and while Veronica worked, I wandered around during the day going for walks. We went to a few roaring parties with her friends, and I could tell she was worried about me. I was keen to break the lesbian thing, and flirted with every guy I could. I was still depressed but at least I was off the speed and not getting beaten up every day. I had no contact with Anita whatsoever and that suited me fine. Upon returning to Perth, I was keener than ever to rid myself of her and our relationship. At a petrol station one day I spontaneously lifted my shirt up and flashed a couple of guys in a nearby car, and they approached me.

"Hey sexy, do you wanna come to a party tonight?" one of them asked me.

I smiled at the one who spoke to me.

"Hey yeah sure," I answered, overjoyed that I was finally getting some male attention.

I called my brother's ex-girlfriend Sarah and asked if she wanted to come with me. It was not really a party, it was just a bunch of guys and me, Sarah and one other girl, but I did not care, I got really drunk and slept with a couple of the guys. Like I said I was desperate to shake off the female relationship thing, and I went home that night and the next weekend the guys invited me out again. Of course, I went, but Sarah refused saying she did not want to do anything as she had a boyfriend. This went on for a few weeks, me meeting these guys and sleeping with them, and sometimes it was the same guys, sometimes different. I was so reckless with my safety; I just did not care about myself at all. My parents were concerned as the phone at home was always ringing.

"Hey Louise's mum," they would say down the phone. "Is Louise around?"

My friends kept asking me what was going on, and my guy friends thought I was wild, but my girlfriends were so worried about me. I just laughed it off, but inside I felt like I was dying. I went on a few 'dates' with guys too, and I would always end up having sex with them, in their cars or in the park, and we were always taking drugs; it did not matter what it was. I fooled myself into believing I was happy, that it was empowering for me to be sleeping with so many men, and that I was in control over who I shared my body with. That much was true, but I was far from happy. I was still having flashbacks most nights and only slept when I was drunk or stoned and when I think back now on my behaviour, I am genuinely shocked. I was so careless and could have been seriously hurt or injured on multiple occasions. Christmas 2000 came and went, and my behaviour was out of control. When I saw my friends, I was not a particularly good friend at all, especially to my female friends. I would flirt outrageously with my guy mates, some of whom were dating my girlfriends, but I was so far gone by that stage that I did not care who I hurt.

One day around February 2001, I was walking our dog in the local park, when I met a tall, good-looking guy with a huge dog. We got talking and instantly hit it off and we went back to his place to smoke weed. Tom was gorgeous with surfy kind of hair, and he was charming and easy to talk to. We ended up sleeping together, and I fell for him straight away, so we spent the next few months together and I stopped seeing all the other guys. Sometimes the guys would call the house, or my phone and I would ignore them. Tom had separated from his wife, but her stuff was still at his house which was a little weird, but we got along well, and I introduced him to Tania. We would spend time together at his place, smoking and drinking and even Dylan came over a couple of times. I was still working driving the van, and Tom was a welcome distraction from my parents. We dated for a few months and my feelings for him grew stronger. Tom's parents were wealthy and we even house - sat for them one weekend. He was the black sheep of the family, as he had a huge bust up with his brother over the family business before I met him. I had well and truly fallen in love with Tom, and I thought that he felt the same way about me.

"I love being with you," he would often say, and I took that as a promising sign.

One night I stayed at his house and when we had sex, we decided to do it for a while without a condom, Tom ended up pulling out at the last minute, but I knew straight away that we may have conceived. After Tom fell asleep, I wandered around his house for a while convinced that we had made a baby. Then I told myself I was being dramatic, and I forgot all about it. A few weeks later I got sick and could not stop vomiting, and I did not realise that I could be pregnant, I just thought I had a bad case of flu. I was so exhausted I could barely get up out of bed, and when I went to Tom's house, I would always fall asleep early.

"What's wrong with you?" Tom would ask me.

"I don't know," I would answer sleepily.

Eventually mum ended up taking me to the doctor as I could not look at food without vomiting. I had a blood test and went back to the medical centre two days later, and as I sat in his office, the doctor looked at me.

"Ah yes, you're pregnant, aren't you?" he said, and I was so shocked that I just sat there looking at him with my mouth wide open.

"I am?" I managed to stammer, and he gave me a broad grin.

"Yes! You are expecting."

Somehow, I made it out into the waiting room and told mum, and she jumped for joy. Mum was so excited that she ran into the house to tell my dad, but I did not really know how to react, as Tom and I had not been together that long, and he was still married! I sat and called Veronica who cried with me, and we talked for a long time.

"Are you going to have the baby at your mum and dads?" she asked me, and I sat there for a while not saying anything.

"I guess I have no choice," I ended up replying.

I saw Tom the next day and we sat on the couch together.

"I'm pregnant," I told him, but he just sat there not saying a word.

I stared at him. "Did you hear me?" I asked as Tom looked at me.

"Well, you'll have to have an abortion," he said, and I felt my heart freeze.

"An abortion?" I asked him. "Are you f***ing kidding me?!"

I sat there with my mouth open looking at him.

"I am not having an abortion," I stated, and he stared back at me.

"Well, I don't want a baby," he said, and I felt the tears welling up.

"Fine," I said. "I'll have it without you."

I left his house an emotional wreck as that had not gone how I had planned. Perhaps I had thought he was going to suggest we move in together or something. For the next few weeks, I could not do anything without throwing up, the only thing I could keep down was Arrowroot biscuits. When I told Tania she cried with me and then she called me one day crying herself.

"Guess what," she sobbed to me. "I'm pregnant too!"

Her boyfriend did not want their baby either, I could not believe that we were going to have babies together, and we talked every day about how we would support one another. I was so tired all the time that I could barely get out of bed. I chatted to mum, and she suggested I quit my job and go on the dole. I just cried and cried, as I had always worked, sure, I had had my fair share of jobs over the years, but I had always worked to support myself. Ever since I was 15, I had held down some sort of job. It was a big blow for my pride to give up working and I spent most days crying about Tom, and I kept thinking he would change his mind. I also went to see him most nights and we were still sleeping together. I was so slender that I was not showing at all, and I thought that if he was having sex with me, then he might change his mind about the baby. My mum was the most excited, it was like it had given her a new lease on life.

"All I have ever wanted to be is a nanna," she would say, as she came home with endless stuff for the baby.

My dad was equally happy and kept trying to hug me and would often come up behind me and pinch my bum so I tried to avoid him the best I could. I decided to win Tom back by sleeping with him every chance I got, and he never said no, which was confusing for me. I had given up all my vices, even drinking coffee and now only ate healthy food. By four months I was eating again and then I was ravenous, devouring everything in sight, and I began to put on weight. Dana was also so excited, and she and my mum decorated the spare room as a nursery. I read pregnancy books and walked every day, and as I walked, I would rub my belly and talk to my growing baby and began to feel hopeful for our future together. I did pregnancy yoga and tried to be as healthy as possible, and I calmed down a lot and began to feel a lot more at peace. Mum bought things for the baby every week, and I got increasingly excited. Things at home were not that good though, my dad and Dylan were fighting every other day, and I was worried about the tension in the house. But I loved my baby, and I was determined to give us a good life. At twenty weeks I found out I was having a boy and promptly named him Lachlan. I had stopped seeing Tom by that stage as I had come to realise that he did not want either of us, or that it was not meant to be. As Lachlan grew and grew, I felt special and important for the first time in my life. I saw my old friends, and they were so happy that I had settled down, and I spent most of my time with mum and Dana. I talked to Tania a lot too, who was having a boy also, and it was lovely to be able to share pregnancy with her. The nursery at mum's was beautiful with yellow walls and Winnie the Pooh decals, and Dana came with me to prenatal classes as she was going to be my birth partner. I walked our dog often and saw Tom regularly at the park.

"How is your health?" he always asked.

It was infuriating, as that was all that he would say to me, so when I was about twenty-five weeks, I ended up calling his mum Joan.

"Hi, this is Louise, um, I was with Tom for a while," I said, worried she might not remember me.

"Hi Louise, how are you?" she asked as I took a deep breath.

"I don't really know how to say this but I'm pregnant and Tom's the father."

There was a long pause, and to say that she was shocked was an understatement. Joan told me that she had no idea, and it was a weird conversation indeed. That night Tom called me, and he was angry.

"I can't believe you told mum you are pregnant," he yelled at me down the phone.

"Too bad," I said. "She has a right to know, and you weren't going to tell her."

That made him even more angry, but I did not care, they were going to be grandparents whether Tom liked it or not.

Dylan was heavily into drugs my whole pregnancy, and he was always fighting with my dad which made things so tense at home. Tom ended up offering to have Dylan at his place as the arguing was out of control. When dad would go away for work, I was always relieved, as he was still touchy feely with me and I hated it, and I hated him. To be honest, I was not convinced I had done the right thing moving back in with my parents. I had niggles in the back of my mind, but considering Tom did not want me, what else was I supposed to do? Dylan stayed at Tom's for a week or two, and then one day he called me, and he was really upset.

"Sis, I have something to tell you and you're not going to like it."

I listened with disbelief as he told me that Tom had a new girlfriend and he had seen the two of them having sex in the lounge room. I felt my heart drop and as I confronted Tom, he confirmed my worst fears; he had met someone else, and it was over between us. Deep down I kept holding out hope that we would eventually get back together, and everyone kept telling me that once Lachlan was born that he would change his mind about us. But hearing Tom say it was over was like a knife in my heart, and for the next few days I cried an ocean of tears. I kept writing Tom letters telling him how I felt about him, but I never sent them. As the days turned into weeks and months, I knew deep down there was no hope for us. I kept walking every day and singing and talking to Lachlan, and slowly I felt stronger and more purposeful. I washed all Lachlan's clothes, and then washed them again. I packed my hospital bag and then re packed it, and the day before I went into labour I was cleaning the house like a mad woman. Mum kept laughing at me and saying I was "nesting."

Chapter 8

lachlan

On the 13th of December 2001, I went into labour at 5.30am. I woke with cramps and went to the toilet and there was a bloody show in my underwear. I could not believe it; he was finally coming! I ran into mum's room and told her what was going on, and she jumped out of bed and began to make breakfast. After an hour or so I called Tania, and she asked me what the contractions felt like.

"Oh, they're not so bad," I said breezily.

I went and woke Dylan up, who was once again living with us.

"Hey, you need to hold that baby in sis. No way you're having it on my birthday!" he joked.

I called Dana and she came over at about 8am, and by then I was having more contractions, and they were getting a little more painful. A few hours after walking around and breathing through the contractions, Dana drove me to hospital, but I was disappointed to learn I was only 3cms dilated. They gave me Panadol and a valium, and we went to Dana's house where I tried to have a little sleep but was not able to. I got into the shower and stayed in there for around three hours as I was determined to remain upright and active for the whole labour. By this time, it was about 10pm and the pain was getting more intense so Richard drove me and Dana back to the hospital, but I could not believe it when they told me I was only 6cm dilated! It had already been fourteen hours and I was no closer to full labour. The next few hours were tough, the contractions were coming regularly, and they were very painful. I refused to have an epidural, (I have no idea why), so instead they gave me a pethidine injection and I started on the gas. I spent a few hours in the bath glued to the gas, and I was in absolute agony. When they checked me around one o'clock in the morning, I was still only 6cm dilated, and I burst into tears. That is when they decided to break my water to try and get things moving. So, the doctor broke my water, and it was excruciating, and he was so rough and not nice to me. I had to laugh when my amniotic fluid just gushed out of me like a tidal wave and splashed him in the face.

"Goodness," one of the midwives commented. "That's the most amniotic fluid I have ever seen!"

By that time, I'd had so much gas I was giggling like a schoolgirl, and mum had picked this wacky jazz music to play, and at one point I said, "I'm having a lounge bar labour." At 5am they checked me, but I was only 8cms dilated and by that time, I was delirious with pain.

"Where's the drugs? Where's the drugs?!" I screamed.

My sister was amazingly supportive through the whole thing, and she held my hand through all the contractions and helped me stay as calm as I could. By 6am the contractions were doubling up and I was in a bad way, I had been in labour for 24 hours and Lachlan just was not coming. The anesthetist saw me and said,

"You're in a lot of pain, aren't you," but I just yelled at him.

"Where have you been? You've been out playing golf, haven't you?"

I had no concept of what time it was and to say I had gone to another level in my mind was an understatement. I had the epidural, but it was so painful as there was no real break in between contractions. I could not think clearly at all, and finally, the epidural kicked in and at about 8am they checked me again, but I was only around 9cm dilated. I think that's when things started to go downhill, every time I had a contraction, Lachlan's heart rate would drop, and I was absolutely exhausted by that stage and could barely lift my head off the pillow. The doctors then decided that it would be best if I had a caesarean section, but I burst into tears. All my plans of having a smooth birth were going out the window and I felt devastated that things were not going at all how I imagined they would. Lachlan was distressed and confused, and it showed on the ultrasound that his head was disengaging, and he was starting to go backwards up the birth canal. Dana cried and held my hand.

"You have to be brave Lou, we need to get Lachlan out safely and that's all that matters," she told me.

I signed the paperwork with tears running down my face, and Dana was crying too and hugging me. My mum started to get all dramatic at that stage.

"I've got cancer," she announced. "I'm going into the theatre with Louise."

My poor sister, she had been there throughout my whole labour but I was too exhausted and out of it to tell my mum that Dana was going in there with me, and not her. After an entire day and night, Dana would not even get to see Lachlan be born. As I lay on the bed and they wheeled me into the theatre, I could tell when the contractions were coming but because of the epidural, they were not as painful. I was no longer upset, I just wanted it to be over. At 9.40am Lachlan was born, and I could not believe the feeling I got when they put him into my arms. He was gorgeous with dark hair and blue eyes, but unfortunately, he had been stuck in my birth canal and was trying to crown with his forehead, so he had a cone shaped head. I did not care about that one bit, as he was the most beautiful thing I had ever seen, and was a healthy weight of 3.75 kg, a lot bigger than the 7lbs my doctor had said! I felt this rush of love for him, and all the pain of the last 24 hours disappeared. I finally had my baby boy, and I could not be happier.

That night my poor bubba was so exhausted that he fed on my colostrum and then fell into a deep sleep. I slept too, with him lying next to me in his bassinette. The next few days were a bit of a blur, I was in a lot of pain and could not really move around a lot. I was too scared to look at my wound, so I just pretended it was not there. My milk came in and I started feeding him, but it was not easy, and it hurt, so I would grit my teeth as he latched on. Mum and dad came in to see me every day, and they were giddy with excitement, like it was them who had given birth. My friends popped in and Lachlan got loads of presents. On the third day I called Tom and told him Lachlan had been born, and I tried not to cry as he told me he had been on a fishing trip. The next day he came to see us, and it felt so weird seeing him hold Lachlan. Tom seemed so happy, and he sat for ages holding him. After he left, I just cried and cried, and the nurse took Lachlan for me so I could have a sleep. Two days later I was discharged from hospital and mum and dad drove us home. I felt teary but also a sense of purpose that I had not felt before, surely this was the break I so desperately needed after so much turmoil. When I looked at Lachlan, all that I had been through seemed to fade away. It was not easy caring for him after the surgery though, but I was finally able to look at my wound, and it was not as bad as I thought and, to my surprise, the surgeon had not used stitches or staples, but glue. It was a neat little line, and I felt relieved that it was already healing so well. Every day I got stronger, and I was also surprised at how much weight I was losing due to breast feeding. Lachlan was a good sleeper, only waking up once or twice in the night, but I did not like the early wake ups and would sit out in the lounge room just dozing in the chair while he fed. My mum was so happy, and she loved spending time with Lachlan. She was an amazing help to me in those first few weeks, and Dana also came by every day, and she was an enormously proud auntie. My dad hovered over me, but I did not care, I was in love with my baby and that was all that mattered.

My brother was living with us, but his behaviour was unpredictable. He and dad would fight all the time and one night Dylan picked up Lachlan and just screamed in his face, and I was gutted. Even though I loved my brother, Lachlan's safety was the most important thing to me, and it was so upsetting to see the effects the speed had on Dylan. That night dad lost the plot towards Dylan and kicked him out of the house, so he went and stayed with some mates. It was heartbreaking, as I loved my brother, and I knew it was the drugs affecting his behaviour, but I no longer trusted him. Poor mum was so upset, but I think she could see how badly Dylan was behaving and it would be for the best if he left.

Becoming a mum was the best thing that had ever happened to me. After Lachlan was born, I would just sit and hold him for hours, marveling at how I had created something so precious and beautiful. I loved his little face; he was a joy to be around and every day I fell more in love with him.

Tania had given birth to a tiny little baby boy in the first week of January. She had named him Michael, and we would spend time together with our new babies. I treasured our friendship, and we would sit at her place in her armchairs trying to nap when the babies did.

"I'm so tired," Tania said to me. "I've forgotten what sleep is!"

Lachlan reached his milestones early, he sat up at three and a half months, crawled at seven months, and walked at ten months. He was a highly active baby, was so curious, and he loved exploring the park. We spent every minute together and Lachlan talked early, around thirteen months. He had a billion questions to ask me, and I would patiently try to answer them. He loved books and musical videos, and every morning mum would take Lachlan into her garden while I had a nap or a shower, she would show him all her plants and flowers and I saw joy in my mum I had never seen before. Lachlan followed his nanna around everywhere she went, and it was lovely to watch. My love for him seemed to grow every day.

Tom came to see Lachlan most weeks, and he would sit with him in his sandpit, and he seemed to like being a dad. I felt up and down about Tom, I was still in love with him I guess, but a part of me had accepted that he did not want a relationship with me. If he was good to Lachlan, then that was all that mattered. Lachlan's 1st birthday arrived, and we had a huge party for him. Mum and dad went all out and invited Tom's family and all our friends. I loved being a mum and felt so happy for the first time in my life. Tom was also developing a close relationship with our son, and that pleased me a lot. Lachlan continued to develop and grow, and by fourteen months of age could say about 30 words.

I am not sure when things started to change, around the time Lachlan was about sixteen months of age, he started to not enjoy cuddles and cried when he peed. He went on antibiotics and then developed a rash on his groin and bottom. I did not think anything of it and decided to put Lachlan into day care so I could have a break, and he loved it and seemed to really enjoy being around the other kids. I started to chat to a couple of guys on MSN messenger, and one was Martin and he lived in Sydney. He was nice, and we chatted every day for a few weeks. One day I came home from the shops and saw Lachlan on my father's lap, and my dad just looked at me and I froze in fear. I felt like time stood still as Lachlan wriggled out of my father's grasp, ran towards me, and suddenly I just knew that my dad was touching him. I turned and left the room and went and called Martin, and I felt a rush of panic as I paced around outside crying and asking him what I should do. Martin was clear when he told me I needed to come to Melbourne and stay with him, so I called Dylan's girlfriend whose parents owned a travel agency, and she booked me a ticket. My parents were horrified and told me I should not be going, but I did not care and just wanted to be as far away from my dad as possible.

When I got to the airport Martin was nothing like I thought he would be, he did not look like his picture, and I almost ran in the other direction when I saw him approaching. We went to his parent's place for dinner, and it was very awkward. By the time we got to Martin's house, Lachlan and I were exhausted, and I was too tired to care about anything but sleep. The next few days were pleasant enough, but Martin suffered from OCD, and as I had never seen it before, it was hard to live with. We could not really go out much as he would always have to return home to check the locks or the stove. Lachlan was happy though, playing in the back yard and watching his videos. I was not sleeping much and stupidly one night I had sex with Martin. I instantly regretted it and felt bad for deceiving him, as I was not in love with him at all. He also was not that good with Lachlan, getting frustrated with his toys and stuff around. I felt trapped and I did not know what to do. I called my cousin Jayden who lived about an hour or two away and told him what was going on, and his wife Bianca came to pick us up and we went to their house. They had two young children, and Lachlan was so happy to have other kids to play with. I felt bad for Martin, as he was such a nice guy, but had already started talking about marriage and I knew I could not stay. Jayden and Bianca had a beautiful house near the city, and I was so glad to be there, and Lachlan settled in quickly.

During the day we would go out together, to shops and parks, and it was just lovely. Lachlan was so happy, especially when we would walk over to pick my little cousins up from school. After two weeks I knew I had to go home, so I reluctantly booked my flight. My mum was so happy when we got back, as I knew she had really missed Lachlan. My dad was away with work so that made it easier to settle back in, I had certainly not missed him at all, and Lachlan had seemed so happy having time away too.

Once I was home, it was like a switch had gone on in my brain and I could not turn it off, I stopped sleeping and could not let my boy out of my sight, it was awful. I was so anxious that I could not eat either. Lachlan went back to daycare, and I tried to sleep but I could not, as I was in a constant state of panic about my dad. I ended up confiding in the centre director one day, and she said that I had to leave home. That was easier said than done, but I started to look for a place for Lachlan and me to live. I would drop him at daycare and go and look at properties, but there was not much choice as I was not employed. Eventually I found one and I got the bond and two weeks rent from Homeswest.

I went home and broke the news to my parents, mum was decidedly upset, but I was a complete wreck, not able to sleep, or eat; I could not let my emotions cloud my judgement and I had to protect my son. I started packing up all our stuff and mum eventually came around and she went out and brought us some things like sheets and towels. I still had quite a bit of kitchen equipment left over from when I lived with Stephan, so I packed that into boxes.

The day arrived and my friends came over early and helped, and I was so grateful to them as I was a bit of a mess. We managed to get it all done in one day, and that night I collapsed into bed and slept all night. The flat was not great, but it was safe, and Lachlan had his own room. The next few days we just pottered around and settled in, but Lachlan did not like his room much and would often end up in my bed. I did not care though, I loved having him right next to me so I could keep an eye on him. This peace came over me as I finished setting up the flat, and it was lovely to wake up next to Lachlan every day. I got to know the other people in the building, and I made friends with Nadine who lived next door to me. Lachlan went to Tom's every second weekend, which was hard at first, but he was a good dad and Lachlan got so excited when he came to pick him up. I was still a bit of a mess about my dad, but I knew it was important for him to have a relationship with Tom. I liked being on my own, but I was tired all the time, and I spent my alone time sleeping and catching up with my friends. It was hard doing all the chores and washing, but somehow, I managed to keep up. I started dating an African guy, Frank, in our building. He had sponsored his cousins from Uganda, so they were living with him, and I got to know them well and spent many weekends with them. I started toilet training Lachlan, and I got him a potty and he was good at using it. A few times I caught him with his finger inside his bottom. A day or two passed and he was doing it more frequently.

"Sweetie I've noticed you're putting your fingers into your bottom a lot," I said to him, and he looked up at me from the potty.

"Yeah, mama that's what papa does," he said.

My world came to a complete stop, and I sat there in a daze as he ran off to play with his toys. Something broke inside me, as I realised that my long-held fears were true; my father had abused Lachlan. That night I called Tania after I had put Lachlan to bed.

"What am I going to do?" I wailed down the phone to her.

"I think you should take him to the children's hospital," she answered. "Tell them what has been going on."

So, the next morning I called the hospital, and they told me to bring Lachlan in for an examination. I felt like a zombie that day, just going through the motions of getting Lachlan ready and making him breakfast. I felt like I was outside my body watching myself arrive at the hospital and find a car park. I watched two doctors examine my son and I was on the ceiling the whole time. We stayed for hours and then finally we were allowed to go home, but I was so stressed that I called a friend of my brother's and asked him to bring me some weed. I had not used it since before I was pregnant, but I was freaking out and did not know how else to cope. That night when Lachlan was in bed, I snuck out onto my tiny balcony and smoked. In the back of my mind, I had known the abuse had happened, that was why I had moved us both out of there, but I never expected Lachlan to just blurt it out like that. And it was not as if I had coerced Lachlan or told him what to say, it was his own admission to me. The department of communities had assigned us a caseworker and he came over a few days later. He wanted to know everything about my dad, and I talked to him for hours.

"Louise, I think you need to confront your parents and tell them what Lachlan said to you," the case worker said, but I just stared at him.

"Are you f***ing kidding me?" I blurted out, and he smiled kindly at me.

"They need to know about these behaviours. It will give a good indication of your dad's guilt about the situation," he explained.

I sat there nodding, feeling like he had just suggested I go and put a bomb in my parents' house. I did not want to do it; I was so angry with my dad for breaking my trust, how could he have done that to my son? But I was also angry at myself for living with them in the first place.

"Try not to blame yourself," the case worker told me, but I did.

Dylan was supportive of me in those days, and his girlfriend Laura was also amazing. I told my sister about the abuse, funnily enough my brother-in-law said he was not surprised. But it was hard for Dana to cope with the truth, and I felt for her. I guess as a survivor, it was just something that I had become accustomed to. The following weekend Lachlan was at Tom's, so I went to mum and dad's place, and I had a huge lump in my throat as I pulled up outside their house. I walked in and sat on the couch and took a deep breath.

"So," I began, "Lachlan has been displaying these behaviours."

Well, that was it, my dad jumped up and began to yell at me.

"Oh, and I suppose it's all my fault, is it?"

I sat there in shock at his reaction as he paced around yelling at me. I had not been specific about the behaviours at all, but he flew into a rage so much that his whole face was red, and he was shaking all over. Mum was no better, as she started to wipe the kitchen bench frantically.

"You're just a whore and a drug addict," she screamed at me.

By then I realised it was no use; they were not going to listen. I left feeling depressed, and I did not know what to do. My mum was always going to support my dad and I did not know why I thought it would be any different, she had failed to protect me when I was a child, so why would she protect Lachlan now? The next few days my depression got worse, and I found it hard to get motivated and do the housework. When I was awake, I found it hard to focus. Worse, I had to tell Tom and that was hard.

"Are you sure?" he kept asking me one day when I invited him over.

"Yes, I'm sure," I answered him. "Lachlan told me what my dad did, and I believe him."

I also had to tell him about my own abuse, but he just looked at me and did not say much. Tom's mum Joan took Lachlan out for me so I could rest, but all I could do was lie in bed and cry, as the sadness was overwhelming, and I was struggling to comprehend what had happened. Lachlan would be playing with his cars and watching his shows on tv, but I struggled to interact with him. What kind of mother was I? I could not even protect my own son; I had failed him. The sadness got worse and worse and slowly the flat became messy and dirty. Everything felt overwhelming, and I made

Lachlan food, but I barely ate it myself. Nadine tried to help me by coming over and offering to watch Lachlan for me, but I felt myself sinking into a deep depression. Our case worker came over to the flat a couple of times.

"I'm sorry Louise," he said one day, and I felt my heart drop.

"Unfortunately, there is no physical evidence that your dad touched Lachlan sexually. There is no proof it happened," he explained.

I stared at him with tears in my eyes.

"But Lachlan told me himself!" I said but the case worker shook his head.

"Even though Lachlan told you in his own words what happened to him, there is no actual physical proof it happened to him."

I was furious, as was with me, my dad had been more gentle than rough, and it had left no physical sign that it had occurred. I was so disappointed as it had taken a lot of courage to get help and now there was nothing I could do. Due to 'insufficient evidence' it looked like my dad would get away with it.

"That's total bulls*** Lou," Tania said to me that night on the phone and I agreed.

A few days later Mum came to see me, which was rare, as she did not often come to the flat. She sat on the couch not looking at me, and she was fidgeting in her seat and looking extremely uncomfortable.

"I know why you did it," she blurted out and I looked over at her as she played with a thread on my couch.

"I mean I know why you did what you did, you did it for Lachlan and I understand why," she said, and I sat there feeling shocked that she was telling me that she believed me.

Then mum got up and made a cup of tea and that was the end of that. Some days Joan looked after Lachlan for me, so I could attend counselling appointments. One day the counsellor took one look at me and knew I was in a bad way.

"I can't go back home," I sobbed to her.

"Louise, I am going to write a letter to get you admitted to the hospital," she said.

I called Joan and told her I was not coming home.

"I can't look after him," I cried down the phone.

"It's okay Louise, I'll take Lachlan home and we'll figure something out," Joan told me.

I sat in the counsellor's office and waited for my sister to come and pick me up. I was heartbroken that I would have to leave Lachlan, but I could not be a good mum to him while I was so unwell.

Once I arrived at the hospital, I went through a grueling five-hour admission with a psychiatrist, and he wanted to know everything about my life, so I told him. At the end he looked at me for a while without speaking.

"You know I could diagnose you with bi-polar or borderline personality disorder," he finally said as he looked at his pages of notes. "But I'm not going to because you are too smart and too self-aware for that. I think you have delayed post-natal depression."

The psychiatrist admitted me and once I got to my room I fell into an exhausted sleep. The mental health ward was chilled out, and they gave me some of the drug Seroquel for the first time, and it made me feel all floaty and not hysterical. I chatted to the nurses and doctors and for the first time in a few months I slept properly. My sister bought Lachlan to see me regularly, and I missed him terribly, but he was coping okay. I was so grateful for Dana in those first few days as, while being apart from Lachlan, I felt like I was missing an arm. After two weeks I found out mum was also in hospital for a shoulder replacement. The cancer was slowly eating away her bones and she came to see me, but when I saw her, I just felt numb. I met someone while I was in hospital, his name was Shane, and he was younger than me. We started spending all our time together and it felt nice to have someone who cared about me. He had bipolar disorder, but that did not seem to worry me, and after another week or two I decided I was ready to go home, and I discharged myself. I went and picked Lachlan up and he was overjoyed to see me.

"Mama, mama you're back!" he called out to me as I scooped him up into my arms. I had my boy back and that was all that mattered.

I felt hopeful that things would be better, as I was on the Seroquel regularly and it seemed to help me stay calm. A few weeks later I let Shane move in with me, and he was great at cleaning and helped me care for Lachlan. My mum was back in hospital, but I was in denial of how sick she was really was. Things with Shane and I were not that good either, as we had started fighting all the time about bills and money. Worse, I had met someone else in hospital who had ties to a bikie gang, and I had started using speed again. I slept with this guy Callum a few times, but he was abusive and manipulative, and I knew I was only around him for the drugs. Poor Shane knew about Callum but did not say much about it. My mood was so up and down and so was Shane's, but to his credit though, he was particularly good to Lachlan and started to take him to daycare during the day. I was all over the place emotionally and tried my best to stay connected with my counsellor. I desperately wanted to be a good mum to Lachlan as I loved spending time with him. He was so clever and loving and was such a good boy, but I continued to struggle and did not know what else to do to help myself.

Chapter 9

mum

My mum was in hospital again and I knew she was nearing the end, but I was in denial and could not face the reality of losing her. One night Shane and I got into a terrible argument, and he ended up attacking me and throwing the tv through my bedroom window. I called the cops, and an ambulance took him to hospital. They released Shane the next day, but I had packed up his things and told him that he could not come back. But a few days later I let him come back, and someone told Tom about what had happened with Shane, and he was not happy.

"I'm fine Tom," I kept reassuring him. "Things with Shane aren't that bad."

Of course, things were not fine, but I was not going to admit that to Tom.

Mum went home from the hospital and then a few days later she was admitted to a hospice.

"I'm just going to have a little rest and then I'll go back home," she said.

I started to see mum every day, but a few days later she went downhill, so I took Lachlan to see her one last time and I had to fight back the tears as I watched him cuddle her. I took Lachlan's to Tom's house but when I got back, mum had stopped talking. I sat with her and sang softly to her, and I could not believe that she was really going to die, it seemed like some awful dream. Dana had been at the hospice with mum constantly and was exhausted, so she had a little rest, while I sat with mum holding her hand, and dad sat at the back of the room with a book. It was just so bloody typical of him to have his nose in a book while his wife lay dying a few feet away from him.

At one point he looked up and said, "it's time to go Clara."

I hated him at that moment as he could not even come over to her and hold her hand. After a while mum began to breathe more heavily and then noisily, then it was like gulping breaths and then it was rattling, and I knew that mum was close to going.

I squeezed her hand and whispered to her, "I forgive you."

Mum was gasping for air, and I yelled at Dylan to get my sister. Dana came running back into the room with Richard, and mum opened her eyes and seemed to look at every single one of us before she gave a big sigh and then she was gone. After that everything was a blur really and I could not believe that she was dead. It hit me hard, and I struggled to cope. Dana organised the funeral with dad because I was not functioning, and I felt so bad for dumping it all on Dana, but I could not seem to get it together. Tom was looking after Lachlan a few days before the funeral, so I called him to say I was coming to pick him up and Tom said he was not going to let him come home with me.

"What do you mean?" I cried down the phone to him.

"You're not a fit mother," Tom said. "Don't come and get him."

He hung up on me and I called Dylan and Laura, and they came over. It turned out that my sister and my friends had all written letters about me to give to Tom, even my mum had written one before she died. The letters said that I was not capable of looking after Lachlan, and that he should live with Tom instead. Even though I knew deep down that they were right, I felt gutted and that my entire world was collapsing around me.

That night I called the police and asked them to do a welfare check on Lachlan, as he had never been away from me for more than two days. The police called me back saying that Lachlan had seemed okay, but I felt like I could not breathe or function without him, and I kept crying hysterically. By day four I was a wreck and could not sleep. In desperation I ended up calling Anita to ask how I could get Lachlan back. I knew she was experienced with the family court, and I did not know who else to call. On the morning of mum's funeral Anita and I went to the magistrate's court and filed a recovery order. I have to say that Anita was extremely supportive and knew exactly what to do. After a few hours, to my relief, the order was granted. Shane ended up coming to the funeral with me, and we made it with minutes to spare. But I was angry at Tom because I had missed mum's viewing. It was so hot that day and we all crowded around under the marquee. I sang a song to mum, and as I stood there, I could feel her looking down on me and it filled me with peace. My Aunt Francine had come over for the funeral and she hugged me tightly. We had the wake at mum and dads, and it felt so weird being there without her. That evening, I took the recovery order to Tom's, and he finally let Lachlan come home. By then it had been about six days, and he was so happy to see me that he came running into my arms and I tried not to burst into tears when I held him.

"Mama where were you? Why didn't you get me," he kept asking me.

I had to explain to him that Nanna had died, and he was terribly upset. Later Lachlan told me that he had not been to Tom's much at all. He had been sent to a friend of Tom's girlfriend's and I was furious. Tom had taken him from me and had accused me of not looking after him properly, yet he had not even taken care of his own son himself! I was so angry with him, but I decided that I would clean up my act and stop drinking and taking speed, as I knew it was not helping me. A few weeks later Laura's mum asked me if I would like a job as a Qualified Educator at her childcare centre and I agreed. Lachlan and I would get up early and go to the centre and open it up, Lachlan would eat breakfast and watch the tv while I set up all the equipment. It was tiring and the days were long, but after a couple of weeks I was up to date with my rent and other bills. I was still struggling with the housework, but we had our little routine and Lachlan loved being around all the other kids at the centre. After talking to Tom, I agreed to let him start seeing Lachlan again on the weekends. He was not a bad dad, he had acted out of love and concern for his son, and I could not begrudge him that. I also finally had the courage to end things with Shane.

"I can change," he cried down the phone to me, "I'll get better."

But I had to be firm and after a week or two, he stopped calling me. A few months later I started seeing another guy in my building, Isaac. He was sweet, and we spent most weekends together. I started getting closer to Nadine as well and she was supportive. I was still smoking marijuana and Nadine would look after Lachlan, so I did not have to take him with me when I went and scored. I would put Lachlan to bed, and sneak outside and smoke. It was the only way that I could cope with losing mum and the massive responsibility of working and raising my son. Plus, what my dad had done to Lachlan felt like a giant cloud over me.

Dylan called me one day.

"He's selling the house sis; dad is selling the house."

I was devastated, as it was a gorgeous house, and it was the only thing we had left of mum. I could not believe dad could let it go like that, it really hurt. We also found out that dad had a new girlfriend, and we were all in such shock to think that he could move on from mum so quickly. Her name was Miranda, and dad was going to buy the half of her house that belonged to her ex-husband. So, the house was sold, and dad got rid of mum's clothes and shoes. I went over there and saw Miranda packing up our stuff in boxes, and it felt so surreal to see this strange woman in my mum's house going through all her things. I really hated dad at that point, I thought he was weak and had betrayed all of us. I missed my mum every single day and most nights I would put Lachlan to bed and sit on my porch smoking and wishing things could have been different. I was angry that mum had died, and my dad was still alive. It was not fair that she would not get to see Lachlan grow up. I would crawl into bed next to Lachlan and hold him close and cry myself to sleep. I felt empty inside without her, and even though our relationship had been a little fractured at times, she was still my mum and my heart felt completely broken.

Chapter 10

julian

Lachlan's 3rd birthday came and went, and I was still working full time, now in the 0–2-year-old room. I started planning a little holiday down south for Lachlan, Nadine, and me. We booked a couple of nights in a caravan park, and I drove us down in Nadine's car. The first few days were lovely, and we went out for lunch and to the river. Lachlan played on the playground, and it felt good to be away from work. There was another family with us at the campground, and after a day or two I met some kids at the swings and Lachlan started playing with them. They started chatting with me and I was introduced to their dad Julian. He was a lot older than me but seemed nice enough, and we spent the next day together at the river and all the kids got along well. He had two girls and a boy, and it was nice for Lachlan to have other children to play with.

"I'm not sure about this guy Lou," Nadine said to me, but he was older and seemed to have it all together, so I thought it was okay.

Julian told me that the children's mum had died the previous year from breast cancer, and I felt for him being on his own with the kids. We said goodbye at the end of our trip and Julian gave me his phone number. A few weeks went by, and he was calling me most days, and we would talk for an hour or two and he said he wanted me to come up for a holiday to see him. Julian seemed so keen on me, and I was flattered.

"Lou, I'm telling you this guy is bad news, you shouldn't be going," Nadine said to me, but I did not listen to her.

After a few more phone calls and with Julian asking me every day, I finally agreed. I asked dad if I could take his station wagon as I was not sure my old Ford would make the journey. I packed and drove up there with Lachlan, and it was a long drive. Lachlan fell asleep on the way but once we arrived, he was so excited to see Erica, Belinda, and Calvin again. They all ran off to play together, but Julian's house was not what I had expected at all, it was messy and littered with toys and he apologized that he was not a particularly good housekeeper. I decided to let it slide and we sat down and had a coffee and a chat. I knew it had not even been a year since his partner had passed away and again, I felt for him. Julian's adult daughter Amanda was there, and we hit it off immediately. That night Julian expected me to cook dinner which I thought was a bit odd as I was the guest. He did not seem to have much food but showed me two huge fish fillets in the fridge.

"Are your kids going to eat this fish?" I asked him, and he shrugged.

"Probably not," he answered.

I looked through the cupboards, found some pasta, and ended up making spaghetti for the kids. I cooked the fish for Julian and I and we sat down to eat, and I was starting to feel awkward around him, but he raved about what a good cook I was. Calvin was eight years old, he was such a sweet boy with big brown eyes, and he liked to play with his action men outside and preferred to play by himself. Belinda was four and was so adorable, and even though she stayed close to her dad, she and Lachlan were running around chasing each other and that pleased Julian. Erica was seven and was extremely helpful, and she was chatty and quite affectionate towards me.

The kids played together until bedtime and Lachlan, and I went to sleep on the lumpy futon. The next night Julian asked me to put Lachlan to bed with the girls in the other room, but I was hesitant to be away from him. In the end I gave in and joined Julian in the living room. We lay down on the futon, and I knew what Julian wanted but I was not sure, as it was so much to deal with, having all the kids and only just meeting a few weeks earlier.

"We should wait," I said as we kissed.

"Why?" he asked, as we kissed some more. "We know each other now."

As we kissed, he pulled my underwear down and I pulled it back up. He pulled it down again and I pulled them up, and this went on for a couple of minutes, but in the end, he was so persistent that I just gave in and let him do it. Afterwards I went to the toilet and cried and cried, as I felt awful and violated. I knew I had made a mistake coming to see him and we had not even used a condom and I was terrified I was going to get pregnant. I felt trapped and did not know how to leave, so I stayed a few more days and faked being happy, the kids were sweet, but I was expected to do all the cooking and housework and I was not happy. Erica was so lovely but seemed to be looking after her brother and sister, which I found to be inappropriate. I also had not told Julian I smoked weed either and it had been five days, and I was dying. On the sixth day I packed our stuff and left, and I felt bad for the kids, but I had only booked a week's leave from work and had to get back. I finally drove away vowing I would never see him again. I went 100km or so out of town until Lachlan fell asleep, then I pulled over somewhere near the bush, and jumped out and ran behind the car and lit up my pipe with shaking fingers. I was upset and teary, mostly because of what happened between Julian and me, the man clearly had no boundaries and that was a red flag for sure. Plus, I was expected to be a domestic slave and that was not going to be any fun either. But I kept seeing the kids' faces and how Erica had cried as I had left, and I felt so bad for them. The house was chaotic, and I had done nothing but cook and clean the entire trip, but they were such beautiful kids and I felt torn up inside. Lachlan had enjoyed it, and it was nice to see him getting close to the other kids. I cried more, feeling so up and down about the situation, and the next day I went back to work, and I ended up confiding in my boss about Julian.

"So, what you're saying is that he basically forced you?" she asked me as we sat in her office.

"I don't know," I replied as I started to cry. "I kind of wanted to but not like that."

My boss told me I needed to get the morning after pill, so on my lunch break, I went to the chemist. Julian called me later that night, but I refused to speak to him, and he called the next night and the next day until I gave in and spoke to him.

"I had to go and get the morning after pill you know," I said tearily.

I did not say anything about how I felt that he had pressured me into sex, as I felt too ashamed and that maybe I had been mistaken.

We talked for around two hours that night.

"God I am sorry Lou. I just have such strong feelings for you, you know. I want to have a baby with you."

It was the right thing for him to say because the next day I was planning another trip to see him, but then Julian called me to say he was coming down to Perth and had booked a hotel for us to stay in. We stayed in the city and went shopping for a promise ring, and I felt happy, and I ended up telling him about the weed, and to my surprise he said he did not care. I realised I was falling for him too and I felt loved and special that weekend. When Julian left, I felt sad and wanted to be with him again. The sadness and anger I had felt when I was at his house seemed to just fade away and I did not want to be on my own any longer. I was in love with Julian for loving me, and I told myself that was enough.

A few weeks later I took another week off work and drove up to see him again, but this time the house was in even worse shape. As soon as I got into the house I felt on edge and anxious, but the kids were so happy to see us, and Lachlan was beside himself with excitement. As it was the school holidays, the kids were keen to go out together, but Julian was driving in the taxi most nights, which meant I had to keep the kids quiet every morning, which seemed like an impossible task. Lachlan was naturally a very chatty little boy, and he was confused to why I kept 'shhing' him. Julian did not seem to be bonding with Lachlan at all either, which was a bit upsetting, as I went out of my way to connect with his children, and I assumed he would do the same. The second day we were there I mentioned I had gone outside while he was at work, and he started yelling at me.

"You shouldn't be going out the front when I'm not home," he said, and I could not believe what I was hearing.

We got into a huge fight, and he pushed me around a bit. It was very upsetting, but I decided to let it go as Julian was working hard in the taxi every night; I thought it was because he was so tired. Things were not good between him and Lachlan, and he seemed to go out of his way to be unkind to him and gave him the nickname 'bullfrog' as he was so loud. I was anxious all the time and had started burning myself in the shower most days. I felt hysterical inside and could only get relief by self-harming. I was burning my whole body including my face and then I got sick with a fever and had discharge from my eyes and belly button. I drove myself to hospital where they said I had a soft tissue infection from the burning, and I needed intravenous antibiotics. Julian was angry at me, but Amanda came to visit me in hospital, which was nice of her. I ended up calling my dad and telling him about Julian, so he came to pick his car up and flew Lachlan and I home. I went back to work, but I was a bit of a mess. Julian called me all the time, but I did not know if I wanted to be with him. Things at the flat were not great either, it was messy and unorganised and the only things I managed to do were feed and bathe Lachlan and do his washing.

My brother's girlfriend Laura came over to see me and Lachlan one day.

"Hey, my flatmate Emmy is moving out, do you and Lachy want to come and live with me?" she asked.

I made a whooping sound and jumped up to hug her.

"Yeah definitely!" I answered.

Laura's townhouse was nice, and I felt relieved that we could get out of the flat.

"Great, I'll come over and help you pack and clean," she said.

It took a couple of days to clean the flat but somehow, we managed and the first night in the townhouse, I felt happier. Laura's place was a 3-bedroomed house with a nice kitchen and a little courtyard for Lachlan to play in. One night Julian called me really upset, as his adult stepchildren had accused him of sexually abusing Erica, and I could not believe it, as sure, he was a grumpy old man but a molester? No way.

"Why are they doing this to you?" I asked him.

"Who the f*** knows," he replied. "Maybe they have some stupid idea they will get the kids and live off welfare."

The police had come to Julian's house and taken all three kids away, and I was so angry. Being an actual survivor myself, I could not understand how or why people could make that up, as lies like that could destroy lives. Julian got a lawyer who advised him to just tell the truth and be patient, and he said that Julian would eventually get the kids back. After a week of them being in foster care, they let Calvin come back home but the girls were not allowed to. Poor Calvin was so traumatised, he had lost his mum and being away from Julian had been very upsetting for him. Julian and I talked every night, I guess I had forgiven him for his crappy behaviour when Lachlan and I had stayed with him, and I was determined to do whatever I could to help him get the girls back. The police interviewed Erica, and they still were not allowed to go home, but after a few weeks, the lawyer called and said there was insufficient evidence to get a conviction. Erica and Belinda were allowed to go and live with Julian's brother and sister-in-law in Perth. It was good news, and a week or two later Julian and Calvin came down to stay with us. Lachlan was overjoyed to see Calvin and they quickly ran off to play, and Laura went and stayed with Dylan to give us some space. I listened to the transcript of the police interview, and I was disgusted by the way the child protection officer had led Erica to say that her dad had `touched her.'

The girls were enrolled in the local school near where they were staying, so we enrolled Calvin too so they could see each other. I enrolled Lachlan at North Perth kindy as I was still working at the childcare centre. After a few months and many interviews, Erica and Belinda were finally allowed to come home. It had been a long, rough journey and we were all overjoyed to see them. It was a tight squeeze with all of us in the townhouse but some-how, we made it work. Even though I had been determined not to get into a committed relationship with Julian, here I was living with him and his kids. Julian started the day shift in the taxi which was much better than the night shift, and I ended up quitting my job as the school runs alone took a couple of hours a day. To be honest, I was relieved I did not have to work anymore, having four kids was a lot to deal with. Things were not that great with Julian and me and we fought a lot, and I did not like the way he spoke to Lachlan, as he was always blaming stuff on him. I tried to stand up for Lachlan but that usually made it worse. The good thing was that Lachlan was enjoying kindy and seemed to learn new things every day. He also loved having the kids around and was now referring to them as his sisters and brother. Julian and I did not have a lot of money either, but we sur-vived, and at the weekends I would take the kids to the pool and the park.

I could see that they all loved each other, and I was grateful for Lachlan to finally having some siblings. Halfway through 2006 I fell pregnant, and just the same as with Lachlan, I knew the night I conceived. I got morning sickness, but Julian kept telling me there was no way I could be pregnant. I took a few urine tests, but they came back negative, but I knew and after a few more weeks, I got a blood test to confirm it. I was about three months along when Julian told me to have an abortion.

"Just get rid of it Lou," he said nastily.

Oh, here we go again, I thought, and I cried at night when all the kids were asleep. Julian kept asking me when I was having the procedure.

"I'm not having one," I said to him one day, as he stomped angrily up the stairs.

I saw my counsellor and she registered me for a program for expecting mums, to help reduce the chance of getting post-natal depression. Since I had struggled so much after Lachlan was born, the mental health clinic wanted to keep an eye on me, and I saw a psychiatrist every two weeks, which was beneficial. I was determined to be healthier mentally this time around, and he advised me to stay on my medication. With Lachlan's pregnancy I had stopped my antidepressant, but the psych said I should stay on them, so I did. The kids were super excited about the baby and talked about nothing else, and eventually Julian stopped asking me to have an abortion and I was glad about that. Amanda was over the moon and every time she saw me, she would ask me what body parts the baby was growing. At around four months I woke up one day with bleeding and I was convinced I was having a miscarriage. I told Amanda and she looked so sad.

"But the bubba is growing eyebrows this week," she said tearily.

Julian drove me to the hospital but when they put the heart monitor on me, there was a strong heartbeat, and I was so relieved and went home to rest the best that I could. But the next week it happened again, and Julian took me to the hospital, but the baby was fine. I kept resting that week and finally the bleeding stopped. Julian and I kept on fighting and the tension in the house was unbearable at times, the kids hated it when we fought but we just could not seem to stop. One day Julian shoved me hard onto a table and my little finger got bent back and I knew it was broken. I felt like I could not stay with him any longer, as the fights were getting worse and the next week, we had another huge argument and he threatened to push me down the stairs "until I lost the baby." I was terrified and tried my best to stay calm. Amanda had assured me once the baby was born then he would change his mind and be happy about it, but as I drew nearer to five months, it did not look like he was softening to the idea. My psychiatrist kept asking me when I was leaving him, and I did not have an answer for him.

"Louise it's dangerous if you stay," he told me, and I knew he was right.

He asked me if I wanted to go to a women's shelter, and I refused, but I knew I had to act before he hurt me or the baby.

I called Dylan and Laura and asked them what I should do.

"You know you can come and live with us sis because Julian is kinda crazy," my brother said.

Laura had just had their first baby, Ruby, and I still was not sure about leaving, as I did love Julian, but I was tired of the fighting and the way he treated Lachlan. I was also genuinely scared of him and the way he was around me now that I was pregnant.

"It'll be ok Lou, just come and live with us," Laura assured me.

I packed up our stuff and that is when Julian started to beg me to stay, so, I did, but a few days later we had another fight and Julian threatened to kick the baby out of me. That was the last straw, so I packed Lachlan into the car, and we left. The poor kids were so upset but I knew I had no choice. Lachlan was understandably upset too, but I reassured him we would visit soon.

It was not great with Dylan and Laura, as Dylan was a heavy drinker, he drank so many beers every night that their bathroom was littered with bottles. They fought often, and it was very unpleasant, and I tried the best I could to mediate between them, but it was hard. I felt for Lachlan, as the past year had been very unpredictable for him, and I tried to keep things as normal as I could. He was such a lovely boy and every morning he woke up happy and eager to learn new things at school. Slowly we got into a new routine, but I could see that it was not easy for Laura, as Dylan was not functioning well at all and was still drinking heavily. He was so drunk that he could not even hold their baby properly. I could not believe what was happening to my little brother, as we had once been so close, but alcohol was taking over his life. I helped Laura out the best I could, but it was hard now as I was tired all the time. I was talking to Julian, and I took Lachlan to see the kids, but Julian was so angry all the time, and it was just awful. The kids missed us a lot and it was hard for Lachlan to be the only child again and I was more tired with this pregnancy and with Lachlan to look after, I often felt overwhelmed. Lachlan still saw his dad every fortnight which meant I could rest, but as my pregnancy continued, so did the threatening calls and texts from Julian. I never knew how he would be in his messages; at times he was remorseful and would beg me to come back, other times he would threaten me and say that he could take me "and put me somewhere no one could ever find me." I still loved him but felt exhausted from his up and down moods, and I felt trapped with my brother, but I was too afraid to go back to Julian.

Chapter 11

isla

On the morning of the 16th of April, I went into labour a week early, just the same with Lachlan, I had a bloody show and then contractions. A few hours later my friend came over and picked Lachlan up for me, and I met my sister at the hospital. Once again, she was to be my birth partner and I was so blessed to have her support. By then the contractions were getting more painful, so I moved onto the gas in the bath, but I was only 4cm and even though I really wanted a vaginal birth, in the back of my mind I was worried it would result in a cesarean again. But I kept persisting, staying upright, and moving between the bath and shower and having pethidine injections. Dana was amazing with me, counting my breaths and staying so positive, she kept talking about how exciting it was that I was having a girl and how I would get to meet her soon. Laura was also there and at one point I was crying and yelling out that I wanted them to call Julian, but they did not, thank goodness. Julian's behaviour had been so unpredictable leading up to the birth that the labour ward had put me in under an assumed name, and it had been my psychiatrist's idea. The labour progressed and was very tough, after many hours I was only 6cm dilated and

I was exhausted and teary. The contractions were doubling up and I was delirious with pain, and I could not believe it was happening all over again, it was like my body was betraying me. My sister held my hand and we cried together, as the doctor came in at about 7.30pm and said that the labour was not progressing to his liking and suggested it was time to go to surgery. I was devastated as after all that hard work, I was barely 7cm dilated, and I begged them to let me keep trying but, in my heart, I knew it was over. In the end I could not argue anymore, I welcomed the epidural and at 8.40pm my darling daughter Isla was born. Dana was the first to hold her and boy could she cry! When Dana handed her to me, I could not believe how tiny she was, Isla had dark hair and a scrunched up little face, but I fell in love with her. I had to laugh as Isla looked a lot like Julian, and she was so tiny, not even weighing 3kg. I lay on the bed exhausted as I tried to feed her, and Tom brought Lachlan in to see us, and he sat on a chair and held Isla in his arms. Lachlan was smiling all over and kept hugging me.

"Mama," he said. "Her toes look like rain drops."

Dana came the next day and decided she would call Julian and tell him Isla had arrived, but when Julian came to the hospital, he was overly aggressive, and Dana took Isla to see him but afterwards he flew into a rage, and they had to call security. Thankfully, Dana was back in our room with the baby by then. The social worker at the hospital was concerned and suggested that I get a VRO against him, so a few days after leaving hospital I found a Legal aid lawyer, Karen, who began the process. I felt sad and cried in her office, as I had tried so hard to 'fix us' but nothing seemed to work. I did love Julian dearly, but there was nothing more that I could do. Over the next couple of weeks, I went to see Karen and she documented our entire relationship, and every detail had to be recorded. I would sit and feed Isla in her office and pour my heart out to her, it was very tiring and emotionally draining. I would go pick up Lachlan from school afterwards and we would go to the park, and I would watch him play with tears in my eyes. Lachlan had also started counselling and I would take him to his sessions and then we would get a hedgehog slice from the bakery and sit, and he would tell me about school. We ended up in court a couple of times, but Julian had a lawyer too and tried to fight the VRO. Fortunately, my lawyer Karen was very thorough, and the order ended up being granted for two years. I went home and cried and cried, as I could not believe it was finally over. Even though I loved Julian, I knew our relationship was toxic and now I could get on with my life.

It was hard adjusting to having two children on my own, and it was not easy living with Dylan and Laura either. I thought they would be helpful, but they were not, and Isla cried constantly and barely slept, and I quickly became tired and overwhelmed. Laura would drive us to school and then I would come home and try to get Isla to sleep so I could do chores. It was funny but we would get in the car and Laura would have music blasting from the speakers and Isla would go straight to sleep, but as soon as we got to school, she would wake up. Isla also took so long to feed and only slept for half an hour or so at home, and I felt like I was in a bad dream, as I was relying on such little sleep and spent a lot of time crying. The reality of being a single mum was hitting me hard and I struggled to cope. Living with my brother was incredibly stressful, as he was still drinking every night and had terrible mood swings. When Isla was three months old, I accidentally gave her the cold sore virus and she became very unwell. She ended up in hospital having anti-viral medication in a drip, and when we got home her sleep was even worse and I could not put her down without her screaming. I was not able to even leave her for ten minutes to run Lachlan a bath, so I would lie Isla on a towel on the floor of the bathroom while I quickly showered with him. She was having real trouble feeding too, and the nurse told me during our four-month visit she was 'failing to thrive' and I needed to do something about it. Laura kept pestering me to give Isla formula, but I was dead against it. The nurse told me I had to spend a whole 48 hours feeding her nonstop, and if she put on some weight at the end, then she would let me continue to breast feed. So, I sent Lachlan's to Tom's and sat in the armchair and fed her every time she woke up. For two days I slept and ate in that chair, and the second morning I woke up to discover that Isla had rolled off my lap and was laying on my feet, but she was completely fine and still asleep. When I took her back to the nurse, she had put on quite a few grams, and it was enough for the nurse who congratulated me on my persistence. I was more exhausted than ever, but Isla had seemed to turn a corner and was sleeping about three hours at night before waking up, it was a dramatic improvement.

When Isla was about six months old and the VRO had been in place for a few months, Julian started contacting me again, even though he was meant to only text me once or twice a week about the baby, he sent a few texts about how much he missed me. At first, I did not reply but as the weeks went on, I found myself weakening, as Laura was pregnant again and things at home were terrible. She and Dylan would have massive fights, and baby Ruby would cry, and Isla would cry, and Lachlan would hide in his room. Julian sent me the sweetest texts.

"I'm sorry Lou. I acted like a nut. It's only because I love you and Moo so much it makes me crazy."

In the end I replied, knowing I was breaching the VRO as well. I did not want him to get into trouble for texting me, but he kept asking me if he could just see Isla for five minutes and eventually, I agreed. We met at a shopping centre and I was so anxious and teary. Julian held Isla and I sat there and watched the two of them, and I was overcome with emotion and admitted that it was good to see him. I went home feeling so guilty, and I did not tell Laura or Dylan as they were against Julian. A few days later I met up with him again and I could feel myself warming to the idea of us being together, Isla would lay in his arms and gaze up at him and my heart would give a little lurch. I was so bloody tired and sick of being on my own, as everything just felt like one giant struggle, so one weekend Laura and Dylan went away, and I went to see Julian at his house. The kids were overjoyed to see me and meet their baby sister, but I did not take Lachlan as I did not want him to be part of a lie. Julian had a little 3-bedroom place in Stirling and the first night I stayed there I could not believe it, but Isla slept through the night, and I kept waking up and checking that she was still breathing. I stayed for two nights and then went and picked Lachlan up and went back to Dylan's and Laura's and tried to pretend nothing had happened. Laura took one look around the house though and spotted a dead mouse in a trap that she had set before she had left, and she flew into a mad rage.

"I know you've been to see him, haven't you," she screamed at me.

"No, I haven't I promise," I lied to her.

Laura would not let up, and she went on and on at me until finally I told her the truth.

"Yes, I took Isla there for the weekend."

"Get out!" she yelled at me. "Take Isla and Lachlan and get out!"

Something in me seemed to snap so I ran into my room and began to pack but she followed me in.

"I didn't mean it," she said to me. "I just can't understand why you would go and see that idiot."

But I had made up my mind, I was leaving.

"Don't go Lou," she pleaded with me.

"No, I'm going," I said, and I told Lachlan to pack his toys and I started loading the car.

She ran out to me, and Dylan followed her.

"Don't go sis," he said to me, but I was determined.

Surely living with Julian could not be as bad as living with them. So, we went to Julian's and after a day or two I went to the court and got the VRO lifted, and Lachlan was so happy to be back with the kids and I felt like I had made the right decision. A month or two after moving back in with Julian I fell pregnant again, and as usual I knew as soon as it happened.

"S***, s***, s***," I swore as I paced around the lounge room.

How could I have another baby, Isla was still breast feeding and slept in our room in a cot next to our bed. As usual Julian was in denial about the pregnancy, but the kids were so excited. I got bad morning sickness and found it hard to look after everything, but Erica was such a sweetheart and helped with Isla. Julian drove in the taxi every day, so I did all the cooking and the cleaning and school drop-offs. We decided we would move to a bigger house before the baby was born and started looking for rentals. Isla turned one in April, and we had a big party for her, she got loads of presents and it was a wonderful day. So, we moved to Merriwa to a much nicer house with four bedrooms, but poor Lachlan did not have a proper bedroom, but he was a good kid and did not complain much. The house was not close to the kids' school, but it was near to where Julian had to pick up his taxi and was next to a lovely big park.

I found it very overwhelming being pregnant with five children, they were all such darlings, but I quickly got exhausted and very teary. It was about this time that we got a family support worker, she was an older lady, Mary, and was amazing. She would come over and do the dishes, help the kids with their homework and make tea. I was worried about how I would cope once the baby was born, but Mary assured me that she would be around to help me out. I found out I was having a boy, and we all chose our favourite names, and I picked Lukas. Things were crazy in that house, it was never tidy, and someone was always having a tantrum about something, including me! Julian spoilt Isla rotten and would give her whatever she wanted, he did not let me say no to her, and when I did, she would scream and scream the house down. One night we were eating dinner, and we heard this weird scraping noise, and we all turned to look, and we saw Isla on her knees slowly pushing a chair into our room. We followed her in and watched her climb up on it and try to grab the chocolate that I had hidden up on a shelf in the walk-in wardrobe. As usual, Julian refused to let me take it off her, and she ate the whole bar and then did not want dinner. I do not remember many fights in that house as I was so tired all the time that I just ignored most of Julian's crappy behaviour.

I did all the chores and school drop-off and pick-ups, shopping, out-ings, birthdays, and playdates and all the while being pregnant with my third child. When I think back now, I am unsure to how I did all that stuff, I just did. Dana called me one day to tell me that she was pregnant too, and I was so happy for her as she had been trying for a while. I was excited as our babies could grow up together. Isla was not a great sleeper, so she spent a lot of nights in our bed. Most of the time I was too exhausted to take her back to her own bed and I did not know how she would cope once Lukas arrived.

Chapter 12

lukas

I went into labour on the 14th of November 2008, five days before I was due. I was having a planned C section this time and felt so relieved I did not have to go through labour once again. I picked the kids up from school and started having contractions that afternoon, so I went home to clean the house and cook tea and then called Dana who had offered to have the kids. I also called Julian who told me he "had a fare on" and could not come home. So, I spent time together with the kids and packed my hospital bag and tried to stay calm. The contractions were getting a little closer together when I suddenly remembered I was meant to call the hospital! They had told me if I went into labour spontaneously, then I needed to come in straight away to be monitored. Then my sister arrived.

"Have you called the hospital?" Dana asked me.

"No, I haven't," I replied, and she looked at me and shook her head.

"Lou you're meant to call them straight away!"

I quickly called them, and they told me to come in, so Dana called Julian again and told him to come home urgently. By this time, it was around 8pm and the contractions were getting more painful, and thankfully Julian finally arrived, and we left. In the car I was having strong contractions and I told him to drive faster, and when I got there, I received a good telling off by the midwife, and she also told Julian off, which I found funny. I was hooked up to the heart monitor and by then the contractions were strong, so they gave me an epidural. It was extremely painful, and as I had received no gas or pethidine, it was excruciating. After it kicked in, I just lay there and relaxed while they got the theatre ready. Lukas was born at 10pm, but he was not breathing the best unfortunately and was quite blue in the face, so he had to have oxygen as soon as he came out. Lukas was gorgeous with dark hair and beautiful brown eyes, and he did not make one peep and as I held him, he latched onto my boob straight away. Julian did not seem that interested in him, but I was instantly in love with him. He had such a perfect little face and I just lay there gazing at him. That night Lukas fed and then fell asleep all night, and I do not think he cried once until about day three, when I was woken up from a nap by a very noisy baby.

"Gosh I thought," as I woke up. "That mum should feed her baby."

I opened my eyes and looked over and got a shock because it was Lukas making all the noise. I quickly began to feed him and had a little chuckle to myself. Lukas only ever cried when he was hungry, and he was such a placid baby, and he would just lie in my arms looking at me with those beautiful brown eyes and I would feel my heart melt. All the kids came to see me, and they all fussed over who would be the first to hold him. Lachlan kept hugging me and I felt sad as I knew it was a struggle for him when he was away from me. When I got home the reality of it all just hit me, as Julian went to work when Lukas was only five days old. I fed him after giving the kids dinner but did not know what to do with him while I tucked Isla in. She always took so long to settle, so in the end I put Lukas in the bassinette and told the kids to wheel him around if he cried. I waited for all the kids to go to bed that night, and then bawled my eyes out, as I realised the enormity of what I had to juggle on my own. My family support worker Mary came the next day and boy was I glad. She cleaned the house and looked after Lukas while I rested. She even picked the kids up from school, and I was so grateful for her support.

Julian was distant from me and from Lukas, he had not bonded with the baby at all and only seemed interested in Isla. Isla was fascinated with Lukas and nicknamed him 'babydoo,' but it was hard to do stuff around the house as my wound was a lot deeper this time and seemed slow to heal. Ideally, I should have been resting but it rarely happened, and my body was constantly tired, and I felt run down. The kids were all so good and played with Isla and bathed her at night. Little Isla was such a darling and loved playing make – believe with Belinda and Erica and I would cook in the kitchen and watch them play together. Isla was so sweet and loved books, dolls, and her siblings. Julian and I started fighting again and I complained we lived too far from their school, so, in 2009 we moved to a big house near the beach. The house was lovely and backed onto a big park which was so nice for the kids, and they played there every day after school. I had enrolled Lachlan in the other kids' school so that made it easier for me, but I felt for him as it was not easy settling in. Julian ignored Lukas most of the time, and it was upsetting, as he was an experienced parent, and should have made more of an effort to bond with him. Julian had three adult children from previous relationships and five young children and one stepson, that was a lot of kids, and it was sad to see him so detached from his own son. There was no actual nursery for Lukas, which made it hard especially when Julian was on night shift, and one day Lukas was crying, and Julian picked him up out of his cot and just screamed in his face to shut up. I rushed over and grabbed Lukas out of his arms and walked around comforting him and crying silently, as it devastated me to see Julian treat Lukas so badly.

I was becoming increasingly overwhelmed, and was constantly tired and emotional, as it was too much for me caring for all the kids and the house too. I still had my family support worker, Mary, thank goodness, as without her I would have been stuffed. I was constantly anxious and found it hard to sleep, and I was also having a lot of severe flashbacks about my abuse which were awful. One night I regressed back to being a baby and I was unable to talk, and the kids did not know what to do with me. One night I remembered those men hurting me and I just lay on the couch drifting in and out and it was extremely traumatic for the kids. Poor Lachlan kept sitting on my lap, patting my face, and telling me that he loved me. I could no longer function properly with all the flashbacks, and I was constantly disassociated. Julian and I were not getting along at all, and we fought often. One day I called Mary crying.

"I can't do it anymore," I said, and she agreed.

Mary came over to the house and started to pack a bag for me, and called Julian and told him to come home as she was taking me to hospital. All the kids were crying but I was too tired to argue. Lachlan was begging me not to go but as I held onto him, I realised I had no choice, it was not fair to expose the children to my trauma any longer.

"Mary," I said while crying. "What will I do with Lukas? I can't leave him with Julian."

She looked at me as she put my bags in her boot.

"Don't worry, I'll take him home," she said, and I stared at her.

"Mary you can't do that! You won't be allowed to," I cried.

"Watch me," she said as she drove me to hospital with Lukas and some bottles of expressed breast milk.

I could not believe this darling woman who was in her 50's was willing to take my baby home so I could get the help I so desperately needed. I rested in hospital and slept mostly, and they gave me valium for the flashbacks, and I went back on Seroquel even though I was breast feeding. Every day Mary brought Lukas in to see me, and I would feed him and express milk for her to take home. It was so hard being away from my baby, but I knew it was the right thing to do. The kids had another support worker step in which helped me not to worry so much. Julian brought the kids in to see me every couple of days, and Lachlan was finding it hard without me, but he put on a brave face.

"Mama will be ok," I reassured him as I held him in my arms. Poor Isla was so young, and she climbed up onto the bed to see me. I began to cry so Erica and Belinda took her for a walk around the hospital. After three weeks I discharged myself and went home, but things were not good. My repressed memories were back in full swing, and I stopped sleeping again. I was remembering my early abuse which I was horrified to discover, had started in early infancy, so I spent a lot of time on the bathroom floor babbling like a baby and crying in pain. Julian thought I was mad and did not hold back from telling me so.

"You're f***en mad," he would yell at me which just made it worse.

I tried so hard to function and snap myself out of it, but it was no use, he and I fought constantly, and I battled my way through the memories and looking after Lukas. When he weaned himself at nine months I went back to marijuana, it was the only way I knew how to cope. And when I wanted to run away and leave all the kids behind, which I did often, I would send them to the park to play. I would put Lukas in his bassinette, and I would sneak out into the backyard and smoke and try to work out what I was doing. I had started to get weed from a friend of Julian's daughter Amanda. His name was Aiden, and I had met him before when I was pregnant with Isla, and we had gotten along well. His nickname was Dr A, and he was a sweet guy. One night I drove to Aiden's place to get weed, and when I got home, he texted me.

"Hey good to see you tonight. You know you are hot and a MILF."

I cannot tell you how much that lifted me up, as things with Julian were at an all-time low, he was so mentally abusive, and I could feel that it was wearing me down.

"You're a stupid bitch," he would yell at me every day. "You're mad and crazy and useless."

Julian was also becoming a lot more physical with me, and I would just scream and scream at him, and he would shove me around and I would yell and throw things and smash stuff up. I felt so out of control and helpless, and that Christmas we got into a huge argument one night, and he flew at me and put his hands around my neck and began to choke me. I tried to fight him off, but he would not let go. Calvin launched himself at his dad and tried to make him stop and Erica ran next door and the neighbour's called the police. The police arrived and ordered Julian out of the house for 24 hours, and the kids all crowded around me and just cried and cried. I sat there with my throat still burning, dizzy, disorientated, and wishing that I were dead.

Chapter 13

trapped

Two days later when Julian came back, I called Mary, and she told me I had to leave.

"Louise," she said to me. "You know you have to leave, or he'll kill you."

My heart sank but I knew deep down, she was right. Mary told me she would find a women's refuge for me and Lachlan, Lukas, and Isla and even though I did not want to, I agreed.

"Start packing your things," Mary said to me on the phone the next day, and a few hours later she arrived and helped me load everything in her car.

Julian was being super nice and casual, and the other kids were just standing there looking at me. Lachlan and Isla got into Mary's car, and as I put Lukas into the baby seat, I felt numb all over. I hugged the kid's goodbye, and Calvin was angry and ranted at Julian saying it was all his fault, but Julian was unusually calm and just watched us drive away. The refuge was in Fremantle and as we walked in, I felt part of me go on the ceiling. We were shown to a room with three beds and a cot, and I tried to be upbeat for the kids but inside I was dying. That night when the kids had fallen asleep, I sat on the floor and just cried and cried. I had tried hard to make our relationship work but I had failed again, and Julian was calling my phone constantly, but I ignored him. I ended up calling my dad and telling him the whole story, and he came the next day and gave me his car and some money. That night I cooked tea for the kids and when they were asleep, I snuck outside to smoke. I could not believe I was in a refuge, I felt like I was living someone else's life. I was alone with two kids and a baby with nothing to my name. The refuge was a bit rough, but we managed, and the staff helped me to apply for a single parenting payment and a crisis payment from Centrelink. We stayed for a few days, and I could tell Lachlan was happier without Julian. Isla cried and said she missed the girls, but I was determined not to give in. She and Lachlan played outside on an old swing set while I tried to work out what my next move was. I reached out to Aiden to tell him what had happened, and he ended up calling me and we talked for over an hour.

"What are you going to do Lou," he said to me, but I did not have an answer for him.

That weekend Lukas got sick with a high fever, and I stayed up all night with him as his asthma had flared up, but the next day he was worse with a bad cough and his colour was not good. Ever since his birth he had been prone to bronchiolitis which made him terribly ill, and I was worried it was turning into another infection. I took him to the hospital the next day and they admitted him for a few days, so I had no choice but to send Isla back to Julian's, and Lachlan back to Tom's. The refuge had made it clear I was not to have any contact with Julian, but I was desperate and did not know what else to do with the kids. After three days in hospital, I was exhausted, and I went to pick up the kids, and I ended up falling asleep in Julian's bed, and when the refuge found out they kicked me out. I drove around with the kids for half a day not knowing what to do, and then I called Mary, and she organized another refuge, this time in Midland. It was a lot nicer than the Fremantle one and I immediately felt at home there. Poor Isla was so upset that I had to rock her on my tummy to get her to fall asleep. Thankfully, Lukas was such a calm baby and did not mind sleeping in a port a cot, and Lachlan was happy as the refuge had a big playground and an art room which he loved. I enrolled Lachlan at the local primary school, and he liked it, and the principal was very friendly and seemed to want to help us. I took Isla and Lukas to daycare just so I could look for a rental, and Lukas did not mind childcare, but Isla hated it. Julian seemed keen for us to reconcile but I was not convinced, as he was doing his usual trick of sending nice messages, but I did not trust him. The staff at the refuge were so lovely to us and helped me apply for some rentals, and I was shocked when I was approved for a three-bedroom place in Guildford. A few days later I had a Homeswest bond and began to pack up our things.

The house was average though, it was an old railway cottage, but I did not care; it was ours. It had a huge yard which the kids thought was great, and I got some secondhand furniture and tried my best to make it home. Julian brought his kids over to see us, which was lovely, but I was determined not to get back together with him, even though I missed Julian's three so much, I knew I could not let that cloud my judgement.

At the weekends Lachlan would go to Tom's and Julian would pick Lukas and Isla up so I would clean the house and rest. Aiden would come over to visit me and we started dating, he was young, and it was very casual, but I did enjoy his company. The house was a real dump, and it was boiling hot in summer and in winter we all slept in one bed to stay warm. One day Aiden was over, and we decided to go and look in the garage, as it was filled with weird stuff the previous owner had left behind. I told the kids to stay in the house, but we did not realise that Lukas had come out after us, he crawled into the garage to see what we were doing, and the door came down suddenly on his leg. He started crying and I rushed to see him, and his leg was badly bruised so we ended up driving to the hospital. They took x rays but as it was the weekend there was no doctor to look at them. Two days later they called me and said Lukas had two fractures in his shin bone and I had to take him back in to have it put in a cast. Lukas was so brave, and I could not believe it was broken and I had not even known about it. Poor Lukas had to crawl around in the cast but when Isla annoyed him, he would hit her with it. Eventually the cast came off, and then Lukas started walking, which was a delightful surprise.

Julian was texting me constantly and trying to get me back, but I kept stalling with him as I knew that he had not changed and if I did go back, then things would be as they always had been. I knew our relationship was unhealthy and we just seemed to bring out the worst in each other. I was still seeing Aiden, but he already had an on and off girlfriend and I knew it would not last between us. Things fizzled out and then I saw on Facebook Aiden had gotten back together with his girlfriend, and they were engaged. I pretended not to care but I was hurt as I had liked him, and it was hard to be by myself on the weekends. I had lost touch with all my friends, and I was depressed, and I was also starting to get behind in my rent too and I was worried I would be kicked out. Even though I loved being away from Julian, and I was much calmer, he texted me every day. As I read his texts, I could feel myself weakening.

"Just come back home Lou. You should be here with us, as that house is not suitable. It's a dump and I should call the authorities."

He was right about that, as the house was very run down, and it seemed that no matter how hard I tried, I could never seem to make it on my own. In the end I relented and asked Julian's daughter Amanda and her girlfriend to move into the house so I did not have to break the lease. We packed up all our things and moved back to Julian's house and I enrolled Lachlan in the local primary school, and he liked it there. A few weeks later we received a letter from the owner saying they wanted to sell the house, so we had to move again. We found a four-bedroom place in Wanneroo, and it was such a nice house with a huge walk-in linen cupboard and ducted vacuuming. I was not happy in that house, as Julian and I started fighting as soon as we moved in, big ugly fights that would result in him shoving me and me screaming uncontrollably. He was so mentally and emotionally abusive, and he would call me so many awful names and made no effort to keep it from the kids. I stayed connected with Aiden and sometimes I would take Isla and Lukas to see him during the day.

"You have to leave him Lou. He could hurt you," he told me repeatedly and I knew deep down in my heart it was true.

Julian was so abusive towards Lachlan too and it broke my heart to see him suffering, it seemed that Lachlan could not breathe without Julian commenting. I was so depressed, and as the fights kept escalating, I found it increasingly harder to rest properly or eat. I was constantly worried, afraid, and then would instigate arguments with Julian and scream the house down. I was under so much stress that I could not think or act rationally. I fantasised about how I could leave Julian, but what could I do, as my attempts to leave him in the past had failed. I knew I was trapped but I still hoped deep down that once again I would be able to leave him. Julian worked the night shift so I would put the kids to bed and go into the garage and smoke marijuana and try to plan my escape. I would pace up and down and go over everything in my mind, desperate for a solution.

I felt alone, detached from reality, and thought that one day Julian might end up killing me.

Contents

Part Two

AFTER

Chapter 14

salvation
16th March 2012

It was a day like all other days, and I was still depressed and still broke. I had dropped the kids at school and was trying to find a way to get some money for food for their dinner. I had been to The Life Centre before, where you would line up and show your health care card and wait with the other people who were all in the same boat as you. I decided it was my best shot, the volunteers were always friendly and at least I would get some vegetables and fruit and not just cans the kids would not eat. I made my way there, mindful of how much fuel I had and how I could make it last the rest of the week. As I drove, I felt a cloud of exhaustion and sadness that seemed to hang over me. It was heavy and brought tears to my eyes. I felt a wave of hopelessness as I stopped at every traffic light, wondering how it had come to this. My mind was on auto pilot, changing gears, braking, and doing all the things I needed to do to drive the car, but deep down inside, my mind was in a pit. I was alone with three children to care for, and barely had a dollar to my name. I spent most of the time crying and struggling to get out of bed. Most days I had to force myself to take them to school. They were everything to me, my rays of sunshine, but lately the sheer overwhelming responsibility was just too much to cope with. I pulled into the car park and found a space. It was busy, volunteers were unloading produce in the open warehouse and there were people milling about near the front door. I stayed in the car for a few minutes watching people come and go; some stuffing food into backpacks and others pushing trolleys full of groceries. I realised something as I watched them, that like me they all had the same look in their eyes; hopelessness, fear, and a resignation that life would never get any better. I felt tears welling up and I tried to blink them away. My kids needed me to be strong and get food for them, so I had to go inside before the centre closed or it would be baked beans and spaghetti for tea. I walked in and sat and waited for my turn. I avoided eye contact with any-one and was trying desperately not to cry. I felt alone and afraid and that same hopeless feeling was rising in me again. I also felt a numbness about how I really felt deep down. I knew I was depressed, like really depressed. I was a drug addict and could not go a few days without marijuana and lately also speed. I was behind in my rent, choosing to pay only half a week in favour of getting drugs. I always fed my kids, they never went without one meal or school lunch, but I knew my resources were running out. Relying on charities ever since I had left my ex-partner the previous year, meant every day was a struggle as I scraped by, counting dollars and cents to feed and clothe the kids. I had just come out of hospital for the second time since my eldest son was born. I had been okay for a few years since my first admission in 2003, but I had hit rock bottom once again and had to go back in. I had been treated for major depression and trauma ever since that first admission, and I always fought to cope and look after the kids the best I could, but lately it was so hard. I never managed to beat the blues or understand why I was in the state I was in. I had been labelled crazy by my ex-partner and my parents and it was a hard label to shake off. I saw myself as messed up and my brain was always thinking that this was the way I would be for the rest of my life. I also relied heavily on medication, and I had no hopes of ever been able to overcome my desperate situation or worsening mental illness. I had resigned myself to believing that this was my life, and it would always be this way.

When it was my turn, I shuffled into the little room and sat opposite a lady with kind eyes.

"How are you?" she asked me.

I looked down feeling the shame washing over me.

"I'm not great," I finally answered.

"I'm sorry to hear that," she said to me. "What's been happening? Do you have any children?"

I took a deep breath and tried not to cry before I answered.

"Yes, I have three children. They are 4, 5 and 11."

She smiled at me. "You are very blessed then. Do you have your health care card?"

I reached into my purse and put it on the table, and she glanced at it and started to fill out a form.

"We can give you a family hamper today if that would help you?" she asked me.

I felt the tears rising again and I took a few more deep breaths.

"Yes, that would help me out a lot," I said.

She wrote for a few more minutes and then looked up at me.

"Things sound tough for you Louise."

I looked at her and I could see something in her eyes I had never seen before.

"Louise," she said to me. "Would you like to give your heart to the Lord Jesus Christ today?"

I stared back at her, and it was like time stood still for a moment.

"Yes, I would," I finally replied, and she smiled at me once more.

"Do you believe that the Lord Jesus Christ died for your sins and rose again?"

I did not hesitate, "yes, I do."

She beamed at me. "Do you confess with your mouth that he is your Lord and Saviour?"

I looked straight into her eyes.

"I do," I replied.

"Congratulations! You have taken the Lord Jesus into your heart, and He will be with you forever," she announced with a big smile on her face.

I nodded numbly not really understanding what it was that I had done. She reached into a drawer and pulled out a book. She opened the front page and printed my name and date at the top. She wrote for a minute or two and then closed it and handed it to me. I took it and held it in my hand.

"Come on," she said to me standing up, "this is a special day for you. Let's get your hamper," and I followed her out, still feeling numb.

In fact, I was so numb that I did not really see where I was going. She called out through the warehouse door.

"Red ticket please."

She reached into her pocket and pulled out a small leaflet, and smiling, she handed it to me.

"We have two services every Sunday and groups throughout the week, it would be lovely to see you there," she said as she patted me on the arm. "It's going to be okay; you've got Jesus now."

I looked down and noticed for the first time that I was holding a New Living Translation in my hand. I stared at it, a Holy Bible. I could not believe it; I had not seen a bible since I was five years old. It was not the best memory either, I was raised in a Methodist church, with stuffy, boring hymns and scary pictures of a man covered in blood. I shook my head and put it in my bag along with the leaflet. I waited for my hamper and then steered the trolley out to my car. I looked down at the food, there was fruit, vegetables, milk, bread, yoghurt, pastries, chocolate milk and some frozen meals. I felt so relieved that the kids would have some afternoon tea and something for dinner too. As I drove out of the car park, I felt a glimmer of hope. In fact, for the first time in my life I thought that things were going to be okay.

september 2012

"You did what?" my boyfriend asked me, and I looked at him briefly as I sliced up a cucumber for the salad I was preparing.

"A few months ago, I gave my heart to Jesus. While I was getting food at the Life Centre."

He made a loud noise and wrapped me in a huge hug.

"That is so good babe. That means you are born again," he said.

I looked over at him. "Born again?"

He nodded and smiled at the confused look on my face. "Yep Lou, you got saved babe. I got saved when I was 14."

I picked up a carrot and began dicing it.

"The lady gave me that," I said pointing to the bible that was on the table, and he smiled again and made another whooping noise.

"That's so good!" he said as he hugged me again.

That night we did our usual routine of smoking weed after putting the kids to bed, but something was niggling at me. I had opened the bible when I had first received it that day back in March, but I had put it aside and not looked at it since.

"Presented to Louise," the inscription read, "by The Life Centre 16th March 2012. May you always be guided by the Holy Spirit and walk in the steps of our God."

That night I pondered as I lay in bed, was there really a God? And who exactly was Jesus? I did not understand at all what I had done that day, and I did not understand Aiden's excitement or what 'born again' meant, and how was I saved, and from what? How could I understand what it all meant, when the only experience I had was from a church that had scared the heck out of me, and didn't I have to be a good person to believe in God? I was sure Christian people were good people, doing honourable deeds for everyone and not drinking or doing drugs and having sex out of wedlock like me. I was quite sure I did *not* qualify. I'd had three children and never been married, I had slept with whomever I had wanted for most of my life, and I had cheated on two of my long-term partners, so surely that disqualified me! I decided that those questions were too hard for my brain to cope with. Over the next few days, I did not think about the bible, I just put it on the shelf and kept living my life. I was still living in complete poverty, barely getting out of bed to take the kids to school, and some days I just refused to get up. At the weekend I would get the kids' breakfast, then go back to bed, and they would be playing around me and making up games and I would just sleep on and off. I was too depressed to go out except for the park, where I would just sit and watch the kids play and avoid making any eye contact with the other parents. I was so depressed, and I thought that I would be this way forever.

Chapter 15

looking back

A few months before going to the Life Centre I had gotten into a terrible relationship with an incredibly violent and unstable man. It was one of the worst decisions I had ever made. Before leaving Isla and Lukas' Dad in 2011, I had gone out with a friend partying, and she introduced me to her Uncle Perry. I had heard of him a few years back (while dating his sister!), and knew he was really bad news. That was the draw card, he was single, quite charming, and highly intelligent, but you could tell he was slightly dangerous. He was easy to talk to and we hit it off. He had a young daughter who was a bit older than Isla, she was sweet and friendly, and I thought that he could not be that bad if his daughter were living with him. I felt the pull of excitement after eight years with my partner and I wanted some adventure. I found myself wanting to take a risk, so I did. A few weeks after we met, Perry invited me to a club. We went to his house first and he told me he was taking speed. He offered me some and of course I said yes. It was the first time I'd had it in many years, and I just wanted to go out and get off my face and not have to think about my miserable relationship. So that is what I did; I drank the powder in water and ended up dancing at a club for about six hours. I had even ditched my friend's uncle at some point and was hanging out with two young guys who found me particularly enthralling. We somehow ended up at a nearby park and I had made out with one of them. One of them kept pressuring me into having sex and I kept saying no. After two hours of trying to fend them off, I desperately called Perry and to my surprise he showed up fifteen minutes later and took me back to his place. I felt ashamed, and Perry made no secret that he thought I was acting slutty. At his place he offed me more drugs and this time I wanted to use a needle, so I ended up locking myself in his bathroom and shooting myself up. At this point I was already too far gone to think clearly about what I was doing. I tried hard to block out thoughts of Julian or the kids, as the speed hit me instantly and my brain was on a whole new level of not caring. It was around 3am by then and Julian must have woken up and seen I was not home. He started to call me frantically, so I sent him a text saying I would be home around 8am and switched my phone off. I was high as a kite and wandered into Perry's living room where he was watching porn. So, I sat in his lounge room and watched it with him, and it was not long before we turned to each other. I remember him kissing me and asking me if it felt weird or not, I was not feeling anything at this point, so we ended up having sex. Around 7am I finally started to come down and I had a shower, and looked at myself in the mirror and I could not believe how bad I looked. My face was so red and blotchy from the drinking and drugs, I looked awful. I was also starting to feel dirty and guilty about what I had done. I smoked some marijuana and went home. Perry and I had talked a lot that night and I had confided in him about the emotional and mental abuse I had suffered in the last eight years. He had told me to leave Julian, but I knew it was not that simple. I had been where I was before, and I always went back to him. When I got home the kids rushed to greet me and I could see in Julian's eyes that he knew what I had done. Surprisingly, he did not say anything, but a few years later he confessed that he had known what I had done; the drugs and the sex. After that night Perry began texting me, offering to sell me weed so of course I took him up on it. One night I made an excuse to go to the chemist and ended up at his place just sitting on the couch and cuddling him. He was an odd man; you could tell that he had been on speed for a long time. Every part of me knew it was such a bad idea to pursue the relationship, as Perry had been in prison multiple times but that just drew me closer to him. He also had so many issues about what had happened that night when we had gotten together. Funnily enough it was not that I had gone back to Julian, but what I had done in the park with those young men that was a problem for him. It was a few weeks after I left Julian that he had grilled me about it. He said he did not want a slut for a girlfriend, and it was weird as Perry took drugs and did crime but seemed to have strict rules about what woman could and could not do.

Perry said he had a friend who was a real estate agent who had a house up for rent in a suburb near the beach and asked if I was interested? I could not believe it, this guy wanted to help me leave Julian; I had a chance to be free. I was once again smoking a lot of weed when the kids went to bed and Julian was out in the taxi. I would sit for hours wondering if I should go for it, how could I pull this off? I had no money and the thought of being on my own again made me sick. Things with Julian were at an all-time low. He no longer tried with anything, except working every night and watching the news. We fought constantly with loud, ugly fights that would end up with him slapping or pushing me, and I would scream at him while shoving him around and throwing things against the wall. The kids were terrified and would cry and beg us to stop. One day Lachlan had a friend over, and Julian lost his temper with him and held him around the neck and lifted him off the ground with his hands. I remember seeing the terror in my sons' eyes, but I felt powerless to stop it. On another occasion Lachlan and

I were driving alone together, a rare occurrence as Julian had banned me from going out with Lachlan by myself, and Lachlan began speaking to me about our family. It was like time stood still and I was so aware of his voice and what he was saying.

"There's a hierarchy in our house Mama," he said. "There's Julian at the top, then Erica, Isla and Belinda, Calvin, Lukas and then you Mama and the cat, and then there is me."

I felt this huge wave crash into me as I tried to comprehend his words, and it was at that exact moment that I knew I had to do something. My little boy had been so brave to confide in me about how he really felt about our home life, he had spoken from the heart. I knew I could not continue to live with Julian when it was having such a detrimental effect on my son. When we got home, I went into the bedroom and shut the door so I could think about the situation and what Lachlan had told me. It was like this voice in my head was saying, "call Tom's mum Joan. You must call Joan."

I knew deep down that I could not leave Julian on my own, I had to tell someone who would be able to help me. This went on in my head for a few days, then one day I decided that I was going to do it. I knew I was not strong enough to do it for myself, so I did it for Lachlan. I sat on the bed and with shaking hands I dialed Joan's number. When she answered, I broke down, and it was like a dam had burst and the words just poured out of me. I told her everything, the controlling behaviour, the fights, the mental and emotional abuse, and the violence towards Lachlan. Joan listened in silence as I finally spoke of the last eight years and the truth of what had been happening all along.

"I do not have any money, Joan; he keeps all the money. I want to leave, I want to leave so badly but I'm trapped, I can't leave," I sobbed.

It felt so good to finally be able to tell someone the truth.

"Louise," she said to me. "If I help you then you can never go back, do you understand? You cannot ever go back to him, not ever, not when you have told me how my grandson has been treated all these years. Because if I help you and then you go back then you will lose Lachlan, do you understand?"

I sobbed and told her that I understood. Joan said she would help me leave him, and that she would pay for the bond for the new house. I could not thank her enough, and I could not believe that after all this time I would finally be able to leave. I texted Perry and asked him to set up a viewing for the property. Within a few days I had been to see the house and it was perfect, so Joan paid the bond for me and within two weeks we were gone.

I packed our mediocre belongings, and when the day arrived, Julian was quite amicable and drove us to the house. It had not been easy telling the kids or him, he had begged and cried and told me he could not live without me. When I refused to change my mind, he got nasty, he said that I would never survive on my own and that I would be back within a week. Every time I felt myself start to give in, especially when the kids would cry and sob and beg me to stay, I would see Lachlan's face in my mind and remember what Joan said to me, so I kept on going, I kept packing and thinking of Lachlan and how we would soon be free. Poor Isla was distraught, she did not understand what was going on and why she had to leave the only family she had ever known. Julian was calm as we packed the car. He did not let me take many things, I had mine and the kid's clothes, a few toys and only two doonas. He did not let me take any of Isla and Lukas' bedding, only what was Lachlan's and mine. I snuck a carton of milk into the car with a loaf of bread, some cheese, a few snacks, and a toasted sandwich maker. We had nothing; I was leaving it all behind. We had no furniture and no real food. On the drive over Julian and I got into a huge fight, and while he was driving, we started yelling at each other, screaming, and calling each other names. Something snapped in me that day, after all the years of abuse and crap that I had suffered, I felt like I could not take it anymore, so I turned on Julian and began to punch him in the arm. He reached over and punched me on the side of the head, and all the kids were crying and begging for us to stop. I called Lachlan's dad Tom on my phone.

"Hey, can you meet me and Lachlan at the new house?" I asked him as I wiped the tears away.

"Sure," he replied. "I'll meet you there."

When we arrived at the new house Tom was there, so I jumped out of the car and ran over to him and told him what had happened. Being a non-confrontational person, he just told Julian to settle down. Julian stayed in the car while we unloaded our stuff, and the kids all ran into the house to explore. Julian's kids wanted to see the house too, but he yelled at them to get back in the car. There were a lot of tears and yelling so I quickly ran to hug them, and they left.

I looked around our new house in disbelief and I could hear the kids running around and shrieking and claiming bedrooms. Tom lingered around as Lachlan showed him which room was his. I chatted with Tom as I waited for St Vincent to arrive, I had contacted them and told them I was fleeing a domestic violence relationship, and they told me they could help me out. They arrived and brought in a queen size mattress, a single mattress, and a small couch. They also brought over pots and pans, sheets, and stuff for the kitchen like tea towels, plates, and cups. They were so kind to me, and I felt the tears welling up as I realised that I had done it, I had left him. Lachlan was so happy, and I watched him set up his little tv in the lounge so Isla and Lukas could watch a DVD. I wandered into the kitchen, which was mostly empty except for an old fridge, and I put the cheese in it and the bread in the cupboard. Tom and I helped unload all the stuff St

Vincent had brought me, and one of the ladies was so nice to me and gave me a big hug. They also brought in a box of food with cereal, pasta, sauce, milk, coffee, and sugar. I felt so grateful and overwhelmed that we were in our own home. They kept bringing in boxes of supplies and there was a toaster, a kettle and packets of biscuits and fruit for the kids. They had cleaning supplies, shampoo, and conditioner, and it was starting to feel like it could be a proper home. One of the ladies pulled me aside.

"Are you okay dear?"

I shook my head and said, "no not really."

She hugged me and told me I had done the right thing leaving him. She handed me a food voucher for IGA, and I cried even harder.

"Try to focus on the positives dear, you need to be strong for the kids," she told me.

Eventually I calmed down and as I looked around our little home, I felt a glimpse of hope that we could make it this time. I had left him, and I now had a safe home for my children. I helped Lachlan set up his bed and he kept hugging me and telling me how happy he was. I ran a bath for Isla and Lukas and watched them splash around and play. I cooked pasta and sauce for dinner, and we ate it on the couch while we watched tv. We had biscuits for dessert, and we all snuggled up together, the kids all talking excitedly. I made up the queen bed and Isla and Lukas fell asleep clutching my hands. I tucked Lachlan into his bed, and he fell asleep straight away, his blonde hair damp and sticking up from his bath. I wandered into the lounge and rummaged through a bag until I found my stash and crept outside and lit my pipe with shaking hands. I took a deep breath of smoke and tried to calm my nerves. I was in a new house with virtually not a cent to my name, I had a couple of days' worth of food and one voucher. I had called Centrelink and told them I was separated from Julian, and they told me I would be on the single parent pension soon and would be adjusting my rate of pay in a few days. I would have to save most of my family payment for rent for the next fortnight.

I stayed up late that night texting my friend Tania and Perry. Tania told me she would see us at the weekend, and Perry replied to my text, and I invited him over. He came over straight away and we took speed together. I no longer cared if it was the right thing to do, I was exhausted and beaten emotionally, mentally, and physically, and even though I knew in the back of my mind that it was wrong, I did it anyway, not thinking of the long-term consequences. I justified it by telling myself it was acceptable, as I never did it around the kids, they were fed and clothed and were safe so that made it okay, right? As it was the school holidays the next few days were a bit of a blur. DCP had given me a trailer voucher, so I was able to pick up my other furniture from Julian's house. Erica called me every single day begging me to come back, which was heartbreaking. While I loved them all so much, I knew I could never go back, but they cried and sobbed and begged me so much that I ended up texting Julian and asked him to tell them not to call anymore. I knew that it was cruel, but I was only just surviving as it was, we were all still adjusting, and the constant emotional roller coaster of the phone calls was enough to deal with.

Over the next few weeks, I cried an ocean of tears, I felt like such a failure that I had not been able to make our relationship work. I had been Calvin, Belinda, and Erica's mum for eight years and it killed me to be away from them. I had thoughts of taking them from Julian and letting them live with us. I knew that was what they wanted but I could not do it as the kids were not mine legally and I knew I would end up with a huge fight on my hands. Isla and Lukas also kept asking me why we had left and when would the kids be coming to live with us? I felt torn in half, the love that I felt for Julian's kids was enough to make me change my mind, but each time I felt myself weakening and wanted to give in, I would hear Joan's words in my head, and I knew I would never go back. Lachlan was so happy and there was no way I was going to risk losing him. I knew that I had made the right choice and I had to stick to it. When Julian and I spoke or texted each other he always said the same thing, "you're just a crazy bitch. No one is ever going to love you." I would read the texts and feel the tears welling up.

"You're useless and mad and you'll never find a job," he would say.

The horrible thing was that I really believed him. I believed that I was crazy, and no one would ever love me, how could they after all the awful things I had done? I was still depressed and had constant nightmares and flashbacks of my sexual abuse; how could I ever be normal?

Slowly the house came together, and I had beds for the kids, but most nights they slept with me. Lachlan had a desk and his x box set up and we had a dining room table also from the Salvos. We still did not have a washing machine, so we went to the laundromat after school. Lachlan would go to Tom's on the weekends and Julian would come and pick up Lukas and Isla, so I was able to catch up on sleep and relax. I had fallen into a toxic relationship with Perry and spent most weekends with him, where we would take speed and have sex for hours, all of which I would be so disassociated from, I barely knew what I was doing. Because of the speed, I then had to smoke weed to come down. I would drink constantly to cope with the fact I had become a target for Perry's abuse. During sex I would be on the ceiling the whole time and he liked to exert complete control over me. After sex I would become ill for hours, crying and burning my skin in the shower. Perry was emotionally abusive towards me, and as a long-term speed user, he was prone to angry and violent outbursts. He directed a lot of this abuse towards his daughter Abigail too, and she was terrified of him. He was ruthless and an expert manipulator, and I wanted to get away from him, but I was so hooked on his never-ending supply of drugs that I felt trapped all over again. Sometimes at the weekend, the kids and I would stay at Perry's place, but he did not care about exposing the kids to drugs like I did and made no effort to hide it from his daughter. When we stayed over at his house, I would set up a room for Lachlan and Abigail to hang out in. I would set up a bed for Isla and Lukas, but Perry resented them so much, and often told me how 'spoilt' they were. Isla absolutely hated it at Perry's house and would cry often but this would only make Perry angrier, and he would openly call her a 'naughty brat.' Lachlan did the best he could, creeping around Perry just like he had done with Julian, and I would set up his x box for him and then go into the backyard and hang out with Perry's mates, smoking and drinking all night. I tried to forget this awful situation I had gotten myself into, as Perry was becoming even more controlling and emotionally abusive towards me, and we would have epic fights where he would threaten to cut off my supply of speed, saying women could not "handle their drugs." He was obsessed with my every move and monitored where I went and what I did during the day. Because I did not have a car, Perry would come over at 6.30am and beep his horn wildly from the drive-way, and if I did not come running out the front door straight away, he would go crazy at me. I would drop him at work and then I would be free to use the car for the day, but it came with a price.

"Where have you been?" he asked me one day.

"I took the kids to school and went to the shops," I answered quickly, and he glared at me.

"What shops?" He was pacing around, and I started to feel uneasy.

"Whitfords, why?" I asked as he started towards the door.

"Yeah, well we'll see about that," he said as he took off in his car.

About an hour later he was back and stormed into my house.

"You're a f***ing liar," he yelled at me, and I looked up from my phone.

"What are you talking about?" I asked and his face was contorted with rage.

"I just drove that route and it doesn't add up!" he screamed, and I stared at him disbelievingly.

"You did what?" I asked, flinching as he came up close to my face.

"I told you I just drove that exact route and you have driven more kilometres than me, so where did you go, and you better tell me the truth this time!"

We got into a huge argument, and he accused me of cheating and would not shut up about it for days on end. He was also so abusive to Abigail, and it was heartbreaking to watch him yell at her constantly. I was becoming increasingly hooked on the speed and would stay up during the week cleaning the house obsessively, then two days later I would crash and not be able to take the kids to school. Lachlan's attendance was so bad that the school called me and said if it did not improve then they would have no choice but to ask us to leave. After that phone call I knew I had to get the drugs under control, I was also sick and tired of Perry and his aggression towards us, and I vowed to give up the speed so I could get some sort of normality back into our lives. I was becoming weary of the come downs from the drugs and the awful feelings of despair that seemed to follow.

That month the Salvos surprised me by showing up with a brand-new washing machine, and I was so grateful that I gave one of the regulars a huge hug. It was going to make such a difference to our lives, and it meant I would not have to keep using Perry's car to go to the laundromat. St Vincent were still helping me with food hampers and vouchers most months. I continued my relationship with Perry, but I was under increasing pressure from Julian to end it.

"I'll take Isla and Lukas off you Lou," he kept threatening and I believed him.

I cut back on seeing Perry on the weekdays, but I was still trying to convince him to give me the odd bit of speed now and again on the weekends.

Mostly he refused saying it was making me crazy. I was mostly off the gear, but I was becoming increasingly depressed, so was now struggling to clean the house and keep up with the washing. The kids' toys were all over the house, but I just could not seem to keep up with the never-ending dishes and mess. My mood was at an all-time low, I was crying continuously and felt so overwhelmed and unable to cope. I also burned my skin several times a day, which would give me such a feeling of control and calm. It was the only way I coped with the chaos of my life. One day Perry and I got into an argument, and I left his house in tears. When I got home, I was crying and sobbing hysterically. He called me and ended our relationship over the phone, saying, "we're done." I was gutted. I called Julian and asked him to take the kids so I could go back to hospital. He agreed, but poor Lachlan was so upset and begged me not to go. Tom came and picked him up and we had a very teary goodbye.

"Mum needs to go and get better mate," Tom kept saying to Lachlan and I watched them drive away with a pain in my heart.

I was feeling completely out of control and knew I could not keep going the way I was. If I went to hospital, then I was going to get sober from the speed and that is what I wanted. I checked myself in through the emergency department and the staff walked me into the mental health ward. I was ready to give up at that stage, and not motivated to get better at all, so I spent the first week sleeping. While I was in hospital Perry texted me.

"I didn't mean that we were done, we can work it out hey?"

By then I was completely sober, so I called him, feeling calm. We chatted for a while and then I said, "oh by the way, we're done," and hung up on him. It felt good standing up to him and feeling some control come back into my life. I was feeling so much better now that the speed was out of my system. I did not want to be an addict anymore, and I knew if I went back to Perry, then that would happen.

Marijuana was still a huge issue for me, I had even managed to sneak some into the ward and at night I would smoke in the bathroom and blow the smoke up into the exhaust fan. The doctors also gave me Lorazepam every day and I loved the floaty feeling it gave me. I listened to music on my laptop and did a lot of writing in my journal. I ignored Perry's texts which were becoming increasingly threatening. I missed the kids so much and felt bad for leaving them once again. My sister Dana brought them to see me, and we would sit in the hospital garden near the duck pond and watch the kids play. I could tell she thought that I was never coming out and would not be able to be a mother to my kids. This was the third time I had been hospitalized and I was so depressed that I had given up all hope of being able to live a normal life. Lachlan was under so much stress being away from me, and it was a tough time for him. He was staying with Tom but did not like it much. I longed for a time where I could be a proper mum to him. Lukas and Isla were slightly better off, as being with their siblings helped them cope with my absence.

The days turned into weeks in hospital, as I struggled to cope with the intense feelings of sadness and failure. I would have flashbacks and panic attacks and was relying on the Lorazepam to help me get by. The intense feelings of shame about my abuse seemed to permeate everything I did. I lived and breathed the shame and guilt of what happened to me all those years ago, and it seemed I could not escape the past; it was always in my mind no matter what I did. I knew cognitively it was not my fault and on some level that my dad was to blame for what happened to me, but the feelings were so intense, like part of my brain just did not get it. The nurses would listen patiently to me, but I could tell some of them could not understand why I still felt this way after so many years. The abuse felt like a deep, dark monster inside that was slowly devouring me, and I resigned myself to believing that I would always be this way.

Chapter 16

aiden

The one ray of hope for me was my friendship with Aiden. We had not seen each other since I had lived in the old railway cottage with the kids, but we texted often. He came to see me in hospital every single day, coming on the bus from where he was staying. He would show up with some weed and we would go for walks and smoke and chat and laugh. He would stay for hours, and we would listen to music, and he would tell me how special I was and what a great mum I was. It was like a soothing balm to my broken heart and soul. I loved being around Aiden and felt like I was 16 years old again. When he went home, I would walk him to the bus stop, and we would kiss goodbye, and his constant presence in those few weeks was the only light in my dark situation.

After four weeks I began to feel stronger, and I discharged myself from hospital. The kids came home to me, and I was overjoyed seeing them all again and feeling their little arms around me. Lachlan came running through the door and threw himself at me in a huge hug. He held on so tight to me and told me over and over, 'I love you mama."

Poor little Isla burst into tears when she first saw me, and I picked her up and hugged her tightly. Lukas said, "hi mum," and hugged me and then ran off to play with his toys, and just seeing them all was enough to keep me going.

I started to get up in the mornings and Lachlan's school attendance improved. Aiden started coming around to visit me, and at first the kids were so stand-offish with him and overprotective of me. Lachlan did not even let him sit on the couch next to me, but Aiden was like a big kid and loved to play games and do fun stuff so eventually the three of him let him in. It was the medicine that we all so desperately needed, and I would sit and watch them all play together, and it brought such joy to my heart. Aiden and I started dating at that time and then Perry contacted me and showed up in my backyard spying on us. When he saw Aiden one day in my room, he went crazy and called me a dozen times, threatening to kill Aiden. It made no sense; he was the one who had ended things with me and now he was acting like I had betrayed him. At this point I told Perry what happened between us was a huge mistake and it was only the drugs that had lured me in. That enraged him even more and one day when I was home with Lachlan, he showed up at our house, as high as a kite and yelling out threats. I was terrified and locked the door and told Lachlan to hide in his room.

"I could do it Louise," Perry screamed. "I could burn your f***ing house down."

I watched him take something out of his car, and I saw that it was a bottle of clear liquid. He started to splash it over the door and on the front window, all the while shouting, "this is how easy it would be."

I thought Perry had splashed our house with lighter fluid or something similar, so with shaking hands I immediately called the police, but he drove away, squealing his tyres as he took off down the street. A day later they arrested him, and we eventually went to court. Perry had an extensive list of criminal offenses and the DPP told me he was close to going back to prison. Because Perry was a repeat offender it did not look good for him. At the end of the hearing, they found him guilty of threatening mine and Lachlan's lives, and he received a hefty fine and was put on probation. The Magistrate made it clear that if he committed any more offences then he would have no choice but to send him to prison. I filed a VRO, and it was granted for two years. Because we lived close to one other it was going to be difficult for Perry to not come near our house. In the end he had to go around the long way home to avoid breaching the order, which made him so angry that occasionally he would drive past anyway honking his horn madly and yelling out his car window. I called the cops a few times on him, but they said it was impossible to police it, which meant he could do whatever he liked. It took many months to feel safe again, as I would often see his car in the distance, and I would feel my heart start to race.

Aiden was spending more time at our place, which helped me deal with the whole situation, but still I was anxious most days when I went out, expecting Perry to pop up out of nowhere and hurt me. Aiden and I tried to put the whole thing behind us the best we could, and the kids were still going to their dads every second weekend which meant Aiden and I had time to ourselves. Aiden had been living with his cousin and the one night he went back there, I ended up calling him.

"Hey, I miss you so much," I said to him, "come back. And don't leave again."

So, he did. Saturday afternoons when the kids were out, we would get weed and do grocery shopping. Aiden always helped me out with paying for the kids for whatever they needed, and he was amazing with the kids and always let me sleep in. He would take them to the park, make them lunch and he was gentle and loving and was slowly learning how to parent them. As much as we cared for the kids, Aiden and I were both still completely addicted to marijuana. We tried to tell ourselves it did not affect the kids, but the truth was that after paying the rent and buying food, the only other priority was weed. We never smoked in front of the kids, we would go out into our courtyard and try to keep it from them. I could not sleep unless I smoked before bed, and I thought that it helped me stay calm. I knew I had a problem, but I was so afraid of not sleeping that I could not even think about giving it up. When the kids went to their dads', Aiden and I would travel all over in search of weed, and we would wait for hours sometimes at various houses, talking and watching tv while we waited. It was like my life force, and I could not do anything without first having a smoke. Driving, cooking, shopping – I had to have a smoke before I did any of those things.

One night Aiden and I were out in the courtyard smoking when we heard a loud sound like a truck or Ute reversing near our house. Our neighbour's driveway was right next to ours, so we did not think anything of it, as we thought it was him. Suddenly this vehicle connected with my car which was in our driveway and started pushing it into the fence. The sound of metal on metal was deafening and I started screaming because we could see my car coming through the fence and into the back garden bed. We were almost frozen on the spot, trying to make sense of what we were seeing. We heard the Ute change gears and start to go back down the driveway, so Aiden ran out the side gate and saw it speeding off into the night. I stood looking at my car which was now completely crumpled, not to mention the fence which was almost squashed flat. We called the police and they asked who I thought was responsible, and I immediately thought of Perry. He did not drive a Ute, but I was convinced he had someone do it for him to pay me back for pressing charges against him. The next day I got a text from Perry's daughter Abigail.

"Hey, I saw a Ute at dad's place that has a big dent in the back of it and some yellow paint," the text read.

I tried telling the police to go and look for a Ute in the area with yellow paint on it, but they did not really buy it. It was so frustrating, as here was this man who was behaving like such a lunatic and there was nothing that I could do. I was scared all the time, not knowing what Perry would do next. The VRO felt like a bloody joke, and Julian kept putting pressure on me, saying that the kids were not safe, and I tried to tell him that they were okay, but even I doubted they were. He kept saying he wanted them to go live with him for a little while, but I knew that Isla and Lukas would not cope being away from me again.

The cops never did look for the Ute which really annoyed me.

"I'm sure Perry did it," I said to Aiden repeatedly.

"Yeah, I'd believe it," Aiden would reply.

I was without a car, and the situation was such a mess and the poor owners had to put in an insurance claim for the fence. I was so afraid that I barely slept. Lachlan's room faced the back yard, and I would lie in bed at night and go through the 'what ifs,' in my mind constantly. Aiden and I tried to move ahead with things and put it all behind us, but it was hard.

One of Isla's friends had two Maltese dogs that had puppies, so we decided spontaneously to get a dog. He had white fur and brown eyes and was the cutest thing we had ever seen. When we brought him home Lachlan promptly named him Samuel, and he was so small he had to go in the pram when we walked to pick the kids up from school. Lukas was now in Kindy, Isla in Year One and Lachlan was in Year five. Being at a different school made it hard for Lachlan in the mornings but his dad bought him a bike, so he started riding to school as we were still without a car.

I received $2000 dollars from the insurance company, and I decided to try my luck at getting a decent car. Julian agreed to be co-borrower, so I put in an application, using the insurance money as a deposit. It was at that time that Aiden and I started praying together a bit more. Aiden had been a Christian for a lot longer than me and was more familiar with the whole concept of praying, and I had tried praying before but ended up feeling silly, like I was not saying the right thing, or that God did not really care about our needs. But after the whole Perry saga, I decided to give it a go. One afternoon I was praying for God to approve my car application, and the car yard called and said my loan application had been approved! I was overjoyed and proudly drove it home. After that Aiden started saying stuff like, "God is so faithful," and, "God really cares about us."

"We need to join a church," Aiden suggested so we picked one that had helped us out with food in the past few months.

It was a nice church, and everyone was friendly. Isla and Lukas went to the kid's church, but Lachlan did not want to, so I accepted his decision and did not force the issue. I started reading my bible too, and I felt like I was starting to understand that Jesus had died for me on the cross and that He wanted me to be in a relationship with Him. I still felt unqualified for His love, but I tried hard to listen to the sermons and take it all in. Over the next few months, I read all four chapters of the gospel and felt amazed by it all. Someone loved me, and He loved me enough to give His life for me! It was overwhelming to say the least.

Life had improved with the new car, but my mood swings were at an all-time high. Everything set me off and I would constantly pick fights with Aiden. I was always on a short fuse and would blow up over pretty much everything. I yelled, screamed, and threw things, and sometimes kicked holes in the doors and one time I smashed up a beautiful salt ceramic candle holder that Veronica had given me. I was so unpredictable and poor Aiden endured the brunt of my anger. I never hit the kids, but I yelled so much that poor Lukas would go and hide in Isla's room until I calmed down. A few times I attacked Aiden, and he would be forced to defend himself, but when I was calm things were good. We would spend weekends with the kids at the park with Samuel, and I felt like we were a real family. We tried to keep smoking a secret from the kids, especially Lachlan. I knew he had done health education at school, and they had talked about drugs. I was so worried he would find out, so I tried harder than ever to hide it. We had a blue cosmetic case with a padlock on it and we kept our stash in there. One day I came home to find Lachlan with the case, and he had broken the lock. When he discovered the weed, he was so angry and began yelling at me.

"Mama how could you," he sobbed.

He was so upset that he could not look me in the eyes, and I was devastated for him, and Aiden tried to talk to him, but he was too angry. Lachlan locked himself in his bedroom and did not want to talk to me at all. When he came out, he could barely look at me.

"Mama I am embarrassed to know you. I don't know who you are anymore," he said. "I just can't believe my mum is a drug addict."

I pretended not to be hurt, but it cut like a knife. That night when it came to our usual routine of smoking, I went through the motions, but my heart was not in it. I kept seeing Lachlan's little face when he refused to look at me. I kept seeing him with the case in his hands and how angry and disappointed he was with me. Inside I felt crushed, so the next day when he got home from school, I asked him to come outside. I told him to get the big green rubbish bin and bring it into the courtyard, and then I got the case and handed it to him.

"I want you to throw everything away, all of it," I told Lachlan. He stared at me with big eyes.

"Are you sure mum?" he asked, and I nodded.

"I don't want to do it anymore mate, but I need your help."

So together we threw it all out – the lighters, the bongs, the weed and even the scissors. As I saw it all going in the bin, I felt this release I had never felt before, it was so freeing. When Aiden got home, I told him what I had done.

"So, you chucked it all out?" he asked me.

"Yep, it's all gone," I answered, and he was shocked and just stood there looking at me.

"So, do you want me to quit too?" he asked, and I looked at him.

"Yeah, I do, we need to do it for the kids," I replied, and he agreed but I could tell that he was not happy.

That night it felt strange not to smoke, but I also felt peace with my decision. I could hold my head high and more importantly my son was proud of me. The next few days were rough as I found it hard to eat and sleep and I was very cranky. I had hot and cold flushes and felt sick constantly, but I persisted and gradually it got easier and easier. The headaches were becoming less frequent, and my appetite increased. I also did something I had not done since we got the new car, I prayed. I prayed that God would take away my cravings and ease my symptoms, and to my surprise He did. After 2 weeks I no longer craved weed anymore, and I truly felt like I had put it behind me. Aiden quit too and I could tell he was not happy about it, but I felt free. Having the respect of my son was all that mattered to me, and I decided to never go back.

We kept going to church and the services were nice and we slowly got to know people, but to be honest I felt out of my depth. Surely all these people were more deserving than me of God's love and forgiveness. I was convinced they did not have the past that I had, and I could not really understand who God was. I had some sort of notion of Him, but I was not sure that I was deserving of His mercy and His grace. I had done horrible things, shameful things, and I had had horrible things done to me. I had done drugs, been promiscuous and cheated on two of my partners. I read about sinners in the New Testament, and they had all been forgiven by Jesus. I understood it cognitively, but in my heart, I was tainted, and I felt like the love I had for God would never be good enough.

Chapter 17

finding faith

Around Easter time our friend from school invited us to her church, and it was a huge church, but I immediately felt at home. There was a morning and a night service where they served dinner to the kids, so we started going to the 5pm service. Lukas really enjoyed the kids' church, but poor Isla did not really settle. She was always super anxious without me, so it made it hard for me to relax and enjoy the message. At home things were okay but we were always broke and the house was a mess. I was very up and down with my moods; I started seeing a different GP who put me on new medication, it was an anti-depressant with adrenaline in it. I had been on an old one for many years and he thought that the new one would suit my depression better. It was hard at first, but after a few weeks I felt better and less sad. I started to feel something I had not really felt before; hope. Aiden was still on and off with the weed and I decided not to force the issue. He had been exposed to it as a young teenager and it had affected him differently to me. Maybe because I had not started smoking until I was an adult, it was easier for me to give it up, either way it was one of the best decisions I had ever made in my life. It was at this time that I felt God speaking to me about mine and Aiden's relationship. One night I was up late and felt God was not happy with us living together any longer without being married.

"I was praying last night, and I think we should get married, like I think God wants us to," I casually announced to Aiden the next morning. He stared at me, and I laughed.

"We can't live in sin anymore babe. We need to do the right thing."

The look on Aiden's face was priceless, but to my surprise he agreed. So, no romantic proposal, no big shiny ring but it was the right thing to do. We told our families straight away and I began planning what I wanted to do for our special day. We settled on a date which gave us just over three months to get everything ready. One night I felt God speaking to me about our engagement, and I felt like He wanted us to have a proper engagement, and not sleep together until the wedding. Of course, Aiden was not happy about the arrangement, but I insisted it was what God wanted and he agreed. I had an old friend who was a marriage celebrant, and she agreed to do the wedding. We did not have much money, but I felt like the moment that we agreed to the engagement, then God began to bless us financially. Our families told us they would help with the catering and drinks, which was such a relief as money was extremely tight. My sister was a wedding photographer and her business partner said that she would take the photographs and decorate the house for the reception. We chose some gardens in the city for the ceremony, as it was so beautiful and green, and I could imagine my mum approving. Tania called me one day.

"Hey Lou, do you want my wedding dress, I mean I'm not going to need it anytime soon," she said, and I was speechless.

"Are you sure?" I asked her and she insisted.

I could not believe it and cried a little when I tried it on, and Tania hugged me and said that I looked beautiful. Dana was amazing and seemed to know how to organize everything for the wedding, she was a huge support to me when it felt overwhelming. She asked a decorator friend of hers for some chairs and decorations for the ceremony. We booked a tuxedo for Aiden, however as the date drew nearer, we realised we had run out of money, so he had to make do with a Target shirt and pants. Lachlan had the same outfit as Aiden, and Lukas had a little waistcoat and bowtie and looked so adorable. Dana's daughter Evelyn and Isla were flower girls and had matching dresses and little feathered headpieces that I made on mum's old Bernina sewing machine. Dana and Tania were my bridesmaids and after spending half a day looking for the perfect dress for them, we finally found one they both liked. Everything had been coming together in the last few weeks, and I could not believe that we were going to pull it off.

The day was fast approaching, and Aiden and I were fighting a lot. It was so stressful planning all the little details and his family were starting to put pressure on him about the guest list. We knew we had to stick to a budget and could not invite everyone, but they made it clear that they were not happy. I stopped eating properly and made dozens of lists every day. I lost a lot of weight, but luckily my dress had a tie up back or it would have hung off me. To keep costs down we had agreed to have the reception at our place, so I hired some trestle tables and tablecloths for the courtyard. We spent a few days writing our vows and it ended up being a story of how we met, which I thought was romantic and would make up for our short engagement. The day before the wedding Dana and her business partner Amberly came and decorated the courtyard with candles and lanterns, and it looked so pretty. Aiden stayed at his grandma's house that night and I ended up calling him hysterically at one point, completely overwhelmed by the whole thing.

"Babe everything is going to be okay," he reassured me, and I felt a bit better.

Aiden's mum Lorna stayed with me that night.

"It will be great," she told me. "I will do your nails and it will be a girly night for us. You just relax and I'll pamper you."

But that is not what happened at all, as Lorna ended up outside in our backyard smoking and talking on her phone, and we did not bond and there was not any pampering going on. I felt so hurt and anxious that I went to bed.

The next day I woke up at 5am and began frantically cooking, as I was terrified, we would not have enough food. My brother arrived with beer and wine and decorated the car with a white ribbon. My sister arrived with Amberly, who began taking photos of all of us getting ready. We went to the hairdresser and Tania met us there, and as I sat in the chair and watched Isla getting her hair done, I could not believe that we were going ahead with getting married. It seemed surreal somehow and I was so nervous that I had a glass of champagne to try and calm my nerves.

Back at home we had our makeup done and Isla was so excited to get her own little lip gloss to wear. By the time I slipped into my dress I finally felt like a bride. Isla looked so beautiful in her dress, and I tried hard not to cry. Lukas was so cute in his outfit but was coming down with a fever, so I sat next to him in the car and by the time we got to the gardens, he was like a limp rag. I had to carry him down the garden path towards the clearing where all the guests were gathered. I met my sister and Tania and we all walked together, and as soon as I saw Aiden and Lachlan, this lovely peace came over me, and everything felt simply perfect. As we said our vows this wind came from nowhere and it swirled all around us. When we said, "I do," this little shower of leaves fell onto us, and a duck flew in and settled on the pond; it was like God was all around us.

After the photos we went back to our place for the reception, and as we arrived everyone clapped and cheered, it was a wonderful moment. I could not believe how good the courtyard looked and how much food we had! I had been stressing out for no reason at all, and it was like God had blessed us in every way. I had a glass of wine and when I looked away Isla accidentally picked it up and took a long drink, thinking it was apple juice. I was horrified and quickly took it off her. She later claimed that it woke her up and she was 'ready to party' but then Julian arrived to take her and Lukas home with him. Lachlan was going to stay with Tom and our friends had kindly paid for us to stay in a motel near the beach for a few nights.

As we left, I started to get nervous as we had not been intimate together for four months. I felt so anxious and overwhelmed as we arrived at the motel. Once we were inside, we started to open our wedding cards and could not believe how much money we had been blessed with. There was enough for a week's rent and for us to spoil ourselves with dinner out. I promptly burst into tears, as it was all too much to cope with. We lay on the bed and Aiden held me as I let it all out. Afterwards we made love as husband and wife, and it was wonderful. We had such a lovely time on our honeymoon and did not want to go home. Once we arrived the kids came back, and we opened our presents, and we were really excited about what the future held for us.

Not long after the wedding Tania called me and said she had booked two tickets for her and me to go to Bali together. I did not want to go at first, it being so close to our wedding, but Aiden insisted, and I quickly got my passport organised.

"Babe we'll be fine," Aiden said. "I'll do all the school runs and you and Tania have a good time."

My brother Dylan had come to live with us before the wedding as he had separated from his girlfriend Laura, and I felt for him at the wedding as Laura had spent all their wedding savings on drugs, and he was devastated. They had four beautiful children together, but he was not allowed to see them, and it was hard for him to be kept out of their lives. I felt uncomfortable leaving Dylan at home with Aiden and the kids, as he was a heavy drinker and there was tension between Dylan and Aiden.

"Are you sure it's okay if I go?" I kept asking Aiden.

"Lou we will be alright, just go and have some fun."

I headed off to Bali and I was so excited once we landed. Tania had booked us a beautiful resort which was filled with frangipanis, and it was so peaceful, and I immediately fell in love with it. We had such a fun time together, and I was eating, drinking, and stealing the odd cigarette from Tania. We did drunk karaoke and were cracking up so much we could barely sing. We found a friendly taxi driver named Pat who we quickly became friends with, and he took us on a few tours of rice paddies and the bird and reptile park. Bali was beautiful and Pat took us to meet his family. His Grandmother had never seen westerners before, and I was overcome with emotion as he showed us around his family home. One night I decided to get a tattoo, so Pat took us to his friend's shop and after a few shots of Jack Daniels I went in and designed one; it was a frangipani design with Aiden's and the kids' names around the petals, and I was happy with the result and ended up keeping it a secret. When we arrived home, everyone rushed to greet me, and Aiden told me later that things with Dylan were not good.

"He is drinking so much babe. And when he came back from work, he got stuck into Lachlan too, it was bad Lou."

We both agreed he had to leave once he got back from his next swing in the mines. I felt sad, as I loved my brother, but he was angry, distant, and it was not working with all of us living together. If Dylan had his own place, he would be able to work out a custody agreement with Laura and be able to see his kids. I felt for him because he was a good dad, and I knew that his children would be missing him dearly.

The next week the owners of our house told us they were selling the property, so it seemed like a suitable time for Dylan to get his own place.

We found a house on the same street and made plans to start packing. The house was such a mess, and it took us a long time to get everything ready. One of our friends from church brought his van over and helped us move. We were so happy with the new place having air conditioning, having battled through many sweltering summers we were looking forward to some cool relief. Isla was so excited to have her own room and spent days decorating it. The boys shared a room, which was fine as Lukas spent most of his time in the games room with his toys. I felt so happy that things were going well for us. Lachlan was in his last year of primary school; Isla was in year two and Lukas was in preprimary school. We settled in quickly at the new house and the school was just across the road, which made life easier for us.

We were still going to the big church, and we had started going to a connect group at one of the Pastors homes which we were really enjoying. I felt closer to God than ever before, and I was praying every day. Worship music had become a big part of our lives, and we would play CDs and feel the peace that it brought to our home. Even though I was slowly starting to understand more of what Jesus had done for us on the cross, I still felt depressed and ashamed of my past. Some days were harder than others and I relied heavily on medication for sleep, and I was still burning myself when I had flashbacks of my abuse. It was not long before Aiden and I were fighting regularly, as one thing I could not understand was why he kept going back to the weed when I was able to give it up. I did not get why Aiden could not just quit like I had.

"It's different for me babe, I started when I was thirteen," he explained to me. "I grew up with it and it feels normal for me. Plus, my mum used to grow it too."

I decided to leave it and not harass him so much about it. Married life was good, but we fought a lot, mostly about money, and it was usually me who would start the fights. I was critical of Aiden, and picky, and would often fly into a rage over nothing. I would yell and scream and break things, and neither of us were working so money was very tight. Aiden did a forklift course and got a job in a warehouse, with a steady income, but he hated it. It was stinking hot in the summer and freezing in the winter, and he was bullied by the other blokes, but things were better financially for us. Isla was seven and she was such a darling. She and Aiden were close, and he would play make believe with her which she loved. They would play make up salons and doctors and it was so lovely to watch them play together. She would be in her element, bossing him around and making him do math sums in a book. Lukas was tiny and adorable but extremely clever. He loved trains, cars and him and Aiden would watch sports on tv. Aiden taught him how to kick a football and they would play together at the park after school.

Lachlan was still seeing his dad but was becoming more reluctant to visit him. I watched it happen slowly over a couple of months, where he would come home in tears after returning on a Sunday night and be upset for a few days afterwards. It got to the point where he was becoming more distressed on Friday afternoons before going to his dad's.

"It's okay sweetie, you can have a break from seeing your dad if you like," I said to him one day.

The relief on Lachlan's face told me I had made the right decision, but telling Tom and was not easy.

"What do you mean he doesn't want to see me? What about tomorrow then?" he asked when I called him.

Tom could not understand why Lachlan needed a break and the phone call had not gone well, but I could see that a forced relationship was taking a toll on Lachlan, and I could not put him through it any longer.

"I feel like I have to constantly go out with him mama, like we always have to be doing stuff and it's tiring," Lachlan explained.

Tom was not a bad father; it was just too much for Lachlan having to deal with two families and I was 100% behind him all the way. I could see that Lachlan was suffering mentally and emotionally, and I was not going to make him do something that he did not want to do. Tom also smoked weed which Lachlan found hard to deal with, and I did not want him in that environment when I had tried hard to give that up myself. Tom still called every fortnight to see him, but Lachlan refused. Tom cried and argued and got angry and even got his mum involved, but neither of them could understand how Lachlan felt.

"How can you withhold him from me Lou, he's, my son!"

Tom was angry and directed it mostly at me, so I tried my best to stay calm and make it all about Lachlan.

Deep down I felt like I had forced Lachlan into a relationship with his dad from an early age. Everyone had told me how different it would be once Lachlan had been born, that Tom would want him, but he never really did. Tom had never wanted me or Lachlan and that was something my son was beginning to question and understand as he got older. After Lachlan was born, I was told constantly that I had to include the baby in Tom's life, I could not cut him out, that I needed to think about Tom's rights as a father. I had never asked Lachlan if he had wanted to see his dad, I had just assumed it was the right thing to do. I felt guilty for sending him to his dad so I could have a 'break.' As Lachlan grew into a teenager, I realised that I had made a mistake, as Lachlan never wanted a part-time dad who paraded him around to his friends and family. Lachlan later confided in me that after we had left Julian and moved to our new house, Tom picked him up from school one day and they had started chatting.

"Dad did you know that Julian was horrible to me. Like he abused me dad."

Lachlan started to cry in the car, but once Lachlan started crying, Tom started crying too, as Tom felt bad that he had not known about the abuse. Lachlan said he had looked over at his dad and immediately stopped crying, as Lachlan realised from that moment on, he could not receive any emotional support from his dad. I felt sad when Lachlan had relayed this to me, but it also made me think that Lachlan needed support to get through the trauma of the abuse, so Lachlan started counseling and I tried to get Tom to come along but he refused. All I could do was pray and hope that one day their relationship would be restored. Tom was a good person; and I knew in my heart that he just needed to give Lachlan space to grow up and to be healed from the past.

Aiden and I decided that we were ready to get baptised at our church, and a year later Isla and then Lukas followed. It was an incredible decision for all of us, and I felt so much closer to God, and that His hand was on our family.

2015 came and I was suffering terribly with my periods. I was anemic and could not even get out of bed, so I saw a gynecological surgeon who decided to give me a partial hysterectomy. I had the surgery, but it was not pleasant and extremely painful.

"You know it was impossible to cut through all that scar tissue from your C sections," the surgeon later told me. "And I do not know who did your last caesarean, but they were a hack. I had to fix all that up."

In the end my surgery was five hours long and the recovery was equally as tough. There were sixty-year-old women being discharged before me. Once I got home, I was in so much pain I had to have morphine, which helped take the edge off. I had to stay in bed for a few weeks, but gradually I began to heal.

Centrelink wanted me to get a job as Lukas was turning 7, and I was terrified. I had not worked since 2005 and I had no idea what I was going to do. Little Isla was so attached to me and hated to be away from me, and who would employ me after being out of the workforce for so long? There were lots of childcare jobs, but I did not want to do that. I was looking for jobs one day when one caught my eye, it was for an Autism service and seeing how I had lots of experience with special needs, I applied for it. I was not expecting to be considered, but I was at the park with the kids one day when I received a phone call from the coordinator.

"Can you come in for an interview tomorrow?" she asked.

"Uh yes I can do that," I responded quickly.

I was stunned and shocked to say the least, and I was also petrified. I had been out of the workforce for so long, and I was convinced I would never be able to return to work. The day of the interview came, and I felt positively ill from anxiety. On the way I prayed to the Holy Spirit, "Holy Spirit please guide me and help me answer the questions, and if I get stuck then give me the words to say."

Even though I had a diploma and lots of experience, I still felt under-qualified for the job, but the coordinator was so lovely and welcoming.

"I haven't had a job in ten years," I explained nervously.

"It's okay," the manager said to me, "we like your resume."

Everything went well and at one point I got so tongue tied I prayed silently for the Holy Spirit to give me the right answer and it worked! The next day they called me and offered me the job. I was so excited and afraid at the same time. It was two days a week to start off with, which suited our family well. I remember the first day clearly, I had been instructed to observe the groups of children and the carers, but the centre was not like any other I had experienced before. Small groups of children were led by educators and there were extremely specific techniques used to guide and care for them. In the first week I learned so much about autism, but I was exhausted. I began my group leader training, and it was both rewarding and tiring. I slowly got to know all the families and I came to really enjoy the job. It was an amazing experience and I just loved it, and I also really liked the other staff members and formed close friendships. I was impressed by how brave the parents were and their utter dedication to improving their children's lives. One mum had not been able to leave the house with her son for almost two years because of his autism. To be able to support his family and give much needed therapy to him felt good. Some of the children went on to attend mainstream schools, sometimes without a teaching aide too. Our program was unique and seemed to make such a difference in these families' lives. I was extremely tired in those first few months, but I began to develop real patience and an empathy towards families that I had not experienced in my years in childcare, but it was hard to balance work and home.

Lachlan was thirteen now and would help babysit Isla and Lukas after school. For a few months we had a dual income and boy that was great. But as my hours increased, so did my anxiety and my fights with Aiden. A few months later Aiden was let go by the 4WD company and he was gutted. I was upset too, as it had been so nice having two incomes. Aiden was really struggling with depression at this time, and he went to see his GP who prescribed a good antidepressant. It did not help that he was still smoking weed most weekends, but the meds helped, and he became a house husband while I worked four days a week.

My anxiety was high, and I struggled to switch off at night. Aiden and I were still attending the same church, but I felt unseen there, and unable to break into the already formed friendship groups. Isla was still struggling with bad separation anxiety which was made worse by me working. Lukas was not really enjoying the kids' church either and said the other kids were not that friendly. At home Isla was very anxious and would not let me out of her sight, and if I did go out without her, she would run down the drive-way crying and screaming.

Lachlan was doing better now that he was not seeing his dad. He joined army cadets and loved it, and he went every week. At the weekends he would go to camps and was learning so many new skills. I was proud of him for joining and he had so much fun on the camps.

Aiden and I were still fighting on a regular basis, and when we were inti-mate, I was just on the ceiling. I tried to be present, but it was impossible for me, as sex triggered me a lot, and I was often disassociated. I trusted Aiden and he never pressured me, not once, but I still could not be present. For days afterwards I would be teary and angry, and I blamed Aiden too. It was not his fault at all of course, it was the abuse that triggered me. I was self-harming with hot water too most days, and I tried so hard to give it up, but I was like a pressure cooker and burning my skin was like letting the steam out. It did not help that Aiden was still smoking and I hated being around him when he was stoned.

Lukas was doing so well at school and joined our local cricket team. I loved watching him learn to bat and bowl and he had a natural talent for it. It was also so good for his asthma to be playing a sport. Aiden was his big-gest fan, and it was lovely to watch them together. Lukas and Isla still went to Julian's on the weekends, but I worried it was not a suitable environment for them. My anxiety was so high, and I had a restless energy which was hard to control. I found it difficult to unwind on the weekends too, even sitting and watching a movie for me was a challenge. I always had to be busy doing something, it was one of my main coping methods.

Aiden was becoming more reliant on weed, and it was costing us money that we did not have. I was becoming angry with him for his addiction and as 2016 approached, I realised that he needed to do something, so I ended up issuing him with an ultimatum.

"Either you get clean babe, or we separate," I told him one day.

I did not want to, as I loved him and he was a great father, but the kids were young and needed him to be emotionally present and sober. I could not see us going the distance as a family if he were addicted.

When I look back now, I downplayed the seriousness of his addiction, I know he did.

"It's just weed," he would often say, but all I knew was that the drugs were getting the best part of him, and that we were second best.

I was praying most days and I felt closer to God, but I could not understand why Aiden just could not give it up. God had helped me quit, so why wouldn't He just do the same with Aiden?

I had a relationship with God, but I was still surrounded by fear and shame and feelings of unworthiness, most of it stemming from my failures as a parent and wife. I needed Aiden to be sober so we could figure out this journey together. We learned about a drug program called 'New Life Recovery' and I once more issued an ultimatum to him, "sign up for the program or leave." This program was at a residential facility, and it was a long way away, but I knew it was going to take something drastic to get Aiden sober, so, he went on the waiting list. I knew if he were accepted that it would be extremely hard for us to be away from one another, we had not been apart since 2012, but I also knew we could not keep going the way that we were. To be considered for the program, you had to call in every week to keep your place, and the person with the addiction had to do it, not a family member, so it was up to the addict to get into the program. That was extremely hard for me, as while Aiden had expressed a desire to get help, it was a big commitment to call every week and keep your place on the list. I prayed every day, and Aiden and I also prayed together.

No one in our church knew what was going on because both of us felt too much shame to reach out to anyone there. Everyone was always so happy in the church, and I was unsure if anyone had dealt with addiction before. The only real support we had was from the intake coordinator, Peter, who we met in person after Aiden went on the waiting list. The months went on and to give Aiden credit, he called every single week without fail. I knew it was only a matter of time before his place in the program would come up. Telling the kids was hard, and Isla and Lukas were so young and did not want him to go.

"I am really proud of you Aiden," Lachlan said to him one night, and that meant so much to Aiden and it gave him the encouragement he needed to keep going.

Finally in June, just before Aiden's birthday, we got the call; Aiden was to leave the first week in July. I was overjoyed and devastated all at once. I could not believe I was going to be on my own again, but I knew it was God taking care of the situation and I had to trust Him. Aiden tried hard to cut back on the weed before he left. He had always found detox to be awful, and he lost his appetite and dry retched a lot, but he had been told it would be much easier than doing a full detox down there.

Chapter 18

on my own again

"I'm going to miss you so much," I sobbed in his arms at night.

"I know," Aiden said, "but this is my chance to get sober and I can't risk losing you and the kids."

The hardest part was knowing that once he was away, then we would not have contact with him for the first two weeks. It was an integral part of the program, to not be in touch with family members, to encourage the participants to fully immerse themselves and not to rely on others to get them through. There was a distinct Christian component of the program too which sounded like just what Aiden needed to heal and get sober. He packed and we cried and tried to spend as much time together as a family. Participants had to be on the dole to help fund the program, so I had to go to Centrelink and tell them Aiden and I were separating, and that was hard. I applied for single parenting payment as it was the only way I was going to be able to pay the rent without him. The feeling it gave me made me ill, but I was determined to support Aiden in getting sober. Even though I felt dread in my heart at us being apart, I knew it was God's plan. It was hard for me to go to Centrelink and formally separate, as I loved being married and after being a single mum in the past, the thought of it happening again left me feeling distraught. I did not know how I was going to survive emotionally either without Aiden, as he was my main support, but I had to trust God and I kept praying that He would make a way. The day arrived and the kids said a very teary goodbye. I drove us to the bus station in East Perth, and as we sat in the car for a few minutes, we were both overwhelmed and crying a lot. I sat and watched Aiden board the bus, which felt surreal, and by the time I watched the bus pull away I was a real mess. I called my coordinator Leah on the way to work.

"I can't do it," I wailed down the phone to her.

"Yes, you can Lou," she told me. "You're strong and the kids need you."

She talked to me calmly and waited for me to stop bawling before encouraging me to come to work. Leah had been so supportive of our situation over the past few weeks, and by the time I got to work I felt better.

The first few days were hard, the kids missed Aiden a lot and there were a lot of tears. They constantly asked when he would be back home. They also had to start before and after school care which was a huge adjustment for all of us. Waking up while it was still dark and going out into the cold so I could get to work by 8am was so hard. I felt numb and disbelief that this was our life now, and I relied heavily on my coordinator who was a fantastic support for me. Leah was a pillar of strength for me for those first two weeks. As I drove to work, I would become overwhelmed, and I would often call her.

"I feel like I can't keep going," I would sob to her.

"You can do it Lou, I believe in you," Leah would say.

When I arrived at work, she would speak words of hope to me, and then she would give me a huge hug. Somehow the kids and I got through those first few weeks, and Aiden was finally allowed to call us, and it was wonderful to hear his voice. We all cried a lot, and then he called me one day crying and saying he wanted to come home.

"I can't do it," he sobbed, "because it's so strict here and it's so hard and I just want to come home."

I took a deep breath before answering.

"Babe," I said to him. "God wants you to keep going and get sober so we can be a family again."

"But I am sober," he replied. "If you let me come home, I promise I won't smoke anymore."

It was so hard for me to stay calm and not yell at him.

"I'm sorry," I said holding in the tears, "but you have to stay."

Eventually we said goodbye, but I felt like there was a knife in my heart.

Aiden was allowed to make regular calls, which was great, but he always seemed to call at the most inconvenient times, like when I was driving or shopping. Sometimes Isla would be having a meltdown and a few times I yelled at Aiden that I was not coping. Fortunately, he was a bit further along in the program and was able to reassure me that everything was going to be okay. Eventually he was allowed to call every Sunday, which suited us much better.

"I am getting so close to God babe, and I'm doing well in the program," he told me one Sunday, and it filled my heart with joy to hear his words.

He told me that students had to read the bible, memorise scriptures, and do lots of chores. I had to laugh when he was put in charge of feeding the chickens when he had a fear of birds. The main emphasis of the program was to develop a relationship with the Lord, and I started to feel hopeful that things would be much better in our relationship.

Aiden had to work out all the reasons of what led him to the drugs in the first place. For Aiden it was several things, his mum had grown cannabis when he was a young teen and that was his first introduction to drugs, and at aged fourteen he began smoking and it quickly became a habit. His mum also had two violent partners, who were physically and mentally abusive towards him, so weed was his escape. On several occasions, Aiden was attacked physically by his stepfather which left him emotionally damaged, and weed was his comforter. Aiden's biological father had abandoned him at an early age, so he had no real memory of him. He also lost his grandad who he was close to, and weed was the answer to his grief.

Aiden's relationship with his mum Lorna was also a very strange one, and she treated Aiden more like a partner than a son and relied on him heavily for emotional support. She never took responsibility for her poor choices during Aiden's childhood, and for how this had impacted him. Lorna chose instead to stay in the abusive relationships and, at one point sent him away to his aunties, saying she could not, "handle him." All these factors contributed to and fueled Aiden's addiction and led to him making some poor choices too. When he was twenty-one, he was charged with aggravated burglary, but fortunately, he was spared a custodial sentence.

Aiden was forced to confront his issues during the program, and a past that had led him to his cannabis habit. Getting to really know God was a crucial part of the program and for his recovery and healing. After a few more weeks Aiden was allowed a home visit, but I was nervous, as I had settled into a routine and was worried how Aiden would fit back in. I was also worried he would also be tempted to go back to the drugs. The visit was okay but not great, and Aiden tried hard to be positive but all I felt was doubt. He kept saying how much he had learned and seemed to really want to stay sober. I thought it was much too early for real change and felt skeptical to say the least, but the kids were so happy to see him which was lovely for them. Although it hurt to admit it, I was relieved when he went back on the bus.

The kids and I went back to our life without him, and I felt overwhelmed most days and relied heavily on God for strength. I too was working on my relationship with Him, and I kept praying that Aiden would be fully healed and we would go back to being a family again. I longed for us to be reunited properly without the addiction lingering over us. It was hard financially and now I was working five days a week; it felt a bit relentless. The house was always a mess, but Julian was helpful, which was nice. He asked me a few times if Aiden was coming back for good and I told him eventually yes, he would. I had the weekends to rest but my anxiety was extremely high, and I was prone to panic attacks too which were awful. Would Aiden be fully healed? Could I trust God that he would not go back to the drugs after returning home? The weeks went on and Aiden was due home for another visit. I was missing him terribly and it had been almost six months. This visit felt different, however, as Aiden was super calm and spent time with God every day reading his bible and praying. I could sense a real change in him, and it filled my heart with joy, as he was happy and settled and spent quality time with the kids.

"Babe," he said to me after a few days. "I feel like I have changed so much. I've grown up and I really don't want to go back. I am ready to come home."

We prayed and prayed for God to guide us and lead us and I could feel that it was the right decision for our family. Aiden was about to enter stage 3 of a 4-stage program, but I trusted God to help him make the right decision. So, Aiden did not go back, and we organised for his stuff to be posted home. That Christmas was truly a happy one.

I was working five days a week again and Aiden was a wonderful stay at home dad, as the house was organised and the kids were happy and so was I. Aiden seemed so different, like a real man of God. He put scriptures up in our room and he prayed over them every day. I could tell his relationship with God had gone to another level and I was both pleased and a little envious. He had the opportunity to go away and fix himself while I was left to 'man the ship.' It is true to say that I felt resentment towards Aiden, and it was not long before I was back to yelling and screaming at him. It was like a switch would go off and I would change in an instant. When I think back now, I can see clearly, I was suffering from PTSD, but at the time I could not see it. Something so small would trigger me and I would yell and throw things. I would go from 0-100 in the blink of an eye, and it was frightening for everyone in the house. Poor Lukas would run and hide when I started up. Lachlan, I think, was used to it, which was a horrible concept, and no wonder poor Isla had emotional difficulties, her mum was hysterical all the time. Isla no longer had separation anxiety, but she would have these meltdowns where she would just cry and cry. She was not able to perform the simplest tasks like brushing her teeth or getting dressed in the mornings, and routines were hard for her, but it was not surprising with such an unpredictable mum. I tried my best to stay calm but often yelled at her. I felt like I was stuck in a loop, and inside I felt so wound up all the time, and deep down I was becoming afraid of my own self. By 2017 I was having panic attacks regularly, only I did not know what they were, and I tried my best to function and keep working.

Lachlan was in year ten in high school, was still in cadets and doing so well academically. Lukas loved sports and was so clever at school. Isla was in year five and was a good student and an excellent sprinter. Aiden was a great stay at home dad and continued to grow closer to God, but I felt like a ticking time bomb. That year Tania was turning 40 and invited us to Bali to celebrate. Somehow, I felt like a family holiday was what we needed, so, I booked the flights for March. It was great fun but also super stressful, as we did not have a lot of money and I could not seem to relax. Worse, one day I left our bank card in the hotel ATM, and I did not realise until Lachlan and

I were out together and then we had to make a mad dash back to the hotel in a taxi. Of course, we got lost and poor Lachlan had to navigate us back to the hotel as I just could not cope. We celebrated Tania's birthday with a lovely dinner and the kids got to hold some snakes, which was great fun.

One of the best things was that we were able to see my friend Pat and his family, and he and his wife and their kids came to the hotel one night, which was special. Another highlight was when we visited an orphanage which was run by our church. It was miles away from Kuta, deep in the forest, and we made our way there in a taxi. The scenery was breathtaking and when we arrived, we were greeted by lots of happy and smiling children. We were overwhelmed with their hospitality and humble way of life. We met with one of the Pastors, who had baptized Isla, and she showed us around. They cooked us a simple meal and even Lachlan said it was his favourite part of the trip. I felt like the Lord was all around us in that place, and I came away feeling inspired and knew we served a mighty God.

As the year went on my mental health deteriorated, as work was endless, and we had a few staff members leave. Even though I had only been there two and a half years, I was considered senior staff, and a qualified educator role came up. I had already been an acting qualified educator on several occasions, but the actual role was a lot more responsibility and pressure. I felt like I was ready for it though, and when the position came up, I decided to go for it. In the months leading up to applying for the job, I started accidentally skipping my dose of anti-depressants, sometimes I would just forget, or I would run out and not fill the prescription for a day or two. I did not realise what I was doing or the effect that it had on me, as I was quite energetic and busy all the time, so I did not notice. I kept skipping them and trying to catch up, and I started to sleep less and had way more energy than usual, like I was high all the time. When I look back, I see how erratic my behavior was, but I could not see it. I felt so energized and capable, like I was flying high, but I could not see that I was becoming increasingly unwell.

Aiden kept telling me to rest and sit down but I did not listen to him. I was working hard training new staff, supporting the families, and trying to do everything at home too. I did not understand what was happening to me, and I was still praying to God too, but they were not my usual prayers or quiet time, it was chaotic, like I was not talking to God but battling something else entirely. I was constantly busy but did not feel tired at all. When Aiden and the kids would go to bed I would stay up and ramble on to God, shout out, and pray all the while doing these strange karate moves, like I was fighting something unseen. I started to feel like I was in a game or movie and that I was being watched or monitored. I was also writing everything down, like recording all my comings and goings on paper, and I kept skipping anti-depressants and then remembering a few days later. With Aiden I was happy and elated and my thoughts were so distorted I started to confuse fantasy and reality. At work I thought other staff were talking about me behind my back and I did not know who to trust. I also went ahead with the interview for the qualified position and thought I did well. My sleep was almost nonexistent by that stage, and I was not eating properly either and Aiden knew something was up.

"Are you okay Lou?" he would ask me.

"I'm fine," I would reply, but clearly, I was not.

I thought I was under surveillance and felt like if I did not follow a certain script or say certain phrases then terrible things were going to happen. I was writing all these weird things down on paper and leaving them all around the house. I was in a constant state of panic, and I am sure my work colleagues noticed. Looking back now I can remember a couple of close friends at work were frequently asking if I was okay.

"I'm fine," I would say dismissively.

I interviewed for the qualified position, but shortly afterwards I remembered that I had not had my meds in around three or four days, and I flew into a panic and raced to the chemist in my lunch break. They organised a prescription for me but by then it was too late, and I must have looked so wild and strange running into that pharmacy and demanding my prescription. I took the right dose but did not sleep that night at all and wandered around the house writing weird stuff on paper. I was paranoid that I was under surveillance, but I still went to work. On the way home one day I called a friend from our church and broke down to her on the phone.

"You have to help me," I sobbed hysterically. "I can't function, everyone is watching me, and I can't escape. I don't know where to go, I don't know what's happening to me. I can't think properly, and everyone is against me, and I need to see you," I sobbed, as my voice wobbled all over the place.

"I'm sorry Louise," she said, "but I'm going on a trip to Bali tomorrow to the orphanage, I can't see you."

I started to wail and cry uncontrollably, as I knew I was in trouble, but I did not know what to do.

"There's a prayer meeting tonight at church, so go there," she suggested to me.

I drove home and then went to the meeting at 7pm. I went inside where everyone was praying, but I could not stop crying and was on the floor sobbing, and I could not get up. A friend came over to me and knelt next to me.

"Get up Louise. You must get up," she kept telling me, but I could not do anything but lie there and cry.

I felt like I was dying, and no one cared, and there was a Pastor there who was praying and pacing up and down and he kept looking at me. I was crying and lying on the floor, and as I looked at him, I was hallucinating that I was the devil, and he was trying to protect his flock from me. I drove home and Aiden kept hugging me.

"What's wrong babe, I know something is wrong. You don't seem yourself."

I lied and said I was okay, but that night I did not sleep again. I went to work the next day, but my mind was so far gone that I could no longer remember how to lead the group of children. I could not remember the order of how things went in the program and kept asking other staff members and students what to do. I am sure my colleagues knew at that stage that I was very unwell.

"I'm going home to get an early night," one of them said to me.

"Yeah, me too, I'm going to have the best sleep," another one commented.

That night Ash told me to make an appointment to see my doctor, but when I arrived the next day, it was a substitute doctor and I felt like I was being recorded in his office. I was so unwell at that stage that I was unable to speak to him at all.

"I can see that you are distressed that your regular doctor isn't here," the doctor said to me.

At that point I felt like if I did not say particular words and phrases in a certain way, then something unbelievably bad was going to happen. The doctor examined me and gave me a medical certificate for a week, but when I got home, I completely lost it. I no longer had any grip on reality, and I ran into Lachlan's room and began yelling at him.

"You have to go, it's not safe. Take Isla and Lukas and run to the church. You know where that is don't you? Take them there, you have to leave now Lachlan, the end is coming and it's not safe!"

"Mama," he said to me as he turned away from his video game, "what are you talking about? Why do I have to go to church?"

I grabbed his hands and looked at him intensely.

"Go now Lachlan. Run to the church! Run!" I cried.

Lachlan ran to get Aiden.

"There's something wrong with mama," he told him.

Isla was trying to organise a sleepover at her friend's house, but my brain was so far gone, I thought that if she went to her friend's house, then she and her friend would be sold into sex trafficking. Lachlan was so worried at that point that he ran to his best friend's house and told his mum that I was sick and needed to go to the hospital. He ran back home and told Aiden to get my things ready.

"I don't want to go," I yelled at everyone.

"Babe you are really sick, and you need to go," Aiden said as he put his arms around me, and I began to cry.

"I can't think," I sobbed. "I can't do it anymore."

Aiden led me over to the couch and I sat down with my head in my hands.

Lachlan's friend's mum Lauren came and drove me to the hospital, but the whole time I thought our conversation was being recorded. Lauren took me to the emergency room and walked me into triage and I sat down and waited but when Lauren left, I suddenly jumped up.

"There's a bomb on a plane to Bali," I yelled. "There's a bomb!"

The hospital staff called security and they took me into a cubicle and restrained me. I passed out from exhaustion and when I woke up, I thought I was Jesus, and I was in hell. I kept waking up and falling back to sleep, as it had been so long since I had slept properly, I thought all the staff were in hell with me, it was horrific. I thought I heard Aiden in the next room being tortured but it was an elderly man who was extremely sick. There were security guards watching me and it was very unsettling. After a few more hours of napping, I woke up and Aiden was there with me, and it was next day.

"Babe," he said to me. "You are still in the hospital. How about you have a shower," but I shook my head and started yelling at him.

"No, I can't, don't make me."

Aiden grabbed my hand and said, "okay, how about we go for a walk outside."

"No, I can't go out there," I cried.

I was still convinced that I was Jesus and thought if I went outside then I would be crucified. My brain was just too far gone and the thought of going outside made me hysterical. Aiden managed to convince me to have a shower and when I got back to the room it was time for me go to the mental health ward. I said goodbye to Aiden, and he was crying as I left.

Chapter 19

gone

I was still very much in psychosis, so they put me in a wheelchair and wheeled me to the ward. I had my own room but when they closed the door on me the panic set in, and I was terrified. I had no idea how to even breathe properly and nothing felt real. I had terrible panic attacks and would feel so dizzy from lack of oxygen that I only slept for a minute or two at a time that night before I would jolt awake from panic and fear.

"God please help me," I cried out.

I had no one else and I was so scared I was going to end up back in that awful place I thought was hell. I lay on the bed sobbing.

"Save me please God," I cried into my pillow. "Save me please."

By then the hallucinations had stopped, but everything seemed blurry around me. So, I poured my heart out to the Lord.

"Lord please forgive me for thinking I was Jesus."

I did not feel real at that point, and I was so panicky and knew that He was my only solution to the mess I found myself in. Slowly, bit by bit, I calmed down and managed to breathe and leave my room, but when I saw people coming towards me, I clammed up and could not say a word. I thought everyone was watching me, so I prayed constantly in my room and carried my bible around with me. I also could not leave my room unless I had my old stuffed rabbit with me. It was so tough for the first few days, and nothing felt real. I had a meeting with my psychiatrist, but I was so panicky I barely remembered it.

"Please I need my meds," I begged her.

"No Louise, no meds," she said and refused to put me back on them.

I kept thinking, 'if I just have my meds then I will feel better.' The psychiatrist increased my dose of Seroquel, and I was allowed to ask for Lorazepam any time I needed it. I was worried I was going to get hooked on it though, so I did not like taking it. I had always preferred to feel 'up' rather than zoned out, but every part of me hurt from the lack of sleep so in the end I did ask for the Valium. After three days I finally came out of the psychosis and I was sleeping a bit better, for around an hour before I would wake up wondering where I was. I talked to Aiden, but I felt teary and overwhelmed with what I had been through. I had no idea why this had happened to me. Eventually I saw the registrar and he told me that skipping doses of my anti-depressants had triggered the psychosis and the hallucinations, and that with the lack of sleep had caused my brain to melt down. I had been on 200mg of the Pristiq which was a very high dose.

I was slowly recovering but it felt like I was running a marathon. I was still feeling panicky, anxious, and struggled with eating and simple routine tasks. I was fortunate that my brain was coming back to its usual state, but I was still terrified of everything. I found it so hard to eat, but because everyone else was, I did too. I had not realised how little I had been eating leading up to hospital, and slowly my appetite came back. I spent a lot of time in my room reading scriptures and praying. I would kneel near the bed and bow my head.

"Lord, I repent for thinking I was Jesus."

I knew this was a sin, even though I had been very unwell I still felt the need to pray for forgiveness. I knew I had to trust God if I wanted to get better. I had fallen into a huge pit of darkness and knew He was the only way out.

I could barely cope with seeing the other patients and felt paranoid and anxious any time someone spoke to me. I constantly checked the time as it seemed to go so slowly, and I felt like I could not make it to the next minute without feeling this crippling anxiety. I worried about whether I would make a full recovery and I knew Aiden was worried about that too. For the first time since becoming a mum I found it hard to think about the kids. I had always put them first, no matter how bad I was feeling, but every time I thought of them, I went into a mad panic inside. I felt detached from reality so I kept telling myself that Aiden could look after them and they would be okay. When I spoke to Aiden, I knew he was wanting to hear some sort of reassurance that I was going to be all right, but I could not say the words because in my heart I did not believe it. He was looking for the old me who would have said, "babe I'm going to be okay," but she was not there anymore. I felt overwhelmed by simply existing, so how was I meant to reassure him?

I felt so sad that I had ended up in hospital yet again. I was making the same mistakes repeatedly, and I felt like I would never get better, and even if I did go home, that I would just end up back in hospital at some point again, because that is what I did. The other thing I could not seem to do was talk to my sister Dana. In the past she had always been there for me and supported me, but now I wanted to isolate myself from her. I knew it was hurting Dana, and when she sent me texts of when to visit me, I felt myself shutting down, unable to reply to her. I felt like I needed to do it on my own, and I did not want to be rescued this time. I had to find my own inner strength to face this and fix this on my own.

I struggled with routine things like making my bed and brushing my teeth, and I worried constantly about 'what was happening next.' This made my days drag on, and I could not sit still, even though I tried. Every morning would begin with a group meeting at 9am, where they would outline the activities that they had on offer for the day. The activities ranged from walks to art therapy, to mindfulness. I tried to participate in the sessions, but it was hard at first as I found it so difficult to talk to people. I had been a social person all my life, I had always been so confident both with individuals and in crowds, but now, the panic started every time I found myself face to face with another person. Now I had crippling social anxiety and it floored me. How could this have happened, and why now? The panic followed me everywhere I went, as soon as I opened my eyes in the morning, I would feel it grip me like some monster and it would stay with me the entire day. It felt like its own entity. At night I would fear going to sleep, and I would be stuck in what I began to call my 'fear space.'

Looking back, I think I had always had this space, but now it had a name. When I entered a room now, I would be gripped with anxiety and panic, I would start to sweat profusely, and I worried about what I would say, what people would think of me and whether they would think I was crazy. Slowly after joining in a few activities, I began to talk to people. There were other women there and as I began talking to them, I felt some of the panic slip away. I talked to Aiden a few times a day, and he said that friends from school had been helping him out, but the kids missed me terribly. It was still hard to think about the kids, so I told myself they were okay. I prayed every day and read my bible, and I chatted to God and told Him how afraid I was. I listened to worship music and going to sleep was particularly difficult. I would lay down with my headphones in and try to just breathe in and out, and eventually I would drift off to sleep.

The other weird thing was that I felt responsible for all the other patients in the ward, and I worried constantly about them all and it was hard to switch it off. Chores were difficult to achieve, and I would think about doing my washing at 9am and at 2pm I would finally do it. Things I had taken for granted before were now so hard to do. One day Lachlan came to visit me. He rode his bike to the train station after school and found his way to the hospital, getting lost on the way. It was amazing to see him, and we hugged each other tight.

"You'll be okay mum," Lachlan said, and I struggled to keep the tears in.

He told me Aiden was doing a wonderful job with Isla and Lukas and when he left, I cried and cried, as I wanted so much to get better. I started highlighting scriptures in the bible and I would read them every day:

2 Corinthians 5:17, "This means that anyone who belongs to Christ has become a new person. The old life is gone, the new life has begun!"

Romans 8:1, "So now there is no condemnation for those who belong to Christ Jesus."

"John 3:16, "For this is how God loved the world: He gave His one and only son, so that everyone who believes in Him will not perish but have eternal life."

Ephesians 6-10, "The armour of God... The belt of truth, the body armour of God's righteousness, for shoes, put on the peace that comes from the Good news.. hold up the shield of faith to stop the fiery arrows of the devil, put on salvation as your helmet, take the sword of the spirit which is the word of God."

Isaiah 41:10, "Don't be afraid, for I am with you, don't be discouraged for I am your God. I will strengthen and help you; I will hold you up with my victorious right hand."

Philippians 4:13, "I can do everything through Christ, who gives me strength."

Each time I read them I would feel a flicker of hope and that kept me moving forward. When I read the scriptures, I could feel God surround me, and I began to have moments where the anxiety was not so overwhelming. I was still panicking all the time, but I began to feel that God was beside me, as a tangible being. The more I spoke the scriptures and played the worship music, the less the panic had a hold over me. I would have half an hour where I was able to sit and do some colouring or talk to someone, it was a massive breakthrough.

I was very worried about my job, and it was causing me a lot of anxiety thinking I had to go back. There was a lovely social worker at the hospital who helped me call Leah and discuss my situation.

"Management have given you three months leave Lou, so you can just concentrate on getting better," Leah said on the phone, and it was such a relief and a weight off my shoulders.

Every time I thought of work, I would have a massive panic attack, as working while being so unwell had been an awful thing for me, and it was such a good feeling knowing I could just relax and focus on getting better. The social worker also helped me apply for sickness benefit. She said it would take a long time to be approved so applying now was a good idea. That night I called Aiden and cried to him.

"I'm so sorry babe," I sobbed. "I didn't mean to get so sick."

"It's okay," he replied. "Just focus on getting better."

He reassured me that he was taking care of everything, and I just had to concentrate on getting well. That night when I hung up the phone I cried and cried, as I was starting to feel guilty for landing up in hospital once again. I was starting to miss the kids.

We organised for Aiden to bring Isla and Lukas for a visit, but that day I was ridiculously anxious. We went into the family room where there was drawing and puzzles for them to do. It was the first time I had seen Aiden since the night of my admission, and it was emotional for all of us. Isla and Lukas were so happy to see me, but I felt extremely overwhelmed. I kept focussing on silly things like the kids not putting the caps back on the pens and them making too much noise, and I felt hysterical inside and ended up yelling at them. It was not a very pleasant visit and once they left, I had a complete breakdown and had to have a some of my medication. Aiden and I talked later that night.

"I don't think I'll bring them back babe, that was too stressful."

We agreed it was too soon for any more visits, and I felt so sad that I had let everyone down.

"It's okay, you're not letting us down. Just relax Lou, I've got everything under control," he said.

The second week of my stay I had a meeting with the psychologist who questioned me about the trauma I had been through as a child. He said I had all the symptoms of PTSD which was funny because I had never really considered that that was what I had been suffering from for most of my life. He said the flashbacks and the constant state of panic were classic signs, and he also suggested that my fight or flight response was permanently switched on, something I had never considered either.

"Have you ever heard of schema therapy Louise?" he asked me.

"No, I haven't," I answered.

"Schema therapy is highly effective in treating trauma. Your brain is stuck back when you were a child, and schema can help you move into the present."

"Whatever it is," I said to him, "I want to try it."

He agreed and said he would organise a referral for me. I was intrigued to say the least, as I had received a lot of Cognitive Behavioural Therapy in the past, but I did not feel like it did that much for me. I knew cognitively that the abuse had not been my fault, but I still believed it in my heart. I struggled with shame and guilt so much that the emotions almost crippled me, plus, the trauma of the abuse was always with me, it followed me around everywhere I went.

So, I continued with the activities, and I slowly started to feel less anxious. I made some friends in the ward, and they shared their stories with me. At the end of the week, the psychologist decided I should try going home for a visit, but it did not go very well. I was hyper-focussed on the state of the house and did not enjoy seeing the kids. I kept noticing things like how the dog's water bowl was not filled up properly and how Aiden had bought generic brand margarine. I ended up having a full meltdown and had to call a friend to come and pick me up and take me back to hospital. I immediately felt calmer when I arrived back on the ward, and I met with the psychologist again who said I was not ready to go home. I kept going to art classes and walks in the mornings, and I had short periods where I could sit and focus on a crossword or watch tv. I could see small improvements and that gave me hope. I kept on praying and reading scriptures and I finally felt like my relationship with God was becoming more real. I had repented a lot for thinking I was Jesus, but I felt no condemnation from the Lord, only acceptance and understanding.

When I spoke to Aiden on the third week, I was calmer and less hysterical, and I began to ask about the kids and felt less detached from reality. The psych told me he had put my referral in to see Dr Jacob Browning, and I was determined to give the schema therapy a go. This had been the most intense and awful hospital admission out of all of them, as I had never experienced psychosis before and never wanted to go through it again. I was so tired of being anxious and panicky and I was sick of the traumatic memories controlling my life. I knew deep down that I was a good person and that I deserved to be free of the pain of my sexual abuse. I had a wonderful husband and three beautiful children who loved me and wanted to see me get well. Later, Aiden confessed to me that he thought I was never going to recover from my breakdown, and he was terrified that I might never come home.

The day arrived of my release, and I was so anxious, but I just kept telling myself that I was safe, and I was going to be okay. Aiden had been going to a new church while I had been in hospital, and they were connected to New Life Recovery. One of the ladies Aiden had met came with him to pick me up from hospital, I had never met her, but she came anyway, and I did feel quite anxious. Her name was Kayla, and she was lovely, but it felt surreal getting into her car and driving home. The kids were at school which meant I could relax for a few hours before they came home. Once I got home, I tried to not focus on the house being messy, as Aiden had done such an amazing job with looking after everything, and I tried to just be in the moment and not stress so much about trivial things. He went to pick up the kids from school and they came running through the door to see me. I held onto them tightly and tried not to cry. Lachlan came pedalling up the driveway a brief time later and ran into the house. I finally had my babies back all around me and I was so relieved, it was so lovely to be able to kiss and hold them again and not feel that awful, disassociated feeling. Lukas talked my ear off about all the things he had been doing, but Isla the poor darling, was so overwhelmed seeing me again that she cried and cried. That night I put her in the bath, and I was so sad to see how bad her eczema had gotten since I had been away. I lay with her in our bed and tried to reassure her that I was home, and I was not going away ever again.

The next few days were hard, and I was panicky a lot of the time. I could not seem to relax or switch off at all, and I wanted to keep busy so that is what I did. Aiden took the kids to school in the mornings, and I cleaned the house, but I had trouble eating and was burning once again in the shower. I felt the panic chasing me around and I tried desperately to control it. We were so short on money, and I was worried how we would pay the rent. It was Julian who suggested I apply for income support through my superannuation, and it was a two-hour phone call to put the referral in. My sickness payment had yet to be approved and we were back at the Life Centre for food.

The day of my first therapy appointment came and I was so anxious, that Aiden and I had a big fight on the way, instigated by me. I felt myself disassociating, and by the time we arrived, I was hysterical. When I walked into Jacob's room, I felt small like I was watching myself from afar. Jacob was Kiwi, which I thought would be triggering for me, but it was oddly comforting instead.

"Hi Louise, I'm Jacob. Would you like to tell me what has been going on?" he asked.

It was a simple enough question, but this tidal wave of emotions came over me, and I burst into tears and Jacob waited patiently for me to calm down. I explained through sobs about my hospital admission and what had led up to it. He was a particularly good listener and just let me speak.

"That sounds like a very difficult time for you, and a frightening one too," he said.

It was the first time that anyone had acknowledged that properly, and it made me cry harder than ever. Jacob explained some of his background and what therapy would look like for the next few weeks.

"I am also going to test you for personality disorders and ADHD," he said.

For the rest of the session, we mostly chatted about my background, and he asked me lots of questions about my family and childhood. When I left, I felt anxious but hopeful that the therapy would be what I needed to get better, and finally free me of the trauma that had haunted me for so long. Things at home seemed to be up and down. In a few weeks it would be Christmas and I was worried about money and how we were going to pull it off. One day Aiden got a phone call from his stepfather, and he asked if we would go around to see him, so we did and to Aiden's surprise he ended up apologising for what he had put him through as a teenager and gave us $1500. Aiden took the money and when we got back into the car, we both looked at each other and said, "what the heck just happened?" Christmas was covered that year!

That was when Aiden told me that he would not be returning to our church.

"I've decided to go to this new church I visited when you were in hospital," he said but I was upset with him.

"We can't just leave," I yelled at him.

"Why not?" he asked me. "They never helped us when you were in hospital, and I am not close to anyone there Lou, why would I go back? Look how they treated you that night of the prayer group. You were so sick, and they did nothing!"

But I was adamant that I was staying at our old church.

"Fine, you can go but I'm not," I said and stormed off to our room.

As I sat there in silence, I could feel something stirring inside of me. I started to pray and felt God say to me that it was okay to go to the new church, that the season at the old church was ending and it was what He wanted.

On Christmas eve we went to the service at the new church. The church was small, and it was in a hall, not a huge building, and everyone was so nice and friendly, and I felt like we were coming home. The lead pastors Jason and Melinda both had an interesting past, they were reformed drug addicts, and had both completed their rehabilitation at New Life Recovery. I felt something different that night, I felt an acceptance I had not felt before at our previous churches. Aiden and I went home feeling a joy we had not felt in a long time.

Christmas day came and it was lovely, and I felt a lot calmer which was great. A week or two after Christmas I went back to therapy, and once again, I picked a huge fight with Aiden in the car, this time over a carpark space, but as I got into Jacob's room, all the anxiety melted away. This time we were screening for disorders and there were a lot of questionnaires for me to take home and bring back the next week. We also talked about schema therapy, and he explained what it was.

"We all have schemas," he said. "A schema is a pattern of thought or behaviour about us and our relationships, it can be a positive type of thought or behaviour, or a negative one. Negative schemas develop in early childhood and some of them are very rigid and resistant to change. There are many schemas, and this shapes our behaviours and thoughts. Some of the schemas are mistrust and abuse, abandonment, defectiveness, vulnerability, dependence, enmeshment, and failure," Jacob explained, and I stared at him not really understanding what he was saying.

"So," he continued, "you may believe that because you were abused then you deserve to be treated badly or you may mistrust everyone that you encounter, or because you were not protected from harm at an early age, then you may feel like everyone leaves you, that is the abandonment schema, one that is very common in survivors of abuse. As we learn more about the schemas, you will come to understand your emotional needs and how you can heal your inner child."

We talked more about the schemas; and I began to understand what they were and how mine affected the way I felt about myself and others. He gave me a list of schemas and told me to fill out the personality questionnaires and bring them to the next session. I left feeling empowered and excitedly shared my news with Aiden. He was such an important emotional support for me, and I wanted him to know that I was committed to getting better. We had not been intimate together since my hospital admission and I was worried about our marriage.

"Lou it's okay," he assured me. "What kind of husband would I be if I left you because you can't make love right now?"

That made me feel better and I sat and filled out the forms. Things at home were better but I was still anxious all the time. We barely had any money and we both felt the strain. I could not believe Centrelink had not processed by sickness benefit claim yet as it had been over eight weeks since my admission. A friend suggested I try and call our local MP to see if she could do anything, so, I did, and she was supportive and could not believe Centrelink had not paid me anything. The next day the MP called me back and said she had spoken to someone in the Human Services Department, and they reassured her that my claim would be approved soon. I felt discouraged but then I got a call from someone at Centrelink and to my surprise she said my claim had been approved! I fell to my knees and prayed my thanks to God.

I was still struggling with social anxiety and Aiden had to accompany me to the shops most days. My sleep was also very up and down which made it hard. Every time I thought of returning to work, I was overcome with waves of fear, so I tried to avoid thinking about it. The next session with Jacob was interesting, as he looked at my questionnaires and to my utter surprise told me I had tested very highly for ADHD, and I could not believe it, as no one had ever picked that up before. Interestingly he also made a comment as to why speed had been my drug of choice.

"It probably calmed your brain down in a lot of ways," he said, and I was gobsmacked.

"No wonder I can't sit still some days too," I joked.

It also made me realise how similar Aiden and I were, as he had been diagnosed with ADD at aged fourteen, so no wonder we clashed at times.

"So, you do not qualify for borderline personality disorder, but only just," Jacob said, "and you also scored very highly for PTSD."

Jacob was very experienced with PTSD and said that schema therapy was highly effective in treating it. We talked about breathing, and he asked me to breathe in and out for me, while he observed.

"You know that your breath is really shallow," he said. "It looks like you're a chest breather, not a diaphragm breather."

I had no idea what that meant until he explained it, and with some coaxing and demonstration, I was able to take some breaths from my diaphragm which felt very weird.

"There's a huge correlation between breathing and panic attacks," he explained.

I was an expert at having panic attacks, but I had no idea that my breathing was fuelling them. He gave me print outs to read about the panic cycle and breathing. That night I sat and prayed and read the handouts. Even though it felt like I was dying when I had panic attacks, I was grateful you could not die from them. The information was particularly useful, and I began to see how my breathing was not helpful when I was panicking. During the next session he taught me how to breathe effectively using my diaphragm and showed me how to count my breaths and hold them.

"Set a timer when you're at home so you can time your breathing," he suggested.

I tried it when I got home. Every time I got distracted and stopped counting, I had to start again and put it all down in a breathing diary. At first it was almost impossible to not get distracted, but I kept practising, determined that I would get better the more I did it.

The next session we talked about 'child modes' and how they affected my thinking and behaviour.

"Child modes are the parts of yourself which come into being in childhood, as a response to the parenting you received," Jacob explained to me. "There are many child modes, including the angry child, vulnerable child, impulsive or undisciplined child and the contented child."

I realised I spent a lot of time in the vulnerable child mode. We talked a lot about my parents, and it was hard to admit that they really did not know how to parent me, especially my mum. Jacob explained that many parents have a 'skills deficit' when it comes to parenting, that their experiences and schemas influence the way that they parent, and that in turn affects their children. It all made complete sense. It was devastating to me to finally be able to deal with how my mum did not keep me safe, that she had wanted to at some point, but was so overwhelmed emotionally that she could not stand up to my father. We also talked about 'adult modes' too.

"Some of the adult modes are compliant surrenderer, detached protector, over compensator, punitive parent and demanding or critical parent. There is a healthy adult mode too," Jacob explained.

It was like a giant light bulb going off in my brain. I spent a lot of time in detached protector mode and punitive parent mode, and I always tried to overcompensate when people hurt me or did not meet my needs, it all made perfect sense.

"Louise, can you tell me more about your abuse?" Jacob then asked me.

As I began speaking, I felt myself drift away at times through the hard parts, but Jacob was gentle and walked me through it slowly, and he made sure I was present at the end and not disassociated when I left his office. Jacob sent me home with another task; this time I had to write down all my arguments with Aiden and what child mode I was operating out of and what adult mode too. He wanted me to think from a healthy adult point of view at the end to show me how I could react differently next time. At first, I dismissed this activity, but then a day or two later I picked a fight with Aiden and afterwards, I shut myself away in our room and filled in the form. By the end of it I had a real epiphany, I had acted like an angry child at first and then the vulnerable child. I had acted out of the punitive parent mode and then the detached protector mode. At the end of the task, I wrote out how the healthy adult would deal with the situation and was impressed by the revelation. I could not wait to see Jacob again and tell him what I experienced.

I also kept doing the breathing exercises, and it was difficult for me to just sit down for ten minutes, but I struggled through them and made a promise to practice again the next day.

So, Lachlan was in year eleven at school, Isla in year six and Lukas in year four. They were all growing up so fast and I sometimes felt emotional just looking at them. Lachlan was struggling with increasing anxiety and decided to quit cadets. He had started the year by doing 5 ATAR subjects but halfway through the term had dropped all but one. He had his eye on joining the army, something he had wanted since he was 12 years old, and he had picked a role that was very tough to get into, combat engineering. He would need a lot of discipline and courage to pass the aptitude test but more importantly, the psychological assessment.

"Do you want to wait until you finish year 12 mate?" I asked him.

"No mum," he replied. "I want to do it now."

Isla was doing so well at school and had been chosen by her peers to be school captain. She was also doing gymnastics one day a week and seemed to have a natural flair for it. Lukas was playing in under 10's at the cricket club and was a good little bowler. Life at home was better, but I was still anxious all the time. Every time I thought of my hospital visit, I would have a panic attack and similarly, thinking of work brought on the attacks too.

I had also discovered with Jacob's help that I was afraid all the time. The fear followed me to the shops and out with the kids, and it followed me when I showered, which led to me burning myself. It followed me to bed at night and sat beside me as I tried to sleep. I do not think I ever noticed before just how constantly afraid I was. *The fear was with me wherever I went.* Night time was especially hard, as I would lie in bed for hours sometimes just stuck in my fear. To me it was not just an emotion, but a tangible force, capable of devouring me at times, as my heart would pound, and I would feel sweaty and overwhelmed. Most of my life I had feared bedtime, and it was still the same as an adult; I hated it. I had never had the courage to face this fear that haunted me. Now that I had God and Jacob, it was time to deal with the fear and I was terrified of it, but I was willing to face it while I had the support of a kind and knowledgeable therapist. Thankfully, my application for income protection from my superannuation came through and that improved our finances a lot. I talked to my coordinator, and she agreed to extend my period of unpaid leave. I was so thankful I had a caring workplace, and so relieved I did not have to worry about work for now.

The therapy continued, and it was time for me to have some corrective emotional healing. I would close my eyes and recall a traumatic memory, and at some point, Jacob would then insert himself into my memory and protect me from harm. I thought it sounded terrifying, but I was willing to give it a go. I closed my eyes and allowed myself to go back to when I was about eight years old. Night time was an awful time back then, and after dinner is when I would just start to feel ill and anxious. I would lie in my bed after my mum had tucked me in and would feel frozen in fear. Would he come in? It was awful when he did come in and it was equally awful when he did not.

"Now imagine yourself in your room, in your bed," Jacob said to me.

I pictured my bed spread and where my bed was positioned, and I could feel my teddy bear pressed up against me.

"Now what is happening?" he asked me.

My heart started to pound, my skin broke out in a sweat, and my mouth went dry.

"Everyone is asleep," I said quietly, "and now the light in the hallway is on and..."

"Yes, Louise, what is happening now?" Jacob asked me gently.

I fidgeted in my seat. "He's coming in," I murmured.

"Who is coming in?" Jacob asked gently as I sucked in a breath.

I could feel the sweat dripping down my back.

"He is coming in. My dad is coming in..... he's coming to hurt me; he's going to hurt me!" I yelled out and I felt frozen on the spot, unable to move. "No, no, no," I said, "not again, not again."

I was glued to my seat and felt like a trapped animal.

"Okay," Jacob said. "Now Louise, I want you to know that I am here. I am walking into your room, and I am turning on the light and I am here, and I am going to take you somewhere safe. Where would you like to go?" he asked but I shook my head.

"I, I, I don't know," I stammered.

"It's alright," Jacob said calmly. "How about we go into the lounge room?"

"Yes," I answered. "Take me there."

"So, we're in the lounge room Louise and I want you to know that I have called the police, and they are coming to arrest your father," he said as I started to cry.

"And now I am going to speak to your father," Jacob said. "Oliver, what you have been doing to your daughter is wrong and illegal. You have been abusing her and it is disgusting. I have called the police, and you are going to be arrested so you will not be able to hurt her anymore."

I was sniffling and crying hard.

"Louise," Jacob said, "the police are going to take your dad away and he won't be able to hurt you ever again."

I nodded my head, as the tears streamed down my face.

"What do you want to do now Louise? What do you need?" he asked as I sniffled again.

"I want my mum to cuddle me," I whispered.

"Okay," Jacob said. "I will get her for you."

I sniffed and wiped my nose on my hand.

"Clara," Jacob said. "I know this is hard for you, but Louise needs you to hold her now, Louise, will you let your mum hug you?" he asked, and I nodded.

"Okay Louise, when you are ready you can open your eyes."

I took a deep breath and opened my eyes. Everything was blurry for a few seconds, then Jacob came into focus, and I felt myself coming back into the room. I took another deep breath and fixed my eyes on him.

"How do you feel?" he asked me.

I reached for a tissue from the box and wiped my eyes and looked around the room.

"I feel okay," I said eventually, but I felt lightheaded and a little queasy.

"I want you to do something nice for yourself when you get home," Jacob told me.

I nodded and left his office feeling very strange indeed. On the way home I felt teary and overwhelmed, so I shut myself in our room and lay down and cried and cried. I cried for that little girl who was hurt so badly, I cried for all the years that I suffered because of my dad's poor choices, and I cried because my mum did not have the skills or tools to keep me safe.

GONE

When the sad feelings subsided a bit, I began to feel angry. I was angry that he had hurt me so much and no one did a thing! I was angry my mum did not protect me, what type of mum ignored her daughter's abuse? All the feelings that I had repressed, swallowed, and buried deep for so many years all came flooding back, and it was bad, and I was crying an ocean of tears. After a while I sat up and got my bible out. I opened it and began to pray. I knew that I needed the heavenly Father's love and healing, He was the only one who was going to get me through this therapy. As I prayed, I felt God leading me to scripture.

Lamentations 3:22-24, "The faithful love of the Lord never ends. His mercies never cease. Great is His faithfulness, His mercies begin afresh every morning. I say to myself, the Lord is my inheritance, therefore I will hope in Him."

I knew that I had to have hope in Jesus if I was to fully recover from the memories. I knew that if I did not turn to him then I was at risk of being completely overtaken by them and they could destroy me once again. God led me to Jacob to have the schema therapy and that he had hand picked him so I could get better. I also knew that God had mighty plans for my life, why else would I have survived what I went through?

Jeremiah 29:11-13, "For I know the plans I have for you, says the Lord. They are plans for good and not for disaster, to give you a future and a hope. In those days when you pray, I will listen. If you look for me whole-heartedly, you will find me. I will be found by you."

That afternoon as I kept praying and speaking scriptures over myself, I realised that I still felt so much shame and guilt about the things that had happened to me as a child, that my shame was thick like a blanket covering me. I felt like my old life still dictated how I felt about myself, and I longed to be free of the shame! God kept leading me to scriptures and I wrote them out and put them on the wall.

Psalm 34:4-5, "I prayed to the Lord, and He answered me. He freed me from all my fears. Those who look to Him for help will be radiant with joy; no shadow of shame will darken their faces."

Isaiah 61:7, "Instead of shame and dishonour, you will enjoy a double share of honour. You will possess a double portion of prosperity in your land and everlasting joy will be yours."

God was telling me that I did not have to feel the shame about my abuse anymore, and that He was going to bless me.

Job 11:13, "If only you would prepare your heart and lift up your hands to Him in prayer! Get rid of your sins and leave all inequity behind you. Then your face will brighten with innocence, and you will be strong and free of fear."

That night as I sat and ate dinner with my family, I realised that I was at a turning point in my life, and I had to stay close to God so I could heal properly and have the strength to look after the kids and go back to work. Things at home were much better but I was still anxious a lot of the time, and I still instigated arguments with Aiden. I tried to be calm, but everything still stressed me out so much. The kids' routines seemed to have improved so at least that was something. Aiden and I had made love for the first time in months too, and it was a lot more enjoyable for me, and I felt less disassociated which was lovely. I was still doing my breathing exercises, but they were hard. Part of the exercise was to record the number of times I lost concentration on the counting, and that part I was not doing so great in, but I was determined to keep doing them and improve.

A few months went by, and I had more corrective healing, this time it was about the abuse I had suffered at the hands of my father's friends. I still had so much fear and shame attached to those nights, and I longed to be free of the horror of what they did to me. The day after that therapy session I felt so liberated, and that night when I went to bed, I fell asleep within half an hour which was normally unheard of for me. I did not feel any fear at all, and I wanted to scream from the mountain tops that I was free, that those men no longer held any place in my heart or head.

I kept on praying and reading my bible and I felt closer to God than I ever had before. A few weeks later I discussed going back to work with Aiden and then Jacob. To my surprise it no longer made me feel afraid. I chatted to my coordinator, and we agreed that I would go back two days a week in May, and I prayed and prayed that God would be with me, and He sure was. The day arrived and I was so calm, and it was amazing to be able to return to something that I really enjoyed doing. I thought it would be weird, but it was not. I was over the moon to see all my old work colleagues and meet the new families, and it was such a relief to be earning some sort of income again.

In June Aiden was offered a job at a high school as a cleaner. One of our friends from church was the head cleaner so she showed him the ropes, and Aiden was so happy that he was working again and as the kids were getting older, it seemed to work out okay. Later that year I booked us a holiday to Lancelin for Christmas. It had been a rough year and I thought it would be nice to enjoy some time away. My therapy ended, and I felt so proud of what I had achieved, as Jacob had been an integral part of my healing, but it was time to move on. Before the end of our last session, he made an audio clip of his voice talking me through some steps to use if I became overwhelmed. There were many times I pressed play on that recording, and just hearing his voice was often enough to soothe me and get me through the next few minutes, until I would feel calm again.

Lachlan was starting to talk about wanting to enlist in the army, so he decided that it was the right time for him, and we attended a YOU session at the recruitment centre in the city. That night he seemed more determined than ever to sign up.

"Do you think that you should wait until you graduate?" I asked him.

"No, mum, I want to do it now," he insisted.

A few months later he got his appointment date for his psychiatric interview. He was so anxious and as the day drew closer, he became even more nervous. We caught the train into the city on the morning of his interview, but when he came out, I could tell from his face it had not gone well and he was on the verge of tears. We waited a while and then had a chat to a Seargeant.

"Why do you want to join now?" he asked Lachlan as we sat down in his office.

"It's the only job that I am interested in," Lachlan replied.

"I think you should wait until you finish school. You need to go and live your life a little, get a job, get some life experience, and then come back when you are done with school," the Seargent explained.

We went away and had lunch in the city, and Lachlan was understandably upset. But after chatting with me for a while it became clearer to him that he was not quite ready.

"Hey, they haven't said a definite no," I said to him as we ate our sushi. "Just wait until you have finished school and have a part time job. You will be almost 18 by then and you can give it another shot."

That made sense to both of us, and we went home, but for the next few days Lachlan seemed a bit down.

"I really wanted this mum," he said to me.

"I know mate," I consoled him, "wait until you finish year 12 and then try again."

Chapter 20

plans of the enemy

That Christmas was such a happy time, and we went on our trip to Lancelin, and it was so much fun. One day we were at the beach, and it was extraordinarily windy. Aiden and I got into a fight, and I decided to go swimming with Lachlan. He suggested we swim out to the pontoon, and I stupidly thought that would be a good idea, knowing full well that I was a terrible swimmer.

"Stuff you Aiden," I thought as I started swimming.

A little while into the swim I knew I was in trouble, but Lachlan was a strong swimmer, so he was fine. I considered turning back at one-point and sure wish I had, but I kept on swimming and a few more metres out, I started to panic. The wind was fierce which made it impossible to judge how far away the pontoon really was. Lachlan kept looking over at me.

"Are you alright mum?" he asked but I was not.

"No," I answered. "I don't think I can do this."

Lachlan looked back at me again. "You'll be ok mum, just keep going."

I kept on swimming, my movements becoming slower as I became increasingly tired. The wind was relentless, and I felt like I was getting nowhere. What had I been thinking? I was an awful swimmer and now I was in big trouble. I started to panic even more, and every muscle was screaming at me.

"Lachlan," I panted, "I can't keep going."

I was so out of breath and fighting the wind, and the waves were starting to wash over my head and my panic went up a notch.

"I can't do it!" I cried out.

"Mum," said Lachlan as he slowed down to swim next to me. "You're okay, just keep going, we're nearly there," he encouraged me.

I swam a little further, but the water was going over my head and I thought to myself, 'you're going to drown,' so I cried out again.

"Lachlan! Help me. I'm going to drown!"

He swam closer to me. "Mum," he said calmly, "you're not going to drown; you just need to keep going."

I gulped in air as another wave came over me. 'Oh Lord,' I said to myself, 'please do not let me drown.' I kept on, the panic becoming more intense, but it felt hopeless, I was not strong enough to swim through the wind, it was so powerful that it was blowing us off course.

"Lachlan," I sobbed, "I can't keep going, I can't do it, I'm going to drown."

My movements had slowed to a doggy paddle, and I was struggling to stay afloat. The waves washed over me, and I thought, 'this is it.'

Lachlan's voice cut into my thoughts, "mum, turn over on your back," he said, but I did not hear him properly.

"What?" I asked him.

"Turn over!" he called over to me. "Turn over onto your back and do backstroke."

I turned onto my back and started propelling myself along.

"That's it mum," Lachlan said. "We're nearly there!"

It was slightly better on my back, and I was able to take a breath in. I sculled along on my back and tried to focus on Lachlan's voice.

"God," I called out, "please don't let me drown."

Lachlan was swimming next to me. "That's it mum," he said, "pray!"

So, I did. "Lord," I called out, "please save me! Please do not let me drown."

I kept on paddling on my back through the waves, and as the water washed over my face, I tried not to panic.

"Mum," Lachlan called out. "I can see the pontoon!"

I almost cried with relief, and I kept on, the wind blowing all around us.

"You're doing great mum," Lachlan said to me as I kept on going and praying aloud.

"Mum, turn over!" Lachlan called out to me.

I flipped over and I saw him holding on to the pontoon. He reached out his hand to me and I swam right up to him, but my legs were so shaky I could barely make it up the ladder. Lachlan boosted me from behind and I flopped onto it like a fish. I just lay there sobbing and sobbing with him patting me.

"It's okay mum," Lachlan lay down next to me. "We made it."

I made a snorting noise. "I nearly drowned!" I cried out, and Lachlan reached over and hugged me.

"Yes, but you didn't," he said, "we made it."

I just lay there crying and I felt so out of it, like I was not even there. We lay there for a while, and I shivered in the cold.

"Mum how will we get back?" Lachlan asked me but I did not answer him. "Can you swim back?" he asked and my whole body went cold.

"No!" I yelled at him. The wind was blowing, and I was shivering.

"Okay," Lachlan said. "I'll swim back and get help."

I sat up and looked over at the beach and I could see Aiden on the sand with Isla and Lukas.

"Are you sure?" I asked him in a shaky voice, "what if you drown?"

He hugged me. "Mum I'm not going to drown," he said. "You know I'm a good swimmer. I will go and get some help mum; you just stay here."

I did not like the thought of being left alone, but I knew I could not stay on the pontoon forever. He slipped into the water, and I felt dread at the sight of him bobbing up and down.

"I'll be back shortly mum, love you," he called out as he swam off.

I lay back down on the pontoon and sobbed. I had been so convinced I was going to drown, it had been like a voice telling me in my head, and I shivered again and sat up. I could see Lachlan swimming quickly toward the shore, and I watched him exit the water and run over to Aiden. I could see Lachlan's hands going in all directions as he told Aiden what was going on. Lachlan looked out at me, and I waved to him. Isla and Lukas were jumping up and down and waving at me too, and I waved back, wishing I were back on the beach with them. Then I saw Lachlan take Aiden's phone, and Aiden tried to snatch it back off Lachlan, and to my dismay it looked like they were getting into an argument. I felt my heart sink, as Aiden was not the best in a crisis, and I could see they were yelling at each other. Aiden turned and started to walk up the beach towards a small dingy that was up near the grass, surely, he was not thinking of paddling out in that. Lachlan followed him up the beach and once again they were arguing. Lachlan threw up his hands and started his way back towards the water. I watched him start to swim back towards me, and I felt the tears coming again, what was I going to do? I knew I could not swim back. Lachlan was almost at the pontoon when he spotted a man swimming nearby, and he called out, and the man swam over to him. Lachlan came up the ladder towards me and spoke to the man.

"Excuse me mister but my mum is stuck on the pontoon and can't swim back. Do you think you could help her please?"

The man pulled up next to us. "Sure," he said.

I died of shame but boy was I glad to see him.

"I'll go back and get you a boogie board," the man said, and I was so relieved.

"Thanks so much," Lachlan replied.

Lachlan and I sat together on the pontoon and watched the man swim back towards the shore.

"What were you and Aiden fighting about?" I asked him.

"Oh, mum I got angry at him because he wasn't being helpful or trying to find a way to rescue you. He just wasn't helpful," Lachlan said.

I reached over and hugged him. "You know he's not good in a crisis." I said and Lachlan looked at me.

"You think?" he said.

"It's not his fault mate. Are Isla and Lukas, okay?" I asked him.

"Not really, they are really worried about you."

I looked over at them on the beach, and they were running up and down and looking at us. I felt bad for getting into this situation, as I knew what a terrible swimmer I was, and I should never have done it. A little while later we saw the man coming back down the beach with a boogey board and a pool noodle. I felt relieved as he swam out to us and offered me one. I held onto the boogie board and eased myself into the water, but just getting back in made me shudder. The man started swimming ahead of me as I paddled behind him, and Lachlan swam next to us. I felt like such a fool, but eventually we made it back and I staggered up the beach.

"Thank you so much," I told the man.

"Thanks for rescuing my mum," Lachlan said.

"No worries, glad you made it back safely," he said as he jogged up the beach.

Isla and Lukas ran up to me, "mama, are you okay?" they asked hugging me frantically.

"I'm okay," I said. "I'm so glad to be back on dry land."

Aiden came up to me and hugged me. "I'm sorry," he said, "but I didn't know what to do."

"It's okay," I said as I hugged him back and felt the tears come again. "It was my fault."

We all walked up to the park, and I sat huddled in a towel, trying to process what had happened. I felt in shock and disassociated, and I could not believe I'd almost drowned. And while on holiday! That night we went out to a restaurant for dinner, and I tried to laugh it off, but when we went out into the beer garden, I glanced out at the pontoon, and I was shocked to see how far away it was. What had I been thinking? That night I found it so hard to settle, and my heart kept fluttering and I was having flashbacks of the waves over my face. We all sat and watched a movie, but I could not concentrate on it. Poor Lachlan was so tired from all the swimming that he went to bed early. That night I finally drifted off, but I had nightmares of drowning. We enjoyed the rest of our holiday, going sand boarding which was great fun and I tried to put it all behind me. When we got home, all that week I kept having flashbacks and nightmares of the incident in the water. It was like my brain just could not turn it off, and it got so bad that I ended up calling Pastor Melinda for a chat.

"Wow," she said to me after I had told her about what had happened. "The enemy was really gunning for you. Thankfully, God had other plans!"

After I hung up, I considered what she had told me. It was true, I had almost drowned, but in the end the Lord had the victory. I found scriptures in the bible.

Psalms 118:17, "I will not die; instead, I will live to tell what the Lord has done."

Genesis 50:20, "You intended to harm me, but God intended it all for good."

I spent a few days meditating on those scriptures and felt the fear dissolve. That Christmas was a happy one and I felt grateful and blessed to be alive.

2019 began and Lachlan was in year 12, and it was Isla's first year in high school, and I could not believe how grown up she was. The day arrived and she was so anxious, but fortunately, she had a big brother to hold her hand. My babies were getting older, and I felt a range of emotions watching Lachlan and Isla walk into school together. Lukas was in year five and I suddenly felt my age. That night Isla was so emotional.

"I can't carry my bag," she sobbed. "It's too heavy."

The next few days were intense and always ended in tears. At night I cried a bit too and kept praying for her. She had been to a small primary school and never really had any problems. As the days turned into weeks, I watched my once smiling and happy girl turn into an anxious and stressed-out mess. Her 12th birthday came and went but she was still so upset every Sunday night at the thought of returning to high school. Isla did gymnastics once a week but that soon turned into a chore as well. I felt so sad for her, she obviously just had not been ready for such a change.

Lachlan was working hard in year twelve and it was stressful for him. I too was finding work difficult, as we had moved locations, and it was a lot further away for me to travel. The new building made it harder to care for the children and I thought I might be ready for a change. I found a job in the same company I worked in and decided to apply for it, it was a community support role and it sounded good. That August, I was picking up the kids from school when someone in a Ute ran into me and tore the front of my bumper nearly clean off. As soon as his car hit mine poor Isla started screaming. My first thought was, 'oh gosh how will I cope with this,' but fortunately, this strength came from nowhere and I was able to reach over and comfort her. It was the other driver's fault, but he denied it, but even the tow truck driver was on my side and told him to admit it. My poor Ford was towed away, and I cried a lot. I prided myself on being a good driver and it was not fair. I got another car to drive through the insurance company as I anxiously waited to hear about the fate of my beloved car. I was at work when I got the call, and I remember going into a quiet spot on my lunch break while I was on the phone.

"Unfortunately, due to the age and condition of your car, it is not repairable," the assessor told me, as I tried to hold back the tears. "And because you still owe money on the car, the payout will go to the finance company."

I started to cry quietly. As I hung up the phone, I felt distraught, as I could not work without a car and had no savings to fall back on. I crouched down against the wall. What was I going to do? The tears fell down my cheeks, but suddenly this wind come and blew gently over me. I looked up and God was there, and He was saying to me that it was going to be all right. I wiped my face, went back to work, and tried not to worry.

That afternoon someone from the finance company called me to say they were happy to let me have the payout and keep paying off my car. I was overjoyed and quickly called Aiden to tell him the news. That weekend we went and picked up my new car, it was a cheap little Kia Rio, but it seemed to run well, and I was happy with it. Once again, the Lord had come through for us and I felt so close to Him. He was such a faithful God.

Lukas was going so well at school and was playing cricket every weekend. It was such a joy to watch him go out there with his mates, he was quite the bowler, and it was so exciting to watch him take wickets. He also developed another passion, ninja warrior. I took him to classes and watched him master the warped wall. Unfortunately, in November he was climbing up the walls in our hallway when he fell and banged his heel on the skirting board. An Xray showed no fracture, but his GP suggested an MRI, and sure enough, he had broken his heel. A few weeks in a moon boot for him and sadly no cricket.

As the year ended poor Isla was still really struggling at school. She had begun to harm herself with the blades from broken pencil sharpeners, and I was heartbroken for her and asked if she would like to talk to the school Psychologist. She refused and I decided to find her a mental health GP. Fortunately, there was a good one at our local medical centre, and the doctor suggested that we attend Head Space, so I made an appointment and Isla said it had helped a little. I felt unqualified to help our daughter and like I was failing her. High school was just so overwhelming for her, and I really did not know what to do. Lachlan graduated year twelve, and we attended his special night, and I was so happy when he decided to invite his dad, Tom. They had not seen each other for several years and I was overjoyed for them both. I felt so proud of Lachlan when he went up to collect his certificate, as he had worked hard, and it was lovely to see him finish school. That December we got an email from the real estate agent that the owner was selling our property, and I was gutted. We had built a life in our little home and the thought of moving made me ill. It was at that time we started to hear about a virus that had hit China, it was spreading rapidly and apparently deadly. Aiden and I prayed that it would not come to Perth. We found a new rental which had 4 bedrooms and 2 bathrooms, and for the first time we organised proper removalists. I had put the money away in muesli bar box in the top of our wardrobe, but when the day of the move arrived, I could not find the box and flew into a mad panic.

"I've lost the money!" I cried out as Aiden and Lachlan came running into our room.

"What do you mean you have lost the money?" Aiden asked me as I frantically searched the cupboard.

"The money for the removalist," I started to cry. "It was up here and now it's gone."

"Mum!" Lachlan said with a worried look on his face.

I kept searching and then realised I had put the money in a different box, and nearly fell off the chair with relief when I eventually found it.

"Sorry everyone," I apologised, and Lachlan hugged me.

The removalists arrived, and even though it was stressful, it all went smoothly.

We settled into our new house and things were good. I had started work as a support worker and had two adult clients. It was vastly different to childcare, but I loved it. I supported them in their homes and in the community, and it was fun. One client I took horse riding and bowling every week. One day I was finishing a shift at one of my client's homes, when a huge storm blew in, so I walked quickly to my car. The wind blew around me wildly and I picked up my pace, and I made it to the car. I unlocked the driver's door and had just sat down when the wind picked up a fourteen-foot trampoline and blew it into the back of my car. It smashed against the boot, rolled over the top of the roof, and came to rest against a tree a few feet away. I was stunned as if I had been a few seconds later coming out to the car, I would have been crushed. I sat there for a while breathing heavily, and eventually I went into my client's house and told his mum what had happened. We went and notified the neighbours, and as I drove away, I burst into tears, as I kept thinking that I could have been seriously injured. The wind was crazy as I drove home, debris from trees blew down the street and people's rubbish bins were blowing across lanes of traffic. When I got home, I hugged my family and told them what had happened, and that night I thanked God for saving my life once again.

Lachlan started the new year with enthusiasm, as he was keen to get fit for the army and find himself a job. Isla was in year eight and seemed to be slightly happier at school. I could not believe that Lukas was in his last year of primary school. That February Covid hit Perth and we had our first fatality. It was a scary concept that a virus could kill people and in March we started restrictions. Our borders closed as the virus kept spreading, so I did lots of reading about it and prayed and tried not to panic.

It was at that time that Aiden started to have some issues. I had noticed that he was pulling away from me emotionally and did not want to spend as much time with me. He was arguing with his mum at that time, and it was really affecting him. He spent a lot of time on his phone and was disengaged from the family, and I tried not to worry but it was hard, as Aiden was also switched off from the kids. That April the school holidays started a week early and he was home as well. I went to work one day with my home client and sent him a text; "hey babe, I love you and I know we will get through this."

He texted straight back, "I don't feel like I can do this anymore."

I texted back, "I know we can do this together, whatever happens we can work it out. We can fix it with sex, ha-ha," but his reply devastated me.

"No Lou, we can't fix this with sex. I don't want to be married to you anymore."

I felt like a truck had hit me and I could not believe what he was saying. It was like the floor was slipping out from underneath me, and somehow, I kept working and then left in a daze. I did not understand what was happening to my husband. Was he depressed? Was he going to leave me? Instead of going home I drove to the beach, sat in the car, played Cody Carnes, and bawled my eyes out. After half an hour I sat up in my seat. I felt like God was telling me this was another attack from the enemy, and I had to fight, so I prayed right there and then.

"Lord, I know that your hand is on my marriage and that you will help me get through this."

I drove home feeling more determined than ever to fix things. A few days later it was Friday and Aiden went out and refused to come home. I was so upset, as it was exactly what he used to do when he was smoking marijuana, and I had no idea what to do. After the kids went to bed I sat on the couch and cried and tried to contact him, but it was no use.

"Be home Sunday, bye," was his last text to me.

I sat on the couch crying until the early hours of the morning. I finally fell asleep but kept waking up. Aiden came home after a few days and said he had been at his cousin's house, but he was distant and vague about what he had been doing. He went back to work, and I tried to function the best I could. Most nights he was late home and seemed more distant than ever, and I would fake being happy for the kids but inside I was really struggling. I knew I was losing Aiden and I felt powerless to stop it. One night a few weeks later I could not sleep, and I tossed and turned for an hour or two and then got out of bed. I wandered around for half an hour and then felt the Holy Spirit speak to me, "go and look in Aiden's bag."

I froze. Had I heard that correctly? I wandered around for a bit longer, but I kept hearing the same words.

"Aiden's bag, go and look in Aiden's bag."

Feeling like I was half crazy, I tiptoed into the bathroom with his bag. Sure enough, on opening it I found a stash of weed. My heart sank, and I sat on the bathroom floor crying. No, no, no, I sobbed to myself and to God, how could this be happening again, and how could I not have known? I must be the dumbest wife in the world, I wailed to the Lord. I felt a surge of anger rush through me, and I went into our room and woke Aiden up.

"Really?" I yelled at him. "You really thought you could hide this from me?"

Aiden looked so sheepish. "Not now Lou, let's talk in the morning," he said as he rolled over and went back to sleep.

Boy was I angry and did not sleep much that night. The next day Aiden and I went for a drive, and he admitted he had been using for a few months. I felt so angry that he could deceive me so badly. How could he do this to me and the kids? I yelled at him a lot that day in the car.

"But you worked so hard in rehab," I said, trying to keep my voice calm. "So, what now? You're going to throw it all away?"

I tried to stay angry at him, but I was terrified of losing him, so instead, I softened my heart towards him and lowered my voice.

"I will help you through this, okay? Just please don't run away to your cousins again. I cannot handle it when you leave," I said as my voice broke and I began to cry.

Aiden started to cry too. "I just don't feel worthy enough," he sobbed, "like you and the kids deserve more than me."

I assured him that God had chosen us to be together and that he was good enough.

"God forgives you babe for the weed, and so do I," I told him.

Aiden promised me he would not leave again, and that night for the first time in a long time we prayed together.

"Lord," Aiden prayed, "I know I have gone back to the weed, and I lied to my wife. You healed me once before, help me break free of my addiction again."

The next day I asked Aiden to go and smoke the rest of the weed and then throw everything away. I went with him to the local park where he hid behind a tree.

"It's done," he said when he came out, and he went to walk towards the rubbish bin, but I stopped him.

"No, not in there, you could just come back and retrieve it," I said.

I motioned to a large drain in the middle of the park.

"In there," I said to him as Aiden stared at me.

"In there?" he asked, and I nodded in reply.

"Yep, throw it in there, there's no way you could get it out from there."

Reluctantly he agreed and I watched him throw everything away. As we walked home, I felt better. We came up with a plan of what Aiden should do if he wanted to get weed, and we put some ideas on paper and put it up on the wall. He needed distraction techniques, so we thought of some ideas: praying, calling me or a friend, playing music, exercising, drumming, and reading the bible. That night we cuddled on our bed.

"Sometimes I feel rejected by you," Aiden confessed to me. "Like the kids come first and I don't matter. When I feel like that I want to smoke."

I agreed that this was a trigger for him and promised to spend some time with him. We decided to try and pray together as much as we could and go on regular dates. The next few days were hard as Aiden began to detox again, and I tried to be supportive and spend some time with him, but he admitted he was struggling, and I did not really know what to do. I had been sober for so many years, I took it for granted that God had healed me of my addictions. The next few weeks were hard. We tried to pray together but I felt like Aiden was just going through the motions, I felt like he was not genuine in his relationship with God. Aiden had been sober a few weeks when he started coming home late at night again, and he never answered his phone when I called him but seemed glued to it every night. I felt so sad and let down, and I felt like I was drowning and there was no one to save me. I confided in some women friends from church and that really helped. I was so blessed to have such supportive friends. My sister was also supportive and checked in on me regularly. But as the weeks turned to months, I felt Aiden drifting away even further, and I felt unqualified to help my husband.

Chapter 21

not that

One night in June I was reading the bible in bed when Aiden came into our room and shut the door. He looked agitated and was pacing around, and then he spoke to me.

"I've got something to tell you."

I looked up and closed my bible. "Yes?" I answered.

Aiden took a deep breath, looked down and started pacing again. He was sweating and avoiding eye contact with me.

"I can't keep it a secret anymore," he said, and my stomach turned over.

"What is it?" I managed to ask him.

He started pacing again. "I don't know how to tell you this Lou."

I waited for him to finish, "yes?" I prompted.

Aiden looked down again. "Um, I will just tell you, I have to tell you."

He looked up at the ceiling and blew out a big breath.

"I'm having an affair."

I heard the words, but they did not register, so I just stared silently at him.

"What?" I managed to blurt out, and he looked up at the ceiling again.

"I have been having an affair, with a woman from work. I am so sorry I have been keeping this from you, I am so sorry Lou."

Aiden began to cry, and I just sat there, staring at him, but I could not speak, and I felt like I was not even there.

"An affair," I said eventually, "with someone from work?"

Aiden nodded and wiped his face. "Yeah, she's an education assistant, a home economics one."

I just kept staring at him and I felt like I was a million miles away.

"What do you mean you're having an affair? Like you have slept with her? You have had sex with her?" My voice was getting louder as Aiden wiped his eyes and blew out a big breath.

"Yeah, I have slept with her."

I could feel my world slowly start to crumble. How was this possible? Surely this was a joke?

"More than once? You have slept with her more than once?" I said, and my voice was almost hysterical.

Aiden nodded and took another deep breath. "Yep, it's happened more than once," he said.

I stood up with shaky legs. "How many times?" I asked him, "and how long? How long has this been going on?"

Aiden started to pace again. "I'm not sure," he said eventually, and something in me snapped.

"What do you mean you don't know," I was starting to yell at him, "how long? How long has this been going on? Like before the school holidays?"

Aiden nodded at me. "From term one I think," he said.

I sat down again and tried desperately to comprehend what he was saying.

"So, this thing with the weed that started in March and all the times you said you couldn't be married to me, that was part of this? Like the affair has been happening this whole time?" I said, feeling like I was on the verge of a breakdown.

Aiden sat down on the bed and began to cry again. He nodded and I tried to calm my heart which felt like it was going a hundred miles an hour. My brain was churning with so many thoughts, surely this was not really happening.

"Please don't leave me Lou. I am nothing without you and the kids," he cried.

I shook my head. "I am not leaving you. Not right now anyway, I just need time to process this."

I stood up and took a deep breath, not trusting my legs to hold me up. I put my hand on the doorknob and turned to face him.

"Do you love her?" I asked and he shook his head violently.

"Gosh no!" he said as I stared at him.

"You need to end this; do you hear me? You need to end it with her," I gritted my teeth and he nodded.

"Yeah, I know. I will tell her tomorrow."

I turned and left the room and strode quickly to the kitchen. I had to do something, so I began to wash the dishes as my thoughts swirled around my brain. What was I going to do? How would I cope with this? Tears began to fall down my cheeks as I slowly began to realise what was going on, and the reality of his words sank deep into my heart. Aiden had slept with another woman, he had broken our vows, our sacred pact with God. My hands trembled as I kept on washing plates and cups. How could this have happened? Was this my fault? Had I somehow pushed my husband into the arms of another woman? I heard one of the kids approaching and I quickly wiped my tears away. I could not let them see me this upset or find out what was going on, I had to protect them no matter what. Somehow, I said good night to them and went about tidying up the house. I had a shift in the morning with my client, but how was I supposed to act normal and take them out? I was late going to bed that night and I sat on the couch and wailed into a cushion. It did not seem real, I felt like I was living in some awful nightmare. Aiden had tried to say goodnight to me, but I had told him to leave me alone, as I needed time to think about what had happened.

That night I cried out to God to help me, and I knew I needed Him more than I ever had before.

"Lord," I sobbed as I lay on the couch. "Please help me, I can't do this alone. How will I get through this?"

I cried and prayed, and I felt Jesus' presence like a warm blanket. I felt Him say that I had to stay close to Him to get through the next few days. I took some extra medication because I knew I would have trouble getting my thoughts to quieten down. I lay in my bed and the tears fell silently down my cheeks. Eventually I drifted off to sleep but, in the morning, I felt like I had been hit by a truck. Aiden started work at 6am so he was long gone, which was a good thing as I was not sure I would have been able to control myself had I seen him. I staggered into the shower and prayed that I would get through the day. I helped the kids get ready for school and dropped them off, and Aiden had texted me earlier to say he was sorry, but I had not replied. What was I meant to say to him, and what could he say to me that would make up for his actions anyway? That day I went through the motions of looking after my client, but I felt a million miles away. I realised to my dismay that I was disassociating the entire day. When I saw Aiden that night, the anger stirred up in me, how could he have done this to me? How could he have done this to our family? I waited until we were in our room with the door shut and then I let it fly. I yelled at him and struck him, and he just stood there and took it, and eventually I ordered him out of our room so I could cry alone.

The next few days were rough. I pretended everything was normal but inside I was dying, and I could barely stand the sight of Aiden, he repulsed me. Aiden assured me that he had ended things with her, but how could, I be sure? Most nights I cried in the bottom of the shower, and as the days turned to weeks, I begged God to let me end my marriage.

"Please God," I pleaded. "Let me leave. I do not want to do this; I don't want to go through this, help me please!"

But every time He would answer me the same thing, "love him."

"How am I meant to love him God when he betrayed me so badly?" I would wail and cry at God as the water ran over my face, and each time God would say to me, "you are a faithful and loving wife. So, love him."

I would feel angry when I heard God say that to me, so angry! It hurt so very much; the pain was bad, so bad that I would lie on the couch and the agony in my heart was so real, it hurt like nothing I had ever felt before. It was like someone had reached into my chest and pulled my heart out. The feeling was so horrific it took my breath away and, once again I would beg God to let me end my marriage. And every time He would repeat the same words to me, "forgive him as I have forgiven you, love him as I have loved you."

I was in an impossible situation, yet God was asking me to stay. In some ways the pain was worse than what my father had done to me, how was this possible?

Aiden kept his distance from me at my request, but my soul was dying. I had always relied on him for support, and I longed to turn to him but how could I? How could I get comfort from my husband, when he was the one who had broken my heart? I kept on doing everything as I had before, cooking, cleaning, working, shopping but I was just a shell, nothing felt real. It felt like it was all just a bad dream. Slowly I began to realise that God was not going to let me out of my marriage, that even though Aiden had broken his vow with the Lord, I had not. One night Lachlan called me into his room.

"Mama, what is wrong? You seem so sad, has something happened?"

Tears flooded my eyes, as I thought I had been so careful to hide it from the kids, I had forgotten one was already an adult and was super aware of my moods. I sat on his bed and told him about the affair.

"It's so unfair," he said as he held my hand. "What are you going to do mama?"

I wiped my eyes. "I don't want to leave him mate, I think we can work it out," I said but Lachlan frowned.

"Mum, he cheated on you, it's not right," he said sadly.

I nodded my head. "Yes, I know but he is in a bad place mate, he's relapsed and has been smoking weed again. He's not a bad person Lachy; he just made a terrible mistake."

Lachlan hugged me. "You're such a good person mum, it's not fair that this has happened to you."

We hugged again, and I reassured him that I was okay. A few days later I approached my husband, as the Lord had softened my heart, and I could see that Aiden was suffering too, so I let him hold me as I cried.

"Why, why, why?" I kept asking him.

He cried and confessed he had no idea why he had the affair.

"Why don't you leave me Lou? I betrayed you."

I made a noise in the back of my throat. "Believe me I have tried to leave," I answered, "but God won't let me."

Aiden hugged me tighter. "I don't deserve you," he cried, and I sat up and wiped my eyes.

"We have to get some help," I told him. "We can't do this alone."

Aiden agreed.

"Will you come to counselling?" I asked him.

"I will do anything to keep you and the kids," he replied.

While Aiden went to sleep, I went on the internet and typed in 'Christian marriage counselling,' and immediately a page popped up.

"I can help you heal from infidelity," it said.

The page said that the counsellor had personal experience with infidelity and offered marriage and individual counselling. I quickly hit the contact button, as I could feel God was present with me, and this was a crucial step to healing our marriage. That night I went to bed and for the first time since it all happened, I felt a glimmer of hope. I did a lot of praying while I waited for the counsellor to contact us. I was still hurting a lot, and I picked fights with Aiden and threw things at the wall. A few times I attacked him physically, as I could not understand why he had done it. I still blamed myself, I mean we did not exactly have the healthiest sex life, maybe it was my fault. I could barely bring myself to make love to Aiden and if we did, I was usually on the ceiling, and I always burnt myself afterwards.

The schema therapy had helped a lot but deep down, I still felt guilty and ashamed. A few weeks after telling me of his infidelity, I now wanted to know every single little detail of the affair, like how often they had sex and where it happened, and what they did together. Aiden was so ashamed every time I brought it up.

"Why do you want to know Lou?" he would ask me.

"I don't know," I would reply. "I just want to know."

He would be forced to tell me the details and even though it hurt like nothing else, I felt better for knowing. The worst part was that I could not bring myself to tell any of our friends, as I did not want them to judge Aiden. I wanted to keep it between me, Aiden and God.

Things at home were not great for the kids. Isla and Lukas could tell something was wrong, but I refused to tell them. Lachlan was struggling to find a job due to Covid restrictions, but he had put his name down to volunteer at the new museum that was opening later in the year, as he loved history and thought it would be something he would enjoy. Isla was really struggling with anxiety still, and often she would get her dad to pick her up from school early. Isla struggled with the night time routine, and everything overwhelmed her, and she was still having counselling at Headspace, but she said it was not helping much. Lukas, however, was thriving in his last year of primary school and was looking forward to his camp at the end of the year.

Aiden and I were picking Isla up from a friend's place one day when a lady ran into the back of my little Rio at the traffic lights. I could not believe that I had had another accident, but it was not my fault again! There was quite a lot of damage, and Aiden and I went to hospital, as both our backs were sore from the rear impact. My insurance company informed me it was a write off and I was devastated. The car was old, so it was only worth around two thousand dollars, and it was such a small amount of money and I felt conflicted about what to do. I stalled with the insurance company until one night my brother called me.

"Hey sis, you know you can access your superannuation because of Covid. You can get ten grand," he said, and I felt this surge of hope.

I quickly hung up the phone and jumped online and applied. I was approved instantly and two days later I got the money. I was so excited to find a car, so Aiden and I went to view another Kia, this time a Cerato. It was so flash and new looking I nearly cried, after years of driving old bombs, the Lord was blessing me. Only God could turn two write offs into a fantastic car for me.

The marriage counsellor had emailed me back, and we booked our first appointment. I was still crying most nights and felt overwhelmed much of the time. Even though I was committed to doing the counselling, I was still asking God for a way out. Aiden was trying hard to be attentive, but I could tell he was struggling too emotionally. Our first appointment arrived, and I was so nervous. Upon meeting Yvonne though, I was immediately at rest, as she was so lovely and friendly and so on fire for God. She spoke such words of encouragement and hope over our marriage.

"It's possible to come back from infidelity,' she reassured us. "God wants to heal your marriage, the enemy is gunning for you, and you will have to be strong and courageous."

That night I cried but they were tears of relief. Over the next few weeks, we had regular counselling, we learned so much about marriage and the Lord, and we always left the appointments feeling hopeful. We talked a lot about accountability and there were new rules about Aiden and his phone.

"Aiden," Yvonne said, "if Louise calls you, then you answer straight away. If you miss the call, then you call her straight back within five minutes."

This had always been a huge issue for me throughout our entire relationship. I had never realised how much it affected me not knowing where my husband was half the time, and Aiden always had his phone on silent and it really affected my ability to trust him. We also talked at length about the woman who Aiden had been involved in. He admitted that it was more of an emotional affair than sexual. He said that yes, they had slept together, but they had also talked about a lot of different things, that he had turned to her when I was too busy with the kids and my own mental health issues. It hurt a lot to hear that, but I tried to be as understanding as I could. Aiden had confided in me that he owed this woman money for drugs and Yvonne produced a plan to confront her. Aiden had to arrange a place to meet so we could give her the money back. I was so anxious, but Yvonne assured me that God would honour me as Aiden's wife.

"Louise," she said. "You must take back your godly crown!"

Aiden contacted her which made me feel positively ill, and she agreed to meeting him but was not aware that I was tagging along too. Yvonne had given me a script of what to say, and Aiden had organised to meet her at a local shopping centre. The day arrived and I was sick with anxiety, but as we approached the food court, a sense of peace and calm washed over me, and I knew it was the Holy Spirit. The woman was sitting at a table and looked up as Aiden approached. I was standing behind him, so she did not see me at first. Her face lit up with a smile and I was shocked to be honest to see how old she was. Most men upgrade to a newer model, but not my husband! She suddenly spotted me, and I could see the fear in her eyes as Aiden held out the envelope.

"Here is the money I owe you," he said looking at the notes Yvonne had told him to write down. Then he took a step back. "And this is my wife, she knows about our affair, and I want to tell you that it's over, we are done."

I took a step forward. "I know who you are," I said, "and I want to tell you that what has happened between you and my husband will never happen again. I know all about the affair and I am choosing to stay with him and work things out. I am asking you to stay the heck away from him. If you do contact him, then I will have no choice but to tell your husband and the principal of the school."

Her eyes widened at that, and she looked quickly at Aiden.

"But we can talk about this, we," but I cut her off.

"No, we are not talking about this. Aiden has paid you what he owes you, so stay away from my husband, that's it!"

I turned and walked away, and Aiden followed. My heart was beating so fast I thought I might faint, and Aiden hurried to keep up with me.

"Wow," he said. "You really told her."

I kept on walking. "I can't believe I actually did that," I said to him.

"I saw your eyes flash with something Lou, like the Holy Spirit was coming out of you!"

I slowed my pace a little and took a few deep breaths. "I guess I got my crown back," I joked.

That night I sat and prayed quietly that it was the end of her being in our lives. At the next session with Yvonne, we celebrated the victory with her.

"I am so proud of you," she said.

I did feel better about things and in that session, we talked about the reasons why Aiden felt compelled to turn to another woman for emotional support. It was not the first time he had talked to other women and relied on them for help emotionally. In fact, I realised in that session, that he had been doing it for our entire marriage, but I had grown so accustomed to it that it just felt normal. I had learned early on in our marriage that to love Aiden, I had to accept the other women that he was emotionally connected to.

"It was only a matter of time until one of those friendships turned sexual," Yvonne said. "It is also because of Aiden's unhealthy relationship with his mum," she explained, and she was right.

Aiden's mum had parentified him at an early age and used him like a partner in terms of emotional support. He was pulled into her dramas and relationships, and he felt compelled to give her the emotional support she had not received from her husbands, and it had really damaged him. I cried for Aiden, as what an awful thing for a mum to have done, no wonder he had no boundaries when it came to other women. We also talked about generational curses and how these were passed down from generation to generation. Aiden's mum had multiple affairs over the years, and Yvonne believed the spirit of lust and perversion was hanging over him.

Chapter 22

only Jesus

Over the next few weeks, we did individual healing sessions too. Both of us had so much trauma in our past that we needed to be set free of. For me it was the death of Stephan, and of course the abuse I suffered at the hands of my father. But it was also the relationship I never had with my mother and Julian's abuse that held me captive. Slowly but surely, Yvonne walked me through some visual healing sessions with the help of Jesus and the Holy Spirit. I was exhausted afterwards but at the same time I felt free. Sin and shame no longer had a hold over me; I was as spotless as the lamb. Aiden enrolled in a 'Breaking Chains' healing group at a local church and it was life changing for him. He had individual healing sessions too, and I was amazed at the difference it made for him, especially emotionally. It was so eye opening for Aiden to realise the emotional connections that he had with other women had damaged him so much, and that he was simply re-creating his relationship with his mum. That he could be set free of it was such a big revelation for him.

Back in our individual sessions, Yvonne explained to me why it had hurt so much when Aiden had told me about the affair.

"When a man marries a woman, they both become one with God," she explained. "It's like they share a heart, so, when a husband cheats, the pain feels so bad because the heart has been almost cut in half."

It made perfect sense to me as to why I had felt the way I did after Aiden had told me about the affair. Yvonne also encouraged me to think about making love to Aiden.

"The longer you put it off, the stronger the devil's hold is over your marriage," she said.

But I was terrified at the thought of it. I had turned that part of me completely off and did not know how to turn it on again, but I promised that I would think about it.

As the year ended Lukas went on his week-long camp to Busselton, and they had much fun doing different activities every day. It was hard to let him go, as he was still my baby, but I had to trust that the Lord would look after him. I was so proud of Lukas for going on camp, for doing chores and behaving so well. When he returned, he seemed more grown up somehow.

Lachlan finally got a job at Big W, and he was also volunteering at the museum and was loving it. He was still planning on enlisting in the army again the next year, so he was doing a workout programme every other day. Isla was doing better, and the self-harm had reduced a lot which was a relief. After a few more sessions with Yvonne, I told Aiden I was ready to make love again, and to my surprise, I was present the whole time and did not go on the ceiling once. Even more surprising was that Aiden was a lot more present too, and it really was beautiful and afterwards we both laughed and felt the joy of the Lord all around us.

"So that is what married sex is meant to feel like," we both said to one another.

We attended Lukas' year six graduation, and it was a wonderful day with lunch out and a swim at the marina. I could not believe my baby was done with primary school. That Christmas was a happy one, and as the new year began, work was going well for me. I had three amazing clients and I loved being part of their families. The end of January came with a five-day lockdown, and it was our first one in the state and it felt weird. We were still allowed to exercise for one hour a day and do shopping of course, but I must admit that I enjoyed the time off and we happily played board games and binged Netflix.

Lukas started high school in the February, and I was so proud of him walking in there with his big sister. He seemed unfazed by it all and had lots to tell me when he got home. Lachlan was working at Big W and was training hard for the army. He was exercising every other day doing sit ups, push ups and running. He had to submit so much paperwork and it was a lengthy process. The day arrived for his second psychological interview, but this time he was prepared. He had studied up on what his role would be as an engineer and the history of the basic training camp at Kapooka. He knew the timetable and I felt confident he would go well. As he came out, Lachlan said he was more hopeful this time around, as he had not got so tongue tied.

I began to pray several times a day for Lachlan to be accepted into the army. It was the only career goal that he had ever had, and even though I did not want him going away, I knew it was not up to me to dictate what he did with his life. I could not be that parent who held their son back from achieving his goals. I prayed hard for him as he deserved to be a part of something important and special. Lachlan had had a rough start in life, and it would be wonderful for him to go and travel and see the world. Even though I knew his identity was in Christ, I prayed for him to find his purpose in life. I prayed so much that I began to really trust that God would do what was best for our son, and this meant that I had to surrender Lachlan to Him; I had to trust that God knew what was best for him. It was hard, because at first, I wanted to know whether he would make it into the army. I kept asking God to reveal it to me. So much so that I started to feel a bit sick with it all. I would lie in bed and wrestle back and forth with it and one night I felt like I could not do it anymore.

"God, I give Lachlan to you completely and the decision about the army," I said aloud and immediately I felt my heart flood with peace.

Aiden and I continued marriage counselling and started to work on our communication skills, something we were both bad at. But we persevered and with Yvonne's help we were learning how to compromise, and get along properly, without all the resentment. We learnt how to use "I feel" statements and diffuse arguments. I did not realise that I had been prioritising the kids over Aiden for most of our marriage.

"You know that affairs don't happen in healthy marriages," Yvonne pointed out.

After she said that, it dawned on me that I was not putting my marriage first, but the kids. That was a revelation for me to say the least. Aiden was looking for an emotional connection and to be validated as a man, and us spending time together is what made him feel the most appreciated. I learned that for him to feel stable and loved, I would need to prioritise spending time with him. I guess deep down I had always known this to be true, but I had never fully acknowledged it before the affair. I learned to be 'busy' in the home from my mum, but while I was prioritising housework and the kids, my marriage was coming last.

Isla had started year 9, but it was so hard for her to cope with the anxiety, so we went to her GP and talked about anti-depressants. I did not want to go down that road, but I could not watch her struggle anymore with the depression and constant meltdowns, so, she started on them, and we prayed a lot for her. She had a few side effects but tolerated them well. It was heartbreaking to see Isla struggle so much and I desperately wanted to see her come out of the fog that she was under.

My brother's daughter Ruby, my niece, started to come over regularly and I was so happy that her and Isla were close. It was lovely to have Ruby around, but I missed Dylan's three boys so much. I had a couple of early photos of Ben, Ricky and Billy and I would look at them often. Dana's daughter Evelyn had always been close to Isla and Lukas, but I had only seen Dylan's kids a handful of times in the past few years.

Church was going so well for us; Aiden had served on the worship team but was now on the set-up team. Because we did not have an actual building, it was demanding work to set it all up every Sunday. Thankfully, we had a dedicated team to do all that work. I had been serving in the kid's ministry for a few years and loved it. Our two Pastors were keen to meet with us about how our counselling was going, and during the meeting I was explaining how hard it was when I had learned of Aiden's affair.

"There was a part of me that died that day," I said as I looked down into my lap. "Like the physical pain was real, like someone had put a knife into my heart."

There was silence in the room and then Aiden turned to me with tears in his eyes.

"Oh my gosh," he said as he grabbed my hand. "I just felt what you felt. The Holy Spirit just revealed it to me. Oh Lou, I am so sorry, I promise I will never, ever do that to you again."

We sat there and cried and then we prayed with our Pastors. I left feeling hopeful that the affair was in our past and that we were moving on. Do not get me wrong, it still hurt, I would think of the affair and still feel connected to it, but it certainly was not as intense as it had been.

"But I don't trust him yet," I confided to Yvonne, and she smiled at me.

"No, but it will come back, these things take time."

Isla started some more counselling with Yvonne's business partner who offered therapy to young people.

"Mum, I like her, but she keeps bringing up God all the time and I'm not ready for that," Isla said to me one day.

I encouraged her to keep going, as they were working on some early trauma, and I thought it would be beneficial for her to persevere. One day Lukas and I were at the beach waiting for Isla to finish at her appointment when Lachlan called me. It was so windy and a bad line.

"Hi mate," I answered. "What's up?"

There was a silence. "Mum," Lachlan said, and my heart skipped a beat.

"Yes?" I answered. There was another silence and then he spoke.

"I got in."

I started jumping up and down on the beach and shrieking like a lunatic.

"Oh my gosh!" I yelled. "Oh my gosh mate!"

Lukas came running over. "Mum what's going on?" he asked.

I held the phone away from me. "Lachlan got into the army!"

Lukas started whooping and jumping up and down with me. There was a man nearby waxing his surfboard who looked at us with confusion as Lukas and I kept jumping up and down and hugging each other.

"I'm so proud of you mate!" I cried into the phone.

"Thanks mum," Lachlan said. "I can't believe it mum; I can't believe I did it."

I sat down on a rock in the sand.

"Oh, mate, I am so proud of you. I have been praying so much and just waiting for the phone call."

Lukas sat down next to me, grinning from ear to ear.

"Thanks mum, I really appreciate your support," Lachlan said.

We hung up and Lukas and I went to pick up Isla and when Lukas saw her, he quickly told her the good news. She was so happy and called

Lachlan to congratulate him. I called Aiden to tell him what had happened and that night we all hugged Lachlan, and I cried a bit with sadness and relief. I felt like I was in shock, but I was too excited for him to be sad. The next day Lachlan was told he would have to pass a physical test before they finalised his enlistment. At some point, he had also ticked the box that said he had counselling in the past and they wanted to know more.

"Mum," he said to me. "I'm worried I've stuffed myself up and I won't get a job offer."

I reassured him that it would all be fine, that God would not give him the opportunity, only to take it away again. That night I sat and googled what being an Engineer would really entail, and as I read it, I felt my heart sink. It was a dangerous job, and I was dismayed to read that the Australian army had lost more combat engineers than infantry in Afghanistan. Then I sat on the couch when everyone went to bed and burst into tears. Why couldn't he choose another role that was not so dangerous? And I could not believe that he had made it. I could believe it actually; we served a mighty and powerful God! I was now in denial, but wasn't this that I had wanted for my boy, for his dream to come true? And now as I sat and howled at God, I wanted Him to take it back. How dare he give my eldest son an exit out of our family. How could God do this to me? I lay down and sobbed into a cushion. This is what I prayed hours for, and now I couldn't deal with it, was I going mad? I could hear the Lord whispering to me as tears poured down my face.

"Trust me. Give him to me and trust me."

I sobbed a little longer and then I sat up. I wiped my face and bowed my head.

"Lord," I prayed. "I know you love our son. I pray you will guide him and look after him. I give him to you completely and I know that you will protect him and keep him safe. In Jesus' name, Amen."

I finally felt some peace with him leaving and that night I slept well. Lachlan kept up his physical training and I could see it was taking a toll on him. He had to do a beep test, and I helped him train every second day. It was gruelling and I felt for him, especially when he would stuff up the test and become upset. We had the ADF training app on his phone and I would do the workouts with him, which was not an easy job at my age, but I knew he needed me to support him, and I came to enjoy the exercise, sort of. He had to do 40 push-ups, 90 sit-ups and a 7.5 beep test. Lachlan installed a chin up bar in his room and that really helped him to develop his upper body strength. I remember the first time he nailed the 40 push-ups and then did three more just because he could. He looked so proud of himself, and I was too. The day of the beep test arrived, and I took him into the recruitment office. I was so proud of him when he called me to say he had passed, I felt like it was one more thing to cross off the list. The only thing left was to prove to recruitment that he was mentally capable of enlisting, and with the help of his previous counsellor, who now resided in Sydney, he finally got everything done. That night I sat with him, and we both cried a little. All he could do now was wait and pray that a job offer would come up soon.

It was Isla's 13th birthday, but because of Covid restrictions she could not have a party, so, I organised a 'drive by birthday party' for her. Some of her friends drove into our Cul de sac to drop off presents and yell out happy birthday to her from their cars. It was not as good as a real party, but it was the next best thing.

Easter came and Ruby came to stay with us. That night when I was going to bed, I tossed and turned for an hour or two, then I sat up in bed and I had a funny feeling about the girls. I opened Isla's door and found the room empty and the window wide open, with the girls nowhere to be seen. With my heart beating a million miles an hour, I went to wake up Aiden. We jumped in the car and drove off down the street, with Aiden frantically calling Isla, but she was not answering. I felt sick in my stomach, as it was almost 2am and pitch-black outside, they could be anywhere. We kept driving and praying that God would help us find them. I was about to call the police when Isla finally answered her phone.

"Where are you?" I yelled.

"We're at IGA," she replied. I swore at her and then hung up the phone.

I quickly did a U - turn, sped over to IGA and Isla and Ruby were waiting in the carpark. They both got in the car with their heads hanging in shame as I tried to calm my breathing down.

"How could you have done such a stupid thing? You could have been kidnapped or raped!"

But they both did not answer me and were mostly quiet on the way home. I marched the girls into the house.

"Right, you two are not sleeping in the same room. Ruby you will sleep in the lounge room," I announced.

I sent Isla to bed and got Ruby settled in the other room.

"You know, I will have to tell your dad," I said. Ruby looked up at me with a sad look on her face.

"Yeah, I know," she replied.

The next day I dropped Ruby at the train station and called my brother. We both agreed the girls could not be trusted, and they would have a break from seeing each other. That night I had a chat with Isla.

"You're grounded until we feel we can trust you again," I said to her.

She was upset and cried and said she did not mean to do it.

"I know you are upset that you can't see Ruby right now, but it's important that there is a consequence to your actions," I explained to Isla.

A few weeks after that, Lachlan received an email with a job offer, and his official enlistment date was July 12th. We all celebrated that night, but there was so much to be done and I instantly went into planning mode.

There was an extensive list of stuff he needed from rubbish bags to an iron and electrical tape. At night I tried to calm myself but inside I was panicking, as it was really happening, and I could not do a thing to stop it. Lachlan kept up his physical training and got an exemption from looking for work. He asked his dad to help with buying equipment, as there were so many items on his list. We got a big suitcase from a friend at church, and he started packing. Clothes, shoes, a head torch, Fixomul for blisters, lengths of cord and more tape, a shaving brush to clean his rifle, socks, and tent pegs. The list was never ending. The weeks were drawing closer and deep down inside I was in complete denial. I had prayed for this, and God had granted Lachlan the desires of his heart, but deep down I was worried. Lachlan and I had a bond that had been tested and tried in all sorts of ways over the years. We had been through multiple traumas together and I was honestly not sure I could cope without him, but when I said those words aloud, I knew that God had given this dream to Lachlan for a good reason. He was my son and was not responsible for me or my happiness. It was not his job to support me otherwise I would be no better than Aiden's mum!

Lachlan deserved to find himself, and to be set free of the burden he had felt all these years, that he was there to fix things in the family, emotionally and physically. Even though it stung me, I knew I had relied on him long enough. I helped him get everything ready and I stayed strong and positive for him.

I wanted to plan a farewell party, but Lachlan did not want any fuss. I organised a barbecue for our family and a few friends, and I had spent ages getting everything ready including making a cake with army green icing and a plastic grenade on top. When we arrived at the park to set up, I felt stressed and anxious. I ended up yelling at Lachlan and Aiden and I stalked off to sulk. I was so focussed on everything being perfect that I was missing the point of us being together. I came back to the picnic area with my head low and apologised to everyone, and in the end, it was a great farewell party and I felt so happy for Lachlan. Poor Isla and Lukas were emotional leading up to the day, as they both loved Lachlan so much and did not want their big brother to go away. He was always there for them, and they were going to miss him terribly. The week before his departure arrived and we finally had everything packed. Due to Covid we would not be allowed to attend the ceremony at the recruitment office. We were, however, permitted, to meet him at the airport to say goodbye. He would be travelling to Canberra and then on to NSW.

The weekend before his departure Lachlan was very emotional, and he kept checking and re checking everything. A friend of ours had been in the army for many years and she had warned Lachlan about basic training. She said they would get yelled and screamed at a lot, and that he needed to try not talk back to the officers and to just do everything that he was told, no questions asked. She said that it would be brutal physically and mentally, and that he would have to keep his head down for 12 weeks and then it would be over. Two nights before he left Lachlan was very restless, and he sat with me on the couch and cried.

"Mum what if this is all a big mistake? What if I don't have what it takes to make it? What if I fail?"

I hugged him and tried my best to reassure him.

"Mate it's normal to feel worried and overwhelmed. This is a massive thing that you are about to do. But I believe in you, I know that you can do this. And you are not going to fail. You heard what Maria said, you cannot really fail basic training. If there is something you are not so good at, they will just retrain you until you pass."

We sat together and he cried a bit more, but I had to try hard to stay calm for him. I felt like the Holy Spirit was there with me, and that night when he went to bed, I lay on the couch and sobbed silently to God.

"Please look after him Lord," I whispered.

The reality was that although I supported his decision, I did not like the idea of him suffering throughout basic training. I knew he was going to do it tough, but I did not want him suffering unnecessarily. The night before he left, we had dinner as a family and Isla and Lukas looked so sad. Lachlan checked his stuff one last time, then he checked it again. It was late when he said he was going to bed.

"Mum, will you lay down with me until I fall asleep?" he asked.

I lay down next to him and held his hand and tried to calm my beating heart. I took some deep breaths and let them out slowly, I could not believe that he was going away, my boy was leaving.

"I love you mum," he said quietly. "Thanks for being there for me. I better try and get some sleep."

He turned over on his side and I prayed quietly under my breath, knowing that his heart was going faster than mine. I lay there next to him before he finally drifted off, and then I went to bed and prayed.

"Lord, I know you have Lachlan in the palm of your hand. Give him strength to do all he needs to do. Protect him and guide him and be always with him. In Jesus' name, Amen."

Chapter 23

goodbye

It took a long time to fall asleep that night. I knew I had to be strong for Lachlan, but it was hard to switch my brain off. Also knowing we had to be up super early that next morning did not help. Isla, Lukas, and Aiden had said goodbye the night before and I finally got to sleep before Lachlan was shaking me awake and my alarm was ringing next to me. I felt strange as I got out of bed, like it was not really happening, and I was not in charge of my own body. I made my coffee and helped Lachlan load his stuff in the car. He looked so smart in his black pants and shirt and tie. I was going to drop him at the recruitment office, and then go back home and pick the others up so we could meet him at the airport. I felt so anxious driving in the city. I knew the way but put the address into my GPS just in case, as I could not risk him being late. Lachlan was nervous so he was chatty, but as we got closer, he became quieter. There was no place to park so I had to pull up on St Georges Terrace, and he quickly unloaded his stuff. I felt for him as he looked quite stressed.

"Bye mum," he said as he hurried off, pulling his large suitcase behind him.

I pulled out into traffic before I glanced at the passenger seat and saw he had left his phone behind. I swore. Of course, there would be dramas! I did not know what to do, should I call the recruitment office? I quickly pulled into the right lane and tried to do a U - turn, but it was impossible, I would have to go around the block. I swore again and tried to remain calm. A few minutes later my phone rang, and it was the recruitment office. I explained I was still in the city and Lachlan could meet me in the same spot. He looked very unhappy as I pulled up, and he quickly opened the door and grabbed his phone, before running back towards the office. I pulled back into the traffic and burst into tears, my mind going a hundred miles an hour. I took a deep breath and wiped my face on a tissue, as I had to calm down and concentrate on getting back onto the freeway. I put on a worship song and drove home, and when I got there Aiden and Lukas were getting out of bed.

"How was he?" Aiden asked.

"Nervous and a bit stressed," I replied and told everyone about the phone drama, and we had a bit of a laugh.

"Poor Lachlan," Aiden said.

"Mum when can we see him?" Lukas asked me and I hugged him.

"We're meeting him at the airport mate," I replied. I had my breakfast and then woke Isla up.

"Mum, I miss him already," she said as she hugged me.

It was such a shame we could not be there for his special ceremony. I have a beautiful photograph of Lachlan accepting his enlistment certificate at the recruitment office, he looks like he has just laughed at something, and his smile is big and warm. Even now when I look at that photo, I feel such joy.

We piled into the car and headed for the airport, and on the way, Lachlan called me.

"Hi mum," he said, and I was pleased to hear that he sounded in good spirits. "Are you guys on your way? We have already left."

I turned onto Tonkin Highway.

"Yes, mate we're on our way."

Isla and Lukas called out to him, "hi Lachy, we're coming to see you."

"Hi guys," Lachlan said to them.

"Hey Lachlan, how's it going?" Aiden asked.

"How did it go at the ceremony?" I asked him.

"Yes good," he answered. "I was nervous at first, but it turned out well. See you soon."

We drove into the airport and found a parking spot. Lachlan's dad Tom was meeting us there and we saw him as we walked in. We waited around for a while before we spotted Lachlan, and the other recruits arrive. He waved to us before turning back to his group, and he looked so grown up and my heart gave a jump. We waited while he and the recruits checked in and put their bags through. A while later he was allowed to come and hang out with us, and we all gave him lots of hugs.

"I think we're all going to get something to eat before we get on the plane," he said to us.

"Are we allowed to come up with you?" Isla and Lukas asked him, and Lachlan looked nervously at the group.

"I'm not sure," he replied.

We stood around with him chatting and watching the other recruits, and Lachlan informed me that one of the recruits was 17 years old. Wow, I thought, brave parents as I was struggling, and Lachlan was 19. There were members of the defence force there and they said we were allowed to go upstairs with the recruits, so we did, but Lachlan looked like he wanted to go off with his new mates. I was feeling so anxious and said to Aiden I wanted to stay with him.

"Babe let him go. He wants to get some food and be with them, it is time to say goodbye," Aiden said.

My heart lurched in my chest, and we all hugged Lachlan.

"Don't worry about me mum, I'll call you once I'm in Canberra," he said.

I did not want to leave but I could see that he had his mind made up. I kept stalling but he kept looking over at the other recruits. Isla and Lukas hugged him and told him they loved him. He hugged us and Tom, and then he was gone. We all traipsed back to the car, and on the way home I cried a bit.

"I miss him already," I said.

The rest of the day we just relaxed at home, but we all felt sad. I wandered into Lachlan's room and absently picked up one of the many lists we had written together. I hugged his pillow and cried because it smelled like him. I glanced around his room at the clothes he had left behind and at his PC where he had spent many hours gaming and talking to his friends. It did not feel real that he was gone. That night the house was quiet, as there was no loud gaming voice or laughter coming from his room. Lachlan face timed us from the hotel in Canberra.

"Hi mum," he said as we all gathered around the phone.

"Hi mate how's it going?"

Lachlan explained he had landed and took an Uber to the hotel. He had his own room and it looked nice. We chatted and then he asked me to help guide him to iron his shirt and pants for the next day. He was fussing over what to wear.

"I'm nervous mum. Should I just wear the same outfit?"

We decided that his not so formal shirt would be better and his good jeans. We chatted for a while longer, and Lachlan said he was going to the

Canberra recruitment office in the morning, and then from there they were traveling to Kapooka.

"I'm tired and it is a few hours ahead here. I am going to watch You Tube and go to bed," he said, and I tried not to cry.

Later, I tucked Lukas in. "I miss Lachlan," he said as he hugged me. "Why did he have to go away?"

The tears came and I tried to be strong. Isla was quiet and went to bed early, so I sat on the couch and just cried and cried. I had so much built-up emotion. The whole journey had been exhilarating and exhausting at the same time, and I could not believe he was gone, Lachlan, our big boy was gone. I sat in the bottom of the shower and sobbed. I felt our whole lives together flash before me, his birth, mum and dad, the long days as a single mum and the endless struggle for me mentally that had taken its toll on Lachlan. He had always been my protector, and my rock, he had fixed things literally and physically for me his whole life. And now he did not have that burden any longer. I wanted to go back in time and change so many things, as it was not fair what he had been through, why hadn't I protected him more?

I felt God's gentle voice, "Lachlan is strong and brave and all those tough things he faced led him to this moment right now. It made him who he is. And it all lead to him choosing the army. If he had an entitled life, he would not be who he is today. Be proud of him and of yourself. I chose you to be his mum."

I sniffled and stood up. I had to go to work the next day and could not spend all night crying on the couch. As I lay in bed, I knew that God had chosen this path for Lachlan; that the Lord saw the emotional support our son had given all of us over the years, and I knew deep down in my heart that God had set him free. The tears kept coming as I drifted off to sleep. The next day my phone rang early, it was Lachlan calling me from the recruitment office in Canberra but on a different number. I was so happy to hear from him, but he was in a bit of a tizzy.

"Mum," he said hurriedly. "I have dropped my phone down the elevator shaft, here in the building. I was ready to get onto the bus to go to Kapooka and I was about to step out of the lift, and it was gone."

I tried to comprehend what he was saying.

"Oh, no mate that's not good."

He spoke again even more quickly. "I've got to go mum; it will be all right; the bus is leaving now. I will find a way to call you, bye."

He hung up and I sat there in a daze, as not only were our son thousands of miles away and about to embark on three months of basic training, but he was also going without a phone. I burst into tears, as now I had no idea of when he was going to contact me. My friend had warned me that the recruits did not have much contact with their families in the first few weeks, to get them accustomed to army life, and then after a few weeks, they had to earn phone privileges. And how was Lachlan feeling now without a way of contacting us? To drop your phone down an elevator shaft and then immediately get on a bus to another state was a very brave thing to do. Talk about radical acceptance! I racked my brain to how I could help the situation. I started Googling the recruitment office in Canberra and got their number. I knew Lachlan would be embarrassed if he knew I was calling them, but I decided to do it anyway. I spoke to a lovely lady who listened while I told her the story.

"Wow," she said. "That's a real shame for him. I have your details, so if we find it, I'll call you."

I explained that they may need to post it to the base in Kapooka and she agreed that would be the best thing. After I hung up, I prayed and prayed that it would be found and be in one piece. It was a solid Nokia phone and I prayed that it had survived the fall. That day it was hard to concentrate knowing that Lachlan would be soon arriving at the base. I shuddered to think of what sort of welcome they would get. I had heard there was lots of yelling and insults even before they got off the bus, but I knew Lachlan was tough and God was on his side. That night after dinner I heard my phone ringing and I raced to pick it up.

"Hi mum," Lachlan said in a wobbly voice, and I could hear lots of noise in the background.

"Hi mate, how's it going?"

There was a pause, and I could hear him suck in his breath.

"I've got to admit mum, it's a bit rough here," his voice quivered, and I tried hard not to cry.

"They've just shaved all our heads and now we're going to go to the barracks."

His voice wobbled again. "I borrowed Corporal's phone so I can't really talk."

I swallowed hard and I knew he was trying his best not to cry.

"Okay mate, it's good to hear from you. I love you and be strong, okay?"

Lachlan hung up and I burst into tears. Oh, my boy! My heart broke for him, and I called out to Aiden. The next few hours were hard as I imagined how frightening it must be for him. I prayed and begged God to look after Lachlan and protect him. It was the hardest thing I have ever had to do, hanging up that phone. I knew if I had of kept talking it would have been likely he would have cried, and that would have been a disaster. He was on his own. That night I cried a lot and told God I was angry at him; how dare he take away our son away. I tried so hard not to think about how scared he must be. I prayed and prayed they would not be too hard on him. The next few days were a blur as I tried to work and cope, and I worried constantly. Was he sleeping? Was he warm enough? Was he getting picked on a lot or targeted by other recruits? I prayed night and day during those days and did a lot of journalling to God. I was in shock that Lachlan was no longer at home, but I also felt like I was grieving for not having a purpose anymore. I had spent months and months helping him prepare, and now I had the post-event blues. What would I do now? Lukas and Isla missed Lachlan dearly and Aiden also shed a tear or two. We were all miserable and tried to cheer each other up. The worst part was not being able to speak to him, so in my down times my mind went to every worst scenario. Man, it was tough! My sister was amazing and texted me and called me every day.

"It's normal to be so upset sis," she consoled me. "He's still your boy."

It was the worst thing not knowing how he was. Sometimes I felt the grief of the separation like it was crushing me. My brother called me in the middle of the week.

"Hi sis, how's it going?" Dylan asked.

"I miss Lachlan terribly," I sniffed and felt the tears come.

"Ah that's to be expected sis, but he's a tough kid, he'll be okay," Dylan said.

I nodded and reached for a tissue.

"Ruby wants to know if Isla can come over to ours on Friday afternoon?"

It had been a few months since the Easter incident, and I considered it.

"I guess that would be okay," I said.

"Ruby can meet Isla in the city, and they can bus it to mine, I'll be home about 5," Dylan suggested.

It was the first week of the school holidays and I figured it would be good for Isla, and I thought the girls deserved a second chance.

"I guess that would be alright," I answered.

We chatted for a bit longer and decided that we had to start trusting the girls again.

"Great, I'll let Ruby know," he said.

The days crawled on and then came Friday. Still no word from our boy and I tried to be as positive as possible. Aiden's tax return had come in, so we were going shopping for a new couch. I was excited, as our old lounge suites were old and quite horrible. We dropped Isla off at the station and I told her to text me as soon as she was in the city. She also put on her location, on her phone. Lukas came along with us as we proceeded to visit every sofa store in the northern suburbs. I felt in a real tizzy, and Aiden and I had more than one argument. I just did not want to rush into it and regret it, but Aiden wanted to spend the money and buy one. We ended up not finding a suitable sofa and trudged home feeling defeated. Isla had let me know she was safely at Dylan's house. We got takeaway and settled in to watch movies. At about 10.15pm I got a text from Julian, and I could not believe what it said.

"Your brother has gotten Isla drunk, and he's touching her bum."

I felt my heart stop, and it was like everything suddenly went still. I quickly showed Aiden.

"What the heck?" he asked angrily.

I called Julian. "She messaged her sisters," Julian explained to me, "saying, I'm so drunk lmfao."

I started pacing up and down the living room and Lukas looked up at me worriedly.

"I'll go and pick her up right now," I said hurriedly.

Julian sucked in his breath. "I f***en told you Lou to keep her away from that useless prick."

I hung up and turned to face Aiden.

"Let's go babe, let's go and pick her up."

We all scrambled around finding our shoes. My brain switched into a higher gear, and nothing mattered to me but getting our baby home safe.

"We won't tell Dylan we're coming," I said as we piled into the car. "We'll just show up and bring her home."

I pulled out of our driveway and as we began the long journey to his house, a million thoughts were racing through my head. Why, why, why did I let her go there? I looked over at Aiden who had his angry face on. I glanced at Lukas in the back seat. He had a worried look on his face.

"It's okay mate," I said to him. "We will be there soon. Text Isla and tell her we are on our way."

The drive seemed to take forever. I was concentrating so hard that my knuckles were white on the steering wheel. Aiden reached over and put his hand on mine. I had the GPS on, and I looked at it obsessively as every kilometre went by. I glanced at Lukas again and noticed that he had put his headphones on to listen to music. My phone rang and I jumped in my seat. It was Isla and Lukas' sister Erica.

"Isla told me that Dylan got her drunk," Erica said worriedly.

"Julian told me and I'm already on my way sweetie," I tried to keep a calm tone. "We're about 40 minutes away."

I ended the call and stared straight ahead. I felt like a woman possessed, nothing was going to get in the way of us picking up our girl. The minutes ticked by, and I put the radio on to distract me from screaming.

"What did Julian say?" Aiden asked me again.

"That Isla was in a group chat with Erica, Belinda, and Amanda. She told them that she was drunk, and Dylan was touching her." I gritted my teeth as the words came out of my mouth and Aiden swore.

"What on earth was he thinking?"

The kilometres flew by. There was barely any traffic on the road, and we were about thirty minutes away, when Isla called me.

"Mum!" she said. "Ruby and I want to leave; we want to go to the bus stop and go to Ruby's mum's house."

"Isla its 11 0'clock at night, you can't just go to the bus stop, it's not safe. Just stay where you are."

Aiden looked over at me.

"But mum we don't want to be here, even Ruby doesn't want to be here, can't we just go to the bus stop?"

I glanced at Aiden, but he shook his head.

"Look I'm so close bub, we will be there in like 20 minutes. Stay at the house okay, it's not safe to leave this late at night, I promise I am almost there."

She reluctantly agreed and hung up and I put my foot down on the accelerator. Ten minutes went past, and Isla called again. This time she was crying so hysterically I could barely understand what she was saying.

"Isla baby, I'm almost there," I tried to soothe her but her crying just got louder.

"Mum," she wailed, and I looked at Aiden.

"Baby I am so close to being there, okay? Just hang in there darling, we'll be there soon. Is Ruby with you?" I asked her, but she kept on crying and speaking incoherently.

"Mum!" she wailed again, and I took a deep breath.

"Isla honey, I promise we are nearly there. Go and wait out the front, you and Ruby wait for us, okay? We will be there soon," I said as I hung up.

Poor Lukas was looking so distressed in the back seat that I reached behind me and grabbed his hand.

"Hey, it's okay mate," I said. "We're really close now."

Aiden consoled him while I just drove. I felt like a mother lion about to pounce, totally focussed and totally in control. No one messed with my babies, no one! Time seemed to stand still as we finally came into Dylan's street. I floored it up to his house and saw the two girls out the front. I pulled up alongside them and they opened the door. I glanced up and saw Dylan standing on his doorstep. He had the oddest look on his face, as he stood there, completely drunk and swaying all over the place. The girls piled into the car and slammed the door. Isla reached into the front and hugged me, sobbing. I looked up at Dylan again, and his face was so strange. I knew it was my brother standing there, but in that moment, I did not recognise him. I looked up and then I saw Ruby's brother Ricky standing on the front step, and I turned to Ruby.

"I didn't know Ricky was here," I looked at him anxiously. "Will he be, okay?"

"Mum's boyfriend Jason is going to get him. Jason is angry and wants to kill my dad," said Ruby and I felt my heart sink at her words.

"Are you sure Ricky will be all right? I don't think Jason coming over is a good idea at all," I said.

Ruby looked down at her phone.

"He'll be okay, mum just said she'll come to pick him up."

Then I noticed that Aiden had his hand on his door handle, he was staring at my brother and his face was like fire.

"Lou," he said as he kept staring at Dylan. "I think we better go."

Isla suddenly cried out, "yeah mum, just go!"

I did not hesitate and quickly peeled away from the kerb. As I drove away, I did not even look back, knowing full well that Dylan was still standing there watching us. I felt so bad leaving Ricky behind, and I kept asking Ruby if he was going to be okay. It seemed like the longest drive home as Isla just sat mostly quiet in the back seat. Ruby was also silent, just staring down at her phone. Poor Lukas looked so upset and confused. Aiden and I tried to chat to him and act natural. Finally, we made it home and it was close to midnight at this stage. Everyone piled out, except Isla who just sat on the back seat, not saying a word. I told Aiden to take Lukas and Ruby inside and told him that we would be in shortly.

Chapter 24

betrayed

Once everyone was in the house, I got into the back seat with Isla. Then once we were alone, it was like a switch went off.

She suddenly started crying and saying, "mum, mum, mum."

Isla squashed herself behind the passenger seat and began screaming in a high pitch voice. I tried to soothe her, and she looked up at me with wild eyes.

"Mum, mum, mum," she cried over and over.

I reached out to her and tried to touch her, but she flinched, pulling away from me.

"Isla sweetie," I said to her. "It's okay, I'm here," but she just kept on crying, a high-pitched wailing sound.

"What happened bubba?" I asked her.

She looked at me, but it was as if she was not there.

"He, he.. he," Isla began but then stopped.

"I'm right here baby, I promise I'm not going anywhere," I said, and she sniffled and sobbed again.

"He, played beer pong with us mum and he put something funny in my drink."

I felt my heart lurch, but I just took a deep breath and nodded at her.

"Like we were playing, and Ruby and I had Pepsi but then I started to feel dizzy. Then I saw him putting beer in my drink," she said quietly.

I swallowed hard and she sniffed again.

"Then we were doing Tik Tok dances, and he was dancing with us. But he was putting his hands on me and down onto my bum. Then he was putting his hand like down my pants a bit at the back," she explained, and I gritted my teeth.

"I'm so sorry bubba that he did that to you, do you think you were drunk?"

Isla nodded and sniffed again. "Yeah, I was feeling dizzy and sick. And Dylan couldn't stop hugging me and was all over me."

I could feel my fingernails digging into my palms as I tried to stay calm. Isla looked up at me.

"Then Ruby went to the toilet, so I went into her room to try and get away from him."

Isla looked down at her hands and her fingers which were twisting around each other, and she started to cry again.

"Then he followed me into Ruby's room, and he closed the door mum," she started to wail, and her eyes were huge. I felt my heart stop.

"He came up to me and was hugging me and nuzzling at my neck mum, and he kept putting his hands down the back of my pants, and he was lifting my head up to make me look at him. He kept saying, 'look at me, look at me,' but I didn't want to look at him mum, I didn't want to! And then he tried to kiss me. So, I ducked under his arms, and I ran out of there and locked myself in the bathroom and that is when I called you."

Isla began to cry and make loud shrieking sounds, and she began ripping at her neck with her nails.

"Get him off me," she screamed, "get him off me!"

I felt part of me drift away at that point and some other me was there, consoling my daughter and soothing her. I took her in my arms and rocked her like I had done when she was a baby.

"I am so sorry bubba; I am so sorry."

Isla leaned into me while she cried and cried, and we sat there in the car while I held her. After a while she sat up and said she wanted to go in the house, so I helped her out of the car. Once inside something seemed to spring into action within me. I saw Lukas, and he looked up from watching You Tube.

"Hey mate, Isla is okay. Uncle Dylan gave her some beer and kept touching her and it made her uncomfortable. But she is going to be all right. Time for bed little man."

He handed me his phone to put on charge and snuggled down into his bed. I leaned over and gave him a kiss, but his little face was worried.

"Will you look after her mum?" I smiled and bent down to hug him.

"Of course, I will mate, try, and get some sleep now. I love you."

It was so late that he went straight to sleep.

I went into Isla's room, and she said that she wanted a bath. Poor Ruby was sitting on the bed looking stunned. I helped Isla into the bath and gave her a quick kiss.

"I'm just going to check on Ruby and then I'll be back bub," I told her.

Then I went into Isla's room and sat next to Ruby and gave her a hug.

"I am sorry this has happened," I said to her.

She had tears on her face, and she wiped them away.

"Do you know what happened with him and Isla?" I asked and she shook her head.

"I know he gave us beer in our Pepsi, and I think Isla got drunk," she said, and I nodded.

"She's on antidepressants, so mixing that with beer can make you drunk."

Ruby took a deep breath.

"Do you know what happened after the Tik Tok dancing and you went to the toilet?" I asked her but Ruby shook her head.

"Well, your dad followed Isla into your room and shut the door so she couldn't leave. He kept hugging her and touching her bum and then he tried to kiss her."

Poor Ruby's face fell, and I hugged her again.

"I am so sorry and it's not your fault, okay? Your dad has made some bad choices tonight, but it is not your fault," I said, and she nodded sadly at me.

"Has he ever given you alcohol before?" I asked and she nodded again.

"Yeah, he has. And he has touched my bum before too," she said quietly. My heart sank and I hugged her once more.

"Thanks for telling me sweetie, I know this is really hard for you."

Ruby looked so sad and lost that my heart broke for her.

"Are you okay?" I asked and she looked at me.

"Yeah, I am okay," she said, and I nodded.

"Alright well I am going to see if Isla is okay."

I left Isla's room, knocked on the bathroom door and poked my head in.

"Are you okay?" I heard her moving around in the water.

"I guess I'm okay mama," she said.

"I am just going to chat to Aiden quickly and then I'll come back."

I found Aiden who was sitting on our bed.

"What the f*** happened Lou?" he asked me, and I told him, as we sat together, both of us not believing what had just occurred.

"I am so angry at the wanker," he said. "I almost got out of the car to kill him," he said, and I hugged him.

"Yes, I know. Thank the Lord you are a godly man babe," I said, and he shook his head.

"I have never wanted to kill someone like that before Lou. I was ready to jump out and do it. But I heard God tell me to tell you to just drive away," he told me, and we hugged again.

"It doesn't feel real," I confessed to Aiden. "I mean he told me that he would look after Isla and then he does something like this! What was he thinking?"

Aiden made a snorting sound. "I don't think he was thinking at all Lou. He was so drunk he could barely stand up," Aiden said, and I nodded sadly as tears filled my eyes.

"What has he done to our baby? I mean I knew my dad was like this but not him."

I leaned against Aiden and the tears flowed down my cheeks. We sat for a few minutes and hugged each other, then we prayed together that God would heal Isla and get us through the next few days.

"You go to bed hun, I'll go check on Isla."

"Are you sure babe?" he asked.

I told him it was okay as someone needed to get up with Lukas in the morning. It was almost one in the morning at this stage. I went to see Isla in the bathroom, and she was just sitting there in the bath, looking so lost and so small that I wanted to break down and cry for her. But somehow, I held it together and reached out my hand to her behind the shower curtain. We sat there together for a while, the steam from her bath filling up the room.

"Why did he do it mum?" she finally asked me, and I took a deep breath.

"I don't really know I'm sorry bub. He has made a terrible mistake. It sounds like he was trying to get close to you during the Tik Tok dances?"

Isla answered and her voice sounded like she was just a little girl.

"I don't know mum; uncle has always been like super cuddly when he is drunk," she said, and my heart give a little lurch.

"You mean he's been cuddly with you before?" I asked and she put her face around the curtain.

"Yeah, when I have been at his place and he's been drinking, he like hugs me all the time, like long hugs," she explained, and I bit my lip as my world started to slide away.

I dug my fingernails into my palms to help me focus.

"I haven't seen him like that around you before," I said, and Isla nodded.

"Yeah, you haven't been around him when he's drinking."

I sucked in my breath. That was true, as too many years of living with him and the alcohol, meant I tried to avoid it at all costs.

"I just thought it was normal mum, like the hugging. That's what uncle has always been like when he drinks," Isla said, and I hung my head and tried to calm my heart which felt like it would beat out of my chest.

"All I know bub, is that he made some bad decisions and obviously wasn't thinking straight. He has made a bad mistake, and you need to know that you did absolutely nothing wrong and it wasn't your fault at all, okay?" I reached out and squeezed her hand, and Isla nodded and asked me to turn the water off.

"What did your dad do to you mum?" I sat back down on the floor.

"He hurt me a lot bub, like forced me to do stuff with him, like sex," I said.

Isla made a sad face. "I'm sorry mama."

I leaned over and kissed her head. "Thank you, bubba."

"I am ready to get out," she said, "can you hold up the towel for me?"

I helped her out of the bath, and she went into Lachlan's room to get dressed. Poor Ruby was still on Isla's bed just looking lost.

"Hey sweetie, do you want to get ready for bed now, it's late."

She looked up and nodded. I waited for Isla to get changed and then I set up the spare mattress on the floor for Ruby. I felt like I was not connected to my body at all, as the girls got into their beds, and I turned off the light.

"I'm going to have a shower; I'll be back shortly," I said as the girls snuggled down to sleep.

I felt like I was watching myself walk away down the hallway and walk into our ensuite and shut the door. I pulled my phone out of my pocket and sat on the toilet in the dark. With shaking fingers, I dialled the number for SARC, and after a long while someone answered.

"Yeah hi," I said in a quiet voice. "I was wondering if I can speak to someone about an assault." I took a few deep breaths.

Yes, you can talk to me," the person on the other end of the line said. "When did the assault happen?"

I felt the tears well up in my eyes and I grabbed some toilet paper.

"Tonight, like three or four hours ago. It was my daughter."

My hands were shaking so much I was having trouble holding onto the phone. I took a few more deep breaths and tried to steady my voice. I then spent the next few minutes describing what had happened.

"So, this is your brother, Isla's biological uncle?" the person asked, and I nodded.

"Yes, he is my brother. He has been an alcoholic all his adult life, but I thought he was a safe person. Like I have never been worried about that sort of thing, not like ever," I explained.

We talked for a while longer.

"So has he ever displayed this sort of behaviour before?" she asked me.

"No, never, I have always trusted him. I never thought in a million years that he would do this," my voice trailed off and the tears started again.

"Okay well you have done the right thing calling SARC," she said.

We chatted for around half an hour.

"You know it seems like this behaviour could be classed as grooming, like the hugging and the touching," she commented.

"Well, I have never seen it," I confessed.

"Sounds like he has kept it from you, and has only done it when you're not around?"

"Yeah, I avoid him when he's drunk," I admitted.

I asked her what happened next, and she told me that she had a legal duty to report the assault as it involved a family member. I was listening but felt far, far away from it really. I did not understand the enormity of the situation at all, and I was in shock and felt so disassociated.

"Call back tomorrow and see if the counsellor can see you," she suggested.

I hung up the phone and burst into tears. I held onto the wall and just cried and cried. I could not believe what had happened, that my only brother who I had trusted my whole life would hurt my baby like that. It just did not make sense. Why had he done it? And had he planned it or was it a spontaneous thing? My thoughts went around and around and around. I felt like there was a snowstorm in my head. Eventually I pushed myself up off the toilet and went and checked on the girls. By then it was close to 2am and thankfully they were both asleep. I took my night time medication and crawled into bed, but the tears kept coming and I lay there sobbing. My heart was completely broken in half. I felt like it had been ripped out of my chest. Everything I had ever known about Dylan now felt like a lie. And how was I going to tell Lachlan?

The next day was a blur. Isla could not get out of bed, her eyes were haunted, and she barely ate anything. Ruby went home on the bus to her mum's, and I kept sneaking off to the ensuite to cry. Nothing made sense. Aiden and I prayed but my heart felt hollow. I had no idea who to call or tell, so, I did not. I did chores and cooked dinner, but nothing felt real. I had not heard from Lachlan, and it was so hard to think about him doing his first week of training at Kapooka and what he might be going through, and I did not know when I was going to hear from him, or if at all, considering he did not have a phone. Was he getting treated unfairly? Was he eating properly? Was he cold?

I lay with Isla in her bed, and she held my hand and cried. She kept asking me why it had happened, and I did not have an answer for her, I just held her tight and told her that it would be okay. Lukas was noticeably quiet, his eyes were sad, and he said he was worried about Isla. That night Aiden and I prayed and decided that we would hold off telling Lachlan for a few weeks as he needed to focus on training. If we told him now, he would just want to come home and I could not do that to him. Early on Sunday morning I got a call from him, and he was using another recruit's phone.

"Hi mama," he said, and I almost burst into tears upon hearing his voice.

"Hey mate, how's it going?" I sat on the edge of the bed and pulled my dressing gown around me.

"It's going okay. It was hard at first, the first few days I didn't sleep much, and it was horrible, but now it has gotten a bit better," he said, and I felt relieved.

"That's good mate. What's it like there?" I could hear his teeth chattering as he spoke.

"It's bloody cold here and it's hard, we get yelled at a lot. Like really yelled at, and they call us names and stuff. We have to make our beds like perfect, or we get yelled at, and then they pull our beds apart and we must make them all over again."

I took a deep breath as he continued talking.

"When we first arrived, and we were still on the bus they came and started laying into us and calling us all sorts of names and s***. They told us we were useless maggots and screamed at us," I heard him say as his voice cut in and out with the wind.

"Gosh that doesn't sound very nice mate," I said.

"It was hard at first mum, but I just try and keep my head down and don't say anything and I am getting more used to it now, and everything has a timing, like how long it takes us to get out of bed and get to the showers and stuff, it's all timed and if we stuff up, we have to just keep doing it all over again," he explained.

He told me that they only had a brief time to call family on a Sunday and that they had to stand at attention on the parade ground during the call. My heart ached as I talked to him and listened to what he had been doing.

"How are you? How is everyone?" he asked, and I bit my lip.

"We are good mate, just missing you. Have you heard anything about your phone?" I asked.

"No, but I'm hoping someone finds it and posts it to me."

We chatted for a few more minutes before saying goodbye. As we hung up, I started to cry. It had been so hard to not tell Lachlan about Isla, and so hard to listen to what he was being subjected to and not get upset, but I knew that God was with him and that he would be okay. He was a strong kid and he had what it took to make it through it. I was determined to let him keep going with the training rather than burden him with the assault. Aiden turned over in the bed and we cuddled as I told him about my conversation with Lachlan.

That week was one of the hardest in my life. I felt constantly burdened by my brother's actions, and it was all I ever thought about. It haunted me night and day, and I prayed and cried out to God about how could this have happened? How did I let it happen? Was this my fault?

"I've failed her," I wailed to God. "It was my job to protect her, and I failed."

Aiden and I talked a lot and he said he felt the same way, that he was her dad and he had failed her too. Isla just walked around like she was a zombie. She could not go to school; she could barely get out of bed, all she did was take bath after bath, like she was trying to scrub it all away. Her eyes were dead, and it killed me to see her like this. Poor Lukas was sad all week too and had a few days off school. I went to work but I was not present. I tried to focus on my clients, but it was so hard, and I wanted to tell people, but I could not. I wanted to confide in my church friends, but I did not know how to. The next week Lachlan called again, and we chatted about his training. He said that they had started PT, and it was not too bad. He said that he was getting better at making his bed but had made a few mistakes and had been punished, in fact, when someone made a mistake, the whole squad got punished. I did not like that but knew it was the army way. He sounded more settled in, and that made me feel better. The good news was that I had spoken to someone from the Canberra recruitment office, and they had found his phone, and it was intact! Lachlan joked that only a Nokia could survive a fall down an elevator shaft and he was right. It was getting posted to him which was wonderful news.

That Sunday in church we went up to get prayer and we confided in our Pastor about the assault. He prayed with us, and the burden lifted a little. Isla was still really struggling, and we went to see her GP and told her about the assault. The doctor said she could try a small amount of medication, but when Isla took it, she said it made her too dizzy. I also emailed her year coordinator and told her what had happened. Isla said she could not face school and I did not push her. I had heard from DCP, and they said they needed to speak to Lukas and do a risk assessment, but he got terribly upset when I told him.

"I don't want to do it mum,' Lukas said with tears in his eyes. I sat with him and held his hand.

"I know mate and I am sorry, but they just need to prove you are safe, okay?"

It was awful having to force him into it. We went to the Department office, and he started crying and saying he wanted to go home. When he got called into the room, he was so brave and went in without me. It was an anxious wait, and I felt sorry for him having to be questioned like that, but by the time he came out he was smiling, and he said it was not as bad as he thought it would be. DCP emailed me the following week and said there was no reason to believe that Lukas was at risk of abuse or assault. The days went past, and I was struggling so much. Every night I cried myself to sleep. I felt so betrayed by my brother, and I was still in shock and every time I thought about that night, I got a knot in my throat. I confided in my sister and to say she was appalled was an understatement.

"What was he thinking Lou?" she asked me, and I did not know how to answer.

Aiden was struggling and cried with me a few times, as he was so angry at Dylan and hated him. For me it was different, he was my brother and I loved him still, as he had never given me any reason to not trust him with my children up until now.

Isla was so depressed and did not even want to see her friends. Her boyfriend came over a few times, but she was just so sad and would cry when he left. She had lost all interest in anything but lying in her bed. I would sit and pray to God, and I felt so overwhelmed with betrayal and grief. I would remember Isla's eyes and the way they looked when she was describing what he had done, and I would want to tear every limb from his body. What had Dylan been thinking? Clearly the alcohol was a huge factor, but it wasn't an excuse in my eyes, and had he planned it or was it just an impulsive thing? I would remember how he came to our house to see us the weekend before Lachlan went away, how he had made a big fuss of seeing him off and I would scream into a pillow. Did Dylan wait for our son to leave before making his move on Isla? Would he have done this if Lachlan were still around, and how could I have missed this? How could I have not seen that he had predator tendencies like my father? How did I miss it?

Every Sunday I would speak to Lachlan, and he would tell me about his training. He was becoming accustomed to army life, had made some mates, and his phone had been posted to him and slowly they got more phone privileges. I loved hearing his voice every week, but gosh it was hard to keep the truth from him. He was settling in so well to army life and I could not risk him messing up his training because he was distracted by things at home. Isla finally had an appointment at CAMHS, and her mental health social worker Alana was a godsend. She understood Isla and was an amazing support to her. Every week Isla would see Alana and she would help her cope with what had happened to her. Aiden and I were struggling to deal with the reality of what had occurred, and we confided in a friend or two from church, as the burden of the assault was just too much to cope with. Every night I prayed and cried out to God for help, I begged him to take this away from us.

In September I got a call from the police saying they had arrested Dylan and taken him into custody, and it made me feel sick and disassociated. The assault had also brought back so many awful memories of my abuse, and I struggled to distinguish between the two things. I was having nightmares and flashbacks, all the while working and trying to support Isla.

My life no longer felt like my own. I did not feel safe at all, and my sleep was all over the place. Once again, I had failed to protect my child from the men in my family, and I was so depressed and absolutely gutted I had not seen this coming. I went from being in shock, to being angry, to crying my eyes out. I was a mess emotionally and had started burning my hands once again with hot water to cope with the pain inside.

"Why didn't you protect her Lord?" I would sob in the shower.

I was angry at myself that I had not been able to predict it happening, and I cried endlessly to the Lord. I screamed out to Jesus silently in the shower, feeling utterly distraught at Dylan's betrayal. I learnt from the police that Dylan was questioned for a long time but then released on bail. That weekend Aiden and I prayed that we would tell Lachlan what had happened, as he only had a few weeks of his training left and I knew I could not keep lying to him.

That Sunday, he called me, and I had to take a deep breath before saying the words. There was a long silence before he responded, swearing explicitly. My heart broke, knowing how hard it must have been for him hearing how his baby sister had been hurt while he was far away.

"Is there someone you can talk to mate?" I asked him.

"Yeah, there is a Padre here mum, I'll go and speak to him," he said.

That night he called me again and said that he had spoken to the Chaplain, and they had prayed together. I felt a peace I had not felt in months and Aiden, and I hugged and cried together. I was still hopeful that I could attend Lachlan's passing out parade and I started looking at flights and accommodation. A few weeks later I got a call from the detective who oversaw Isla's case.

"Isla needs to come and give a witness statement," she said, and I felt my heart drop. "I know she probably doesn't want to but it's important we get her side of the story."

"I don't want to mum," Isla cried when I told her.

"I'm so sorry bub, but you have to," I said and felt like such a s*** mum for making her do it.

When we arrived, Isla sat in the car and cried and begged me not to make her go inside. I had to swallow my tears as I helped her out of the car. The detective was so nice to us and sat us down and explained what would be happening. I was not allowed in the room with her, which was upsetting, and I felt like I was on the ceiling when they took her away to do the interview. I paced up and down the whole time she was in there, and I was so relieved when she finally came out. The detective said she had done such an excellent job, and I was so relieved that it was over.

A few weeks later I got a call from the Department of Prosecutions saying they had enough evidence to charge my brother with three counts of indecent assault of a child under 16 years of age. Inside I felt like my world was crashing down around me. How could this be happening, and to my brother? I was gutted for him, but another part of me was glad and hoped he would get found guilty and go to prison. I was torn between being Isla's mum and being Dylan's sister. Poor Isla was struggling so much, and she begged me not to let her uncle go to jail. I had to explain that there was not any way that I could stop it, that the DPP were going ahead with charging him and that it was the right thing to do. I kept telling myself that even though he was my brother, he had done something terrible, and that all that mattered was Isla.

I had to show Dylan that I was not going to accept what he had done, that I was not going to turn the other cheek or sweep it under the rug. In short, I was not going to be like my mum. Poor Isla was so hurt when Ruby started turning against her, posting mean stuff on social media about "when I used to have a cousin." Isla was so upset and began cutting herself a lot. I knew deep down she blamed herself for the assault, and I tried to tell her this was all on Dylan. All she knew was that she had lost an uncle and four cousins. I tried searching her room to look for things she could cut herself with, and sometimes I found things and other times I missed them. Isla could not go to school; she just lay in her bed crying and staring at her phone. I was devastated for her, and I was so angry that part of her had been stolen that night and she would never get it back. All I could do was take her to see her mental health worker and pray and comfort her, but it never was enough, I felt like we were all under this giant, dark cloud.

Chapter 25

trauma

One day I picked Isla and Lukas up from school and we had an appointment with her counsellor. I quickly drove home and dashed inside with Lukas to go to the toilet and when I came back out to the car Isla was sobbing hysterically.

"Mum, I've taken some tablets," she said as I stared at her in horror.

"What tablets?" I asked her.

She motioned to an empty packet on the floor of the car, and I could see that it was ibuprofen.

"How many tablets and where did you get them?" I tried to calm my voice as she sobbed in my arms.

"I got them from a friend at school. I took 12."

My heart skipped a beat, and I quickly called Aiden.

"You need to come home babe, Isla has taken a whole packet of Nurofen," I said to him.

I took Isla inside and I called a friend from church who was a nurse.

"Call an ambulance Lou," my friend told me. "I'll come over and look after Lukas."

I sat with Isla trying to keep her from falling asleep and reassuring Lukas that she was okay. My friend came over and said she would take Lukas to her place and give him dinner. After they left, I called the ambulance again, as I could not believe we were still waiting. Eventually I decided to take Isla to the hospital myself, so I helped her out to the car and jumped in the driver's seat and we took off down the street. While I was driving, I kept looking over at her to make sure she was staying awake. Once we hit the freeway, I put my foot down and used the emergency lane, my mind so focused on getting us to the hospital that at one point I hit about 150 km/hr. Everyone was staring at us and beeping their horns as we flew past them. We pulled into the hospital car park, and I helped her walk into ED, and they got her in quickly and Julian came to meet us. I kept thinking that she was going to suddenly stop breathing, but as afternoon became evening, I learned that high doses of ibuprofen are usually well tolerated in the body and if it had been Panadol, it would have been a different story. We stayed at the hospital most of the night and went home in the early hours.

I put Isla to bed and just lay on the couch and cried and cried. I could not believe my baby girl had tried to take her own life, and I felt devastated for her, and I was so angry. Angry at my stupid brother for ruining her life, how could he have been so careless with her? How could he have manipulated her and used her so badly like she was nothing? I took the next 2 days off work to be with Isla and I watched her like a hawk and hid all her medication. A week or two later I got a call from Lachlan.

"Mum it's not looking good about the parade, I don't think you're going to be able to come. Stupid Covid," he said angrily.

I felt tears in my eyes. "That's such a shame mate," I said whilst trying not to cry.

"Yeah, they are going to film it and send all the families a video."

I hung up and burst into tears, as I had held onto the thought of seeing Lachlan and watching the most important day of his life, and now because of a dumb virus I was not able to.

"Stupid covid," I sobbed to God that night. "It's not fair."

The day drew near, and Lachlan was getting extremely excited about finishing. I could not believe that the end was finally in sight for him, he had trained so hard and come such a long way in the three months since he had left. Lachlan had left a scared boy and had grown into a man. I texted him on the day of his parade and felt sad I could not be there for him. That afternoon he rang me.

"Hey mama," he said, and I could hear lots of noise in the background.

"Hey mate, congratulations!"

We chatted for a few minutes. I felt so proud of him, and the tears were welling up again.

"I can't believe you've finished," I said, and he laughed.

"Yeah well, it has been a long journey mum. I must admit at times it felt like it would never end!"

He told me that they were having drinks to celebrate and then all going out together. I could hear the joy in Lachlan's voice, and I felt so happy for him. It had been such a hard journey, and I was so proud that he had finished.

"So how do you feel about finishing?" I asked him.

"Well let's just say that I am so bloody glad that I never have to do that again," he joked, and we laughed together.

That night I prayed and thanked God. "Lord, I thank you that our son has finished his basic training, I praise your mighty name."

One of the hardest things I had ever done was to let Lachlan go to the army, but the Lord had promised me he was going to look after him and He had delivered. It had not been easy for Lachlan though, he had written us letters about harsh discipline and the strict routine, about how they broke every recruit down to nothing and then built them back up. I had become emotional reading about the relentlessness of the training, how Lachlan had felt like it was never going to end. I'd had tears in my eyes after reading the letters and I had had many sleepless nights worrying constantly about him. Lachlan had suffered mentally and emotionally after living with Julian all those years and I had been worried the training was going to destroy him, but it had not. It had made Lachlan tougher and stronger and now here he was, he had graduated and achieved something truly remarkable.

That November Lukas came into my room early one morning.

"Mum, I don't feel well," he said as I sat up in bed.

"What's wrong mate?" I asked and he held out his hands.

"I feel hot, and my hands are all red."

Sure enough, I looked down and they were really red. It was a bit odd, and he did not look well so I kept him home from school. That afternoon I came home, and he was sitting on his bed.

"Mum my hands are really itchy," he said, crying.

His hands were so red that I got a bit of a shock when I looked at them. I ran to get an ice pack and he clutched it between his hands. That night Lukas had an extremely high fever and could not sleep, his hands were incredibly itchy, and he was so hot even though I had given him Nurofen and Panadol. He took a few baths and we managed to get about three hours sleep. I took the next few days off work to look after him, and when we saw the GP, he just said it was a virus and it would go away. I went to the chemist to get him some numbing cream, as the itching was driving him crazy. On the third night I was so sleep deprived I went to the pharmacy and got some Paedamin to try and sedate him. I ended up putting him in our bed, so I could get a few hours of sleep, and it seemed to go on and on. His fever was so high, and his hands were just so itchy, all I could do was put ice packs on them and numb cream while he cried and cried. He lay on the couch barely able to move and could not eat; he lived on apple juice and jelly, and I felt so stressed watching our boy be so sick.

Aiden and I prayed and prayed for him, and Lukas asked us to pray for him so we would lay hands on him and pray for God to heal him. I had been a parent for a long time and had never seen a virus like this before. After a week I took him to the ED at Joondalup hospital, but we waited hours and there were no decent ice packs, so in the end Lukas begged me to take him home. I was relying on giving him three or four times over the recommended doses of antihistamines to keep the itching at bay. At night I gave him melatonin and Paedamin to try and knock him out so he could sleep for a couple of hours. I was exhausted, and he was not getting any better. I prayed all the time, and Aiden and I kept praying together, begging God to heal him. I took him back to the hospital a few days later and demanded they see him. By that time, his whole body was covered in a rash and his glands were very swollen. They took one look at him and said they thought he had the mumps, so they panicked and put him in isolation. The doctors tested him for Covid, and the mumps and I waited hours while he dozed on the bed. He was so lethargic and unwell, and I had never seen him so sick before that I thought for a moment that he was going to die.

I paced around with nervous energy, praying in the spirit. I was so sleep deprived and stressed and I just wanted answers. Eventually, after spending hours poking and prodding him, the doctors said that they thought he had mumps and sent us home, telling me he had to be isolated for 7 days. That night I burst into tears and sobbed and sobbed, as I could not cope with him being unwell any longer. Whatever the illness was, it seemed relentless. Two days later I got a call from the hospital saying that Lukas' blood tests for mumps were negative, and they did not know what it was that was making him so sick. His feet and hands were now peeling, layers and layers of his skin were peeling off, in his bed and all over the floor. After another week Lukas' glands went down, and his fever went down but he had no energy and could only lie on the couch and get up every few hours. Eventually after another week he got better, and after four long weeks, he finally went back to school. I was so relieved that our boy was back to his usual self, and it was such a joy to see him with a cricket ball in his hand again. At a follow up visit to his GP and after a blood test, the doctor said that Lukas' allergy markers were high, and his liver enzymes were elevated. I was so worried that it might be some serious illness, but we went back after two weeks, and his next blood test showed his liver levels had decreased but his allergy markers were still a bit high. Lukas was much better, and the GP thought that the elevated levels were just left over from the virus.

The year was ending, and I felt exhausted and depleted. To make matters worse Lachlan called me from barracks where he was posted to the engineering corps.

"Sorry mum but we've just been told that we won't be getting any leave this year because of Covid."

I was devastated, as I had been counting the weeks until Lachlan was due home and now, we had to do Christmas without him, and who would Lachlan spend it with? I cried and cried and was so mad at God.

"You promised me you would look after him!" I ranted.

A week later Lachlan called and said that he was going to spend Christmas with his mate, and I was overjoyed for him. Christmas came but it was not the same, and I could not sleep on Christmas Eve, so I was exhausted for the entire day. We spoke to Lachlan, and he was with his friend so at least I did not have to worry about him.

Early in 2022 I received a phone call from the DPP, they said that Dylan had appeared in court for a second time and had asked for a continuum. I was gutted and still crying every night about him, and worse, I had to go and give my statement to the detective, which was difficult. Somehow, I got through it and drove home in a daze. That night I prayed that Dylan would plead guilty to spare Isla the trauma of a trial. We had to attend an appointment at the child witness service, and I think that both Isla and I were on the ceiling the whole time.

Isla was struggling so much at school and her attendance had dropped to below 30 percent. After a few meetings we decided that she would leave school and go to Tafe to do general education. This suited Isla much better, and she appeared happier. Tafe was a lot less stressful and seemed catered to meet the needs of kids who struggled with mainstream school. Isla was doing a little bit better, and I felt relieved that she was no longer cutting herself all the time.

In April I began having dizzy spells and vertigo, and I was also having troubles with my balance and chronic headaches. One night I was fast asleep when I was woken up by a flash bulb going off in my head. I sat upright and nearly fell backwards with vertigo. The room was spinning around and around and that day my balance was so bad I nearly fell over a few times. I ended up at the hospital where they diagnosed me with vestibular migraine disorder, and they advised me to change my diet, so no more coffee, and fermented foods like soy sauce. The next few weeks were horrible, as the more I cut back on coffee, the more headaches I got. I had been drinking coffee since I was 13 years old, and it was so hard to give it up. I started doing balance exercises which did help, and slowly I was cutting back coffee and substituting it with decaf but man it was hard. I also had to give up bacon, ham, mushrooms, and products containing yeast. I cried a lot in those first few weeks as my diet seemed so bland. I kept persisting and after a few more weeks on the diet, my balance had improved so much, and I had hardly any more headaches.

I got a phone call from Lachlan shortly after.

"Mum I am coming home on leave," he said.

We were overjoyed and met him at the airport, and there were lots of hugs and a few tears. The weather was just beautiful, and we went to the animal farm for Isla's birthday. It was so good to see Lachlan, and he kept us entertained with tales of his engineering training. It was hard to say good-bye to him afterwards and I went and hid in our room and cried and cried after he left. The next few weeks without Lachlan were hard for me, as I do not think I had really grieved properly when he first left. Maybe it was due to Isla being assaulted that had delayed the sadness, but I spent many nights in his old room, crying into his pillow.

Chapter 26

what God can do

In May I was driving Lukas to school one morning when I was rear ended in the Kia. The impact was so severe that I bashed my head on the back of the seat and blacked out for a few seconds. Lukas started to cry loudly and then I came to, and I reached over and started comforting him.

"It's okay mate, it's okay, we're okay."

It was pouring with rain and our car had been pushed up onto the median strip. Suddenly a man appeared at my window and after a few seconds I put the window down.

"Do you want me to call you an ambulance?" he asked me, but I sat there not really comprehending what was going on, or what he was saying.

He asked a few more times but I just sat there, not saying much, and then a lady opened my door and stuck her head inside.

"Come on," she said to me. "Come and get in my car."

So, we got out, into the rain, and we walked to her car which was parked up on the strip too. I looked back at my car which was completely smashed in, and the stuff from my boot was scattered all over the road. I could see outdoor chairs and my umbrella, sitting there on the road getting all wet.

We squeezed into her back seat, and by this stage I was in complete shock and shaking from head to toe. Lukas dialed Aiden's number on my phone but when he answered I was not able to speak.

"We've been in an accident," I blurted out, handing the phone to Lukas.

The ambulance arrived, and we got in, and after an assessment they said we should go to the hospital.

"No, I don't want to go," I said, and Lukas leaned over and hugged me.

Then the police arrived, and one of them poked their heads into the ambulance and spoke to me.

"How fast do you think you were going when you hit the car in front of you?" the officer said but Lukas quickly cut them off.

"My mum didn't hit that car; she is such a good driver and didn't hit them at all."

The police asked me a few more questions and then left.

"Do you have a friend who can take you to hospital?" asked the paramedic.

I rang my friend Janet, and she took us, but by the time we got there my head was pounding so much that I was feeling nauseas. The doctor put me flat on my back and I spent a few hours there having x-rays. Lukas was cleared, so Janet drove him home. They discharged me saying I had a mild concussion, so I went home and saw poor Lukas, who was so teary and upset too and we sat together and cried. The poor kid was completely traumatized by it all and I hugged him tight and tried to reassure him. I put my insurance claim in, and Aiden and I had to see the car to remove my stuff. That was hard seeing it so crumpled, and I cried, as I realised that Lukas and I could have been seriously injured. I thanked God for days after that, and a week later I found a car, it was a lovely Mazda, and it was a good car. God was so faithful to us, as it was a much better car than the Kia. I was still having terrible headaches every day from the concussion, and it got so bad that I was crawling to the toilet to vomit from the pain. I ended up back in hospital where they gave me another CT scan, fortunately, it was just concussion, but boy were those headaches ferocious. I found I could not do a task and finish it properly, and when I tried to cook, I would miss out the vital steps like putting oil in the frying pan, and I could not seem to even get dressed properly; and found myself walking out of the bathroom with my jeans unzipped. Nothing made the headaches better, and I was tripling up on the doses of anti-inflammatory medication in the hope it would help. The hospital had given me a prescription for Oxycodone but when I took a tablet it made me feel awful, so I threw it into the bin. A few weeks later the headaches started to subside, and I went back to work. I was a nervous wreck on the road though, as I thought that every car was going to plow into me, and I felt stressed every time I drove. Poor Lukas was the same and it was hard for him to deal with, especially as the location of the accident was right near his school. I started physiotherapy and that helped with the pain and the trauma of the accident, and the physiotherapist was so kind to me, and it was nice having someone to support me through my healing journey.

Lachlan was calling more frequently as his combat engineering training became increasingly intense. The squad worked hard day and night, and they did not get a lot of sleep. They had to learn hand to hand combat and I did not like the idea of that at all. He did weapons and watercraft training, and lots of building and construction work. They had to build these huge bridges that were metres long and they did not get much rest in between. Then came the demolition and explosives training and things amped up rapidly. Lachlan was calling home a few times a day and was teary and exhausted.

"I don't think I can take it much more mum," he would say.

Some nights I would stay up praying with him so he could get some sleep. The pressure on him was enormous and I prayed and prayed for him every chance I could. Lachlan called saying that he had made mistakes, and he was down on himself, which is how he had always been when making errors. One day in July he called me, and he sounded so flat and down.

"Mum, I've been told that if I make one more mistake then I will be kicked out," he broke down and cried.

"Oh, mate, I am so sorry to hear that. What are you going to do?" I asked.

He was sniffing and sobbing quietly.

"I don't know mum, but I feel like I can't keep doing this you know," he said.

When he hung up, I broke down to Aiden, as Lachlan only had three weeks to go, and I wanted to tell him to just hang in there, that he had to push himself a bit and it would all be over. Lachlan had worked so hard, and I hated the thought of him quitting now. But I knew he had been pushed mentally and physically and I was so worried he was going to have a complete breakdown. The next day Lachlan called me again crying.

"I'm broken mum," he sobbed.

I listened as he told me that he had decided not to continue with his course, and I felt both relieved and sad for him, but reassured him he was making the right decision.

"Mum, I need to have a meeting with my Seargent and the officers too. I am nervous, what will I say?" he asked.

I told him to be honest with them and to tell them exactly how he felt.

"I want to leave on my terms mum, I would rather quit than be kicked out," he said.

That night Aiden and I prayed and prayed for a positive outcome, we prayed the Holy Spirit would speak for him and soften the hearts of the officers. I did not want to see Lachlan go through any more stress, as I was concerned that he had already been pushed to his limit, and I was not sure that he could take much more. Lachlan rang me the next day saying that the officers had agreed to let him leave the course and go into a holding platoon. His Seargent had pulled him aside and said that he had never seen officers agree with a trainee leaving before due to mental health reasons, and that he admired Lachlan for sticking to his guns. I knew it was God who had made that happen, and I felt so relieved. While in the holding platoon, Lachlan would be able to start some therapy, and I thanked the Lord for looking after him.

I was still struggling with the whole thing about Dylan, as I wanted to forgive him so much, but it was extremely hard. Every few weeks Dylan would have another hearing and then he would be granted another continuum, and I felt frustrated that it was dragging on so long. Plus I was having a lot of flashbacks about my abuse, and some nights I lay in bed, wide awake reliving what my dad had done to me. I had new memories too which nearly derailed me completely. I would suddenly become busy and not want to sit still at all, and it would go on for days, me doing endless chores and working around the house until I was an exhausted, and sobbing mess. Eventually I would give in and lie on the couch where the memories would flood my brain, making me feel wild and out of control. I remembered more of the abuse at the hands of my father's friends, which nearly destroyed me inside. I thought I was done with all of that, and I did not want to remember any more of that crap from my childhood. I felt angry and ripped off with life.

"Please God take my life," I begged. "I can't take it anymore, please come and take me away."

I would sit in the shower sobbing and asking the Lord to come and scoop me up and take me to heaven with Him. Some nights I would burn and burn my skin, desperate for the pain to leave me. I felt exhausted, emotionally fraught and had no more strength to keep on living. Each night I would pray and pray, then crawl into bed and God would bring me peace so I could sleep. The next day He would give me the strength that I needed to be able to wake up and keep going. And every day that Dylan did not plead guilty, was another day closer to poor Isla having to go through a trial.

I talked with Lachlan every day, as he was settling into the holding platoon. He had started to see a psychologist, whom he had already seen when he was younger. I felt so grateful that he had Sonia to lean on and to talk through all that happened. It was hard for Lachlan to be away from us, and I thanked God that he had her for support. Lachlan seemed a lot happier now, and when we talked, I realised he was working through some of his early trauma. He was also working on his sense of self-worth and the therapy seemed to be very beneficial.

Towards the end of the year Isla started going downhill again, and it was such a shame as she had found a little job at an indoor game's venue. She loved working and seemed to be good at it. One night Isla came to me saying she had taken another overdose, but this time it was antidepressants and ibuprofen. I could not believe our beautiful daughter had tried to take her life again. I ended up driving her to the emergency department once again, but they got her in quicky, and Isla lay there on the hospital bed sleeping but moving restlessly around.

"Mum," she said when she woke up. "My legs feel all numb."

I stayed with her all night and eventually we were discharged, and I drove home and crashed into bed, too tired to cry or think about anything. I felt like we were fighting some invisible force that was against our daughter. Aiden and I kept praying and praying for her, but inside I was exhausted and felt so helpless. Isla said her legs were still numb for days afterwards, and I was worried that some sort of toxin was in her blood from the overdose. I was so grateful that I had my church group friends to confide in about what was going on with Isla, it really helped to ease the burden, especially the outcome of the assault and the effect that it had on Isla's mental health. It also helped to know that they were praying for her too. I had been praying for a long time for her to come back to God, but I knew that I could not force her, she had to make the decision on her own. All I could do was tell her I was praying for her every day, and just keep loving her the best I could. I felt like I had to watch Isla's every step, and we bought a safe for the medication, so we could be sure another overdose was never going to happen again. It was also taking a toll on Lukas, and some days he could not get to school. He was so worried about his sister and found it hard to understand what she was going through. He suffered from anxiety and even though I knew I should not, some days I let him stay home from school.

"Hey mate, do you want to start seeing the Chaplain?" I asked Lukas.

"Yeah, okay mum," he answered, and he said that it helped him cope with what was happening to Isla.

The year was ending, and fortunately, Lachlan had been granted some leave, in fact it was going to be around two months, and we were all so excited.

One day Lachlan called me and said he had something to tell me.

"Are you sitting down mum?" he asked. I sat down on the couch.

"I am now," I replied.

"Um, mum this is going to be hard to say. You know how I have been seeing Sonia the therapist?"

"Yes, I know you have," I answered.

"And I have gone through a lot with her mum, I have discovered things about myself I didn't know before, like the therapy has been helpful and I have grown a lot as a person," Lachlan continued.

"Yes, you have mate," I said.

Lachlan cleared his throat and suddenly I wondered, was he going to leave the army for good?

"Well, um, mum I don't really know how to say this, but I am gay," he said.

"Um what?" I asked, feeling confused.

"Yeah, it's something I have found out in the last few weeks, maybe months, I'm gay."

I did not know what to say so I just sat there on the couch feeling shocked.

"I um, ah okay," I said eventually, and there was another long pause.

"I mean didn't you already know mum? Didn't you ever suspect?" Lachlan asked.

I shook my head hard.

"No, I never thought that mate, like I never thought that you might be gay," my voice trailed off and I felt like someone had sucked all the air out of the room.

My head was spinning, and Lachlan's voice sounded like it was far away.

"Oh, okay it's just that Sonia did. She thought that about me back when I was 17," he said.

I did not reply as it felt like someone had stabbed me in the chest.

"Yeah, so I thought that I would tell you because I have known about it for a while," Lachlan said quickly.

I cleared my throat before saying, "well, I appreciate you telling me."

"Are you okay mum?" he asked as I shook my head and tried to process what he was saying.

"Yes, I am okay," I said but I was not.

Lachlan continued, "so, I am dating someone too, you remember Nathan?"

I took another deep breath.

"You mean Nathan from school?" I asked.

"Yeah well, he came out a few months ago and told me that he had feelings for me. So, we're together now, like we are in a relationship," Lachlan explained.

I realised I had been holding my breath, so I let it out slowly.

"Okay, well, as long as your happy mate, that's all that matters," I managed to say.

We chatted for a few more minutes before hanging up. I stood up and walked into our bedroom and sat on the bed, and suddenly the tears came like a flood, and I just sat there sobbing and howling and clutching a pillow. Lachlan gay? No Lord! It could not be true. I felt like someone had punched me in the guts, and I cried an ocean of tears that afternoon, as I could not comprehend what was going on. I called Aiden and sobbed down the phone to him. He was equally as shocked as I was, and when he came home, we hugged and prayed together. To say I was in denial was an understatement, I just could not wrap my head around it. I felt so silly, I had thought he was just a late bloomer, that he had not met the right girl. Him gay? No way! That night I felt unsettled and anxious, and I kept praying that God would make a way for me to understand what was going on.

That weekend I confided in some friends at church who served in the children's ministry with me. We hugged and they told me to just love Lachlan and accept his decision, and I was so relieved there was no judgement, just love and understanding. I felt sad all the time, that something had been taken away from me. I spoke to Lachlan again a few days later.

"How are you going mum, are you okay?" he asked.

"I must admit that it has been hard for me mate. But I am slowly getting used to it," I answered.

When I prayed, I asked God to help me not judge our son, but to just love him. It was not that I was against gay people, I used to live with a woman, I just did not want our son being gay. I also worried how the army would react once he came out. I knew that they gave the impression that they accepted all people, but I was concerned that it was just an image. I hated the thought of him being victimized because of his choices.

The next week I decided to do some reading on the internet about Christian parents with gay children. I typed in a search and many articles came up, and I spent about an hour reading all the different points of view and stories of families who had experienced what we were going through.

One stuck out to me; a story about a Christian family whose son came out to them, and they were shocked to say the least, and right away the parents told him that it was unacceptable in the eyes of the Lord and that their son needed to repent. They forced him to confess to their Pastor in their church and they prayed openly for him not to be gay. This went on for many months, and eventually they talked him into conversion therapy. The son attended but then had a mental breakdown and left the family. He started taking drugs and they lost contact with him, and I could feel the tears start to well up at this time.

The story continued; many years later the son contacted the family and they reunited, and it was a happy time for all of them. The parents realised they had made a mistake trying to force him not to be gay. Then one day the son accidentally took an overdose and he died. At that point I was crying uncontrollably, and I reached out to God and asked him to give me strength and comfort.

"Do not give up on your son," God spoke to me. "Just love him as I have loved him, don't judge him, just keep loving him and accept him for who he is."

I knew in that moment that God loved Lachlan no matter what choices he made. In the next few weeks, I did a lot of praying for Lachlan, both Aiden and I did. It took time but slowly I came to accept his decision, and, in some ways, it made me love Lachlan even more than I already did. There was no way that I would ever reject him and risk losing him. I had to accept our son's decision and that he was a grown man and would not always make choices that I agreed with.

Lachlan came home in November, and we were all overjoyed to see him, and he hugged us all tightly. That summer was a happy one, and we went out to the beach and to dinner and Lachlan took us paintballing which was lots of fun. We also met his boyfriend, Nathan, and I could see that Lachlan was happy and I was happy too. Lachlan went back to the base in late January, and I was not as worried about him as before.

Aiden started a new job in the first term, as a Head Cleaner at a local high school. It was a big responsibility, but I knew that he was ready for it. Aiden was going to oversee fourteen cleaners and he was nervous to say the least. I felt like God had given him this chance and I knew that he would do great and be a wonderful boss.

A few weeks later I got a call from the DPP saying that my brother had finally pleaded guilty to 2 counts of indecently dealing with a child under 16. I sat down with a heavy heart, as the lawyer explained that he had received a 3-month suspended jail term and that she would send a letter explaining everything. Isla was on a break from Tafe and seemed to be more relaxed. I cut my hours at work down to a nine-day fortnight and I was less stressed too. The paperwork arrived from the DPP, but I could not open it, and it sat on the dining room table for a week until Isla noticed it and opened it. There in black and white it stated that there was a lifetime restraining order on Dylan and that he was also on the sex offender's registry for 8 years. I sat there looking at the papers and felt myself drifting away. Isla also reacted similarly, and in the next few weeks, she was emotional and started cutting again. I felt like someone had run me over with a truck and I stopped sleeping. After three weeks of insomnia, I finally relented and saw my GP to get some Valium to calm me down at night, so I could sleep. I saw the effect that the outcome of the sentence hearing had on Isla too and I was heartbroken for her. Once again, she became so depressed that she could not leave her room. I was helping her apply for new jobs as the one at the play centre had ended, and finally, she got a trial at a café in the city, and I encouraged her to go even though she did not feel like it. A few weeks later she got the job, and she was happy. I drove her into the city for her first shift, and she came out smiling that afternoon and I knew that it was a gift from God.

I was really struggling with the outcome of the court case, and even though I was pleased Dylan had not received any jail time, I was also angry that he had somehow gotten away with destroying a part of our daughter's life, that what he had stolen from Isla, she would never get back. It did not seem fair at all, even though I knew that it was a big deal for him to be on the offender's registry. Deep down I hoped that Dylan's life had radically changed and that he was sorry for what he did to her. I was not sure that he was even living with the reality of hurting her or whether he was walking around pretending that he had done nothing wrong. Perhaps he was thinking that I had made the whole thing up, as I knew what my father thought about me, and maybe my brother was the same. Anyway, whatever he thought about it was irrelevant, as I would never get the chance to confront him and ask him what he had been thinking that night, something I also felt robbed of. Did Dylan feel genuinely sorry for what he had done to Isla? Some days I was convinced he deeply regretted it and would give anything to change it, other days I believed that he could not care less and that now I had a true enemy.

Isla got more shifts at the café, which gave her a new purpose, and it got her out of bed and that was an amazing thing. Her GP had given her a medical exemption, so she did not have to worry about school. She had started on a very small dose of anxiety medication, and it was helping a lot.

Aiden and I had been talking and he had decided that he wanted to try and contact his biological dad. His mum had always told him that his dad never wanted him and had been living in the eastern states. Aiden had found out a few years back that he was now living in Perth and was a Pastor at a church. Aiden had felt rejected his whole life from his dad's actions and he decided that now was the time to face him. One night while Aiden was asleep, I did some internet digging and found a phone number for Bradley, his dad. A few days later I told Aiden I had found his number, and Aiden kept saying that he was going to call him but was too afraid. One weekend he decided to go for it, and we sat together as Aiden nervously dialed his number. Unfortunately, we got his voice mail, so Aiden left a message. A few hours later his dad called him back, but Aiden missed the call. Aiden decided that he would call him back and this time, his dad answered.

"Hi, is this Bradley?" Aiden asked with a shaky voice.

"Yes, it is," came the reply.

Aiden took a deep breath, and I reached over and grabbed his hand.

"Um, this is Aiden; I think you're my dad."

There was a long silence.

"Aiden, is it? What makes you think I am your dad?" Bradley asked.

"Because my mum Lorna always said that you are my dad," Aiden explained.

"Okay, well I'll tell you what happened back then Aiden," Bradley said. "I knew your mum years ago and we slept together, but we were also sleeping with other people you know and partying a lot. When I started dating Lorna, a mate told me she was already pregnant and then we stopped seeing each other. Then one day after you were born, she came around and told me that I was your dad, so, I said that I wanted a DNA test, but she left, and I didn't see her for a long time. Then she came around again when you were about 2 or 3 years old, and I was married by then. She said I was your dad, so again I asked her for a DNA test, but she left, and I never saw her again. So, there is no way I am your dad."

There was a long silence and I saw Aiden's face fall, but he chatted with Bradley for a while longer. When he ended the call, Aiden burst into tears, and my arms went around him, and I just held him as he cried. I was gutted for him, as all these years had passed, and now to find out he might not be his dad, well it was just heartbreaking.

The next day Aiden messaged his mum on Facebook, "why did you lie about Bradley?" Lorna sent him a horrible voicemail saying she could not believe Aiden was treating her so badly and, 'what about her and what she had suffered.' She also said in the message that Aiden 'owed her.'

I was not at all surprised at his mum's behaviour, as Lorna was such a toxic person and always turned-on Aiden any chance she got. Then his auntie got in on it and sent Aiden some nasty messages and said that Aiden also 'owed Lorna.' The auntie said that when Lorna was pregnant in the eastern states, she had to run away from Bradley because he was abusing her, that he had locked Lorna in a flat and she had to escape and come back to Perth. I was at work and when I saw the messages on our shared Facebook account, I lost my temper. I messaged the auntie back saying she should be ashamed of herself for treating Aiden so terribly. I asked her why this so-called story had been hidden from Aiden for 40 years? Why hadn't anyone told him about his father? I was so mad at his mum and auntie for hiding the truth about his dad; they did not care about Aiden at all, and instead they had their own agendas. Aiden contacted his dad again, but they ended up having a huge yelling match. Aiden told him he did not want to hear a 'story' but just wanted the truth.

"Let's get a DNA test," Aiden asked him, but Bradley once again denied he was Aiden's father and hung up on him.

The next few days were horrible for Aiden, as he felt so rejected and all the pain and abandonment he had felt as a child came rushing back. It was a good few weeks before he began to feel better. Aiden assumed that Bradley had blocked his number, so Aiden decided to hand it over to God and let the Him deal with it. Aiden had tried to find out the truth and that if they were meant to be in each other's lives, then God would find a way. Aiden was such a wonderful father to our children, and I prayed that God would heal him. I also prayed that if there was anything to be revealed, then God would bring it into the light.

That autumn Lukas started playing outdoor soccer for the first time since he was 6 years old. He said he no longer wanted to play cricket, and as I watched his first game, I was surprised at how physical it was! Lukas got shoved to the ground a few times and I could feel my protective mum instincts coming out. It took a few weeks for me to settle down and not get so worried and angry every time he got tackled. Unfortunately, soccer was on a Sunday so we had to take turns taking him, so we could still serve at church. It was the first time Lukas had played sport on a Sunday, but we prayed together and decided that we would support him. It meant Lukas had to take a break from serving in the kids' ministry with me, which would be the first time since he was in year 7.

"Hey mate, I think it would be a good idea if you only played a winter sport, that way you can still serve at church in the summer," I suggested.

"Okay mum," Lukas said. "I'm happy with that."

I loved watching him play soccer and his skills were improving every week. He scored a couple of goals and Aiden and I were so proud of him.

Slowly I began to accept the consequences of my brother's actions, but I was mourning for him and felt so sad. I missed Dylan all the time and felt like there was big hole in my heart where he used to be. I was also missing my niece and nephews growing up and that made me even more sad. Isla and Lukas were missing their cousins and none of it seemed fair at all. All I could do was keep praying and giving my grief to the Lord, as I knew that He had a plan to turn all our pain into something good. When I looked back on all that God had done for me, I felt hope.

today

Lachlan has been transferred to Melbourne to train in a different field, he is also looking for a rental property as Nathan has agreed to move interstate. His life is moving in a different direction, and I feel excited for him. He has regular contact with his dad Tom, and they have a good relationship. I keep praying for Lachlan's salvation every day.

Isla is starting to move back towards the Lord, she is listening to worship music and asking me a lot of questions about when Jesus is returning. She is praying with me and planning to come back to church. She has a lovely boyfriend whose family embrace and support her. I feel like it has happened all at once; Isla was once miles away from the Lord, but she is now back in His arms. All our prayers for her have finally come true. I worked out we have been praying for her for five years and the Lord is faithful indeed.

Aiden and I are in a good place, we hardly ever argue and if we do, the resolution is always swift. I no longer carry the pain and burden of his infidelity, as God has completely saved our marriage and turned it into something incredibly beautiful. Aiden still feels the pain of his father's abandonment and is currently on a waiting list to have some schema therapy.

Lukas will be 15 soon and is growing up into a wonderful young man. He is doing so well at high school and enjoys sports, photography, creative writing and has an excellent group of friends. Soccer is a big part of his life, and he has such amazing knowledge of the game.

I miss my brother terribly every single day, that hole in my heart has yet to be filled. I miss my niece Ruby and my nephews, Ben, Ricky, and Billy every day too, and long for a time when I can see them again. I think of their sweet faces often, and when I do, I am brought to tears. I am hopeful that one day we will be reunited. I miss my mum and think about her often too. As I am aging, I miss her even more, and many things remind me of her. Apricot coloured roses, gardens filled with pansies and petunias and a particular dress shop all bring back beautiful memories of my time with her. Whenever I see a small child with their nanna or grandma, I always think of my mum and Lachlan and how it filled her with joy to be a grand-parent. My sister Dana and I are close, and we see her, Richard and Everlyn regularly. I am pleased to say that Julian and I are in a good place too; we get along well now and recently he has met someone special, and I am very happy for them.

As for my dad, I have not seen him in over fourteen years. I decided long ago to not pursue a relationship with him, and I am at peace with my decision. I have forgiven him for much of the abuse, but forgiveness is a long journey, and it is something that I am working on, even today.

Like every family, we face challenges, and as I write this we are still rent-ing and, come next year, we will be forced to move once again. The Lord is good to us, and whatever we face, we face with Jesus by our sides, confident that He will never leave or forsake us and one day He will return.

Chapter 27

peace and suffering

As I finish my story, I am feeling a range of emotions. It has been, without a doubt, the hardest thing I have ever had to do. Some chapters took weeks, even months to write, and many times, I stopped sleeping from fear or worry, many times, I refused to write or argued with God about why I had to keep going. This has been over two and a half years in the making, and I am still unsure of what to do next. I have considered publishing this anonymously, as I do not want any attention to be honest, but I know God wanted me to write this, not for my benefit at all, but to give hope to every lost and broken person out there.

For anyone who has been hurt and betrayed, this story is for you. For anyone who has given up on themselves or humanity, I hope my words bring you hope. For anyone who has had their heart trampled on and for those who have caused immense pain to the ones they love, I want to tell you there is a way forward.

In the bible Jesus talks about how people who are well do not need a doctor, and it is the same for you and me. It is the broken person who needs

Him, it is the lost souls who need Him, and it is the people who are so far gone they do not even recognise themselves anymore who need Him!

Many people ask how God can let suffering into our lives, if He really is God, then why does He allow His people to suffer? I do not know all the answers, but I know that if God fixed everything in our lives, then we would be living perfect lives like robots; we would have no room to develop as human beings, and our lives would have no real meaning. I know that if God fixed one person's life and constantly rescued them from harm, then He would need to do it for all of us and we would be nothing more than puppets, or He would have to choose who He saved and who He did not, and how could He choose? It would be like if I asked a parent to choose one of their children to suffer harm or perish, and the other to be spared, how could they choose? It is the same with God. Even though He allows us to go through pain or hardship, He wants to accompany us on that tough journey, and be with us through the heartache, so He can grow, develop, and truly heal us.

Isaiah 43:2, "When you go through deep waters, I will be with you. When you go through rivers of difficulty, you will not drown. When you walk through the fire of oppression you will not be burned up, the flames will not consume you."

Even though it is hard to believe at times, *God will use your pain for good,* but only if we allow Him to. So, what is the point I hear you ask, why does He allow us to suffer? I do not think there is one definitive answer to this question. The world brings us pain and suffering, no matter who we are or where we live, or what kind of upbringing we may have had. I can tell you that trying to deal with all your pain on your own is almost soul destroying and at times, feels completely futile. I believe that if you allow Him to, God will accompany you through that pain and trauma and change your life for the better, and more importantly, He will give you the skills and tools you need *so you can go on to help others get through their suffering too*. God created the universe and created humankind from the dust. He is a Sovereign God, the only God there is.

Genesis 1:1, "In the beginning God created the heavens and the earth."

Genesis 2:7, "Then the lord God formed the man from the dust of the ground, He breathed the breath of life into the man's nostrils, and the man became a living person."

If we give God all the glory and adoration that He deserves, and come into a relationship with Him, then He will use the pain that we have suffered to *transform our lives and the lives of those around us*.

Revelation 4:11, "You are worthy, our Lord and God, to receive glory and honour and power, for you created all things and they exist because you created what you pleased."

God is worthy to be praised and He wants us to trust Him so we can walk with purpose into the plan that He has for our lives.

Jeremiah 29:11, "For I know the plans I have for you," says the Lord. "They are plans for good and not disaster, to give you a future and a hope."

God knows what we suffer, and it is hard to understand why we must go through challenging times. No, God does not stop it, but He does use the suffering for something good, that somehow, He weaves that pain and trauma into something beautiful, and my story is a testimony to this. If we allow Him then He will grow us, heal us, and lead us into a life of peace, purpose, and joy. If we let Him into our lives, if we surrender ourselves to Him, then He will heal every wound in our hearts.

1 Peter 5:10, "In his kindness God called you to share in his eternal glory by means of Christ Jesus. So, after you have suffered a little while, he will restore, support, and strengthen you, and he will place you on a firm foundation."

If I look back on the times I have grown as a person, *it is always after a time of great suffering and hardship*. A lot of people are looking for an easy existence, and that is fine if you want to be the same person for the rest of your life. If you are content to go to work or school, come home and sit on the couch and stare at a screen or do the same thing every week of your life, then go for it; one day you will die and what will have been the point of your life?

But if you want real meaning in your life and to see real change, *then choose to follow Jesus Christ*. If you want to see your loved ones and the people around you be blessed and transformed, *then choose to follow Jesus Christ*. Following Jesus is not an easy road though. When I became a Christian, I thought it was going to be an easy life, that all my problems would just magically go away, but that is not true at all.

Hang on, some of you might say, isn't she trying to sell us this Jesus thing? Yep, I am, but I am here to tell you the truth, following Christ is not for the faint hearted, it takes guts, courage, and real strength to stay on the straight path to Him. Why do you think so many people have abandoned their faith? I have faced real opposition from Satan since following Jesus Christ. Like I said, life is not devoid of heartache and pain once you follow Him, but I will tell you this; I would much rather face challenges and hardship with Jesus by my side, *than to face it alone*. You see, God has this way of shielding us from life's pain, we will still go through those late nights and health scares, the bad phone calls, and financial difficulties, but the Sovereignty of God will be our strength and our power.

2 Samuel 29-31, "For you are my lamp, O Lord; the Lord shall enlighten our darkness. For by You I can run against a troop; By my God I can leap over a wall. As for God, His way is perfect; The word of the Lord is proven; He is a shield to all who trust in Him."

Many of you will question at some point in your lives whether God exists, does He exist? And does Jesus exist? You have read my book; you have been on this journey with me, by worldly standards I should not be forgiving my father for what he did to me, or my mother for that matter. In the world's eyes I should not be forgiving Aiden for the affair; how could I have stayed with him? And what about my brother, how could I forgive him, and does he deserve to be forgiven? How could I forgive all these people who have hurt me so badly?

I will tell you how and why because *God loves and forgives me, so now I must do the same.* Because God exists and has shown me His mercy, then I must now do the same to those who hurt me. *I will love them and forgive them.* I do not want to hold on to past hurts, pain, and regrets, what is the point when it is only going to cause me to suffer overall? It makes no difference to my dad if I do not forgive him, and the same for my brother, *all it does is make me bitter and angry inside.* If I hold onto past hurts and regrets, all it will do is stunt my growth as a person. I have worked hard over the years to forgive everyone who has ever hurt me. I have had to work at forgiving myself also for the mistakes that I have made. Forgiveness has been a long, hard road. It is not human nature to forgive people, if they make you suffer; you want to make them suffer! I can tell you that one of the most rewarding, exhilarating, and freeing experiences I have ever had is to *truly forgive those who have caused me pain.*

There is much argument that God exists, just within my book. You have read of the suffering I have encountered in my life, but you have also read of the healing and the miracles that have taken place because of that suffering. And not just me, my family too. How can Isla continue to grow, heal, and move forward after what happened to her? *Because of God.* How can Aiden and I be free of the drugs and the pain of our pasts? *Because of God.* How could our marriage be healed? *Because of God.*

You might say, well Louise is a strong woman, she battled her way through the trauma and healed herself, but that is not true at all. I tried it on my own, I tried it without God in the picture and I failed. You see, I am a strong person, however I am not strong enough to heal myself or forgive others, or do it on my own, but *God gives me the strength to overcome; it all comes from Him. Everything I have is because of Him.*

Philippians, 4:13, "For I can do everything through Christ, who gives me strength."

I may be naturally a strong person, but the real strength comes from knowing God and loving Him and surrendering to Him, especially when the unexpected happens. Life is a crazy ride, and we must hold onto Him tightly!

Chapter 28

the hard truth

I want to tell you the truth about God, but in doing that, I must also tell you the truth about Satan. He is not the cute, red, fluffy devil with the pitchfork and horns you see depicted at Halloween; he is much more than that.

Lucifer was once God's most beautiful angel in heaven until one day he made a fatal mistake, he wanted to be God.

Isaiah 14:13-14, "For you said to yourself, 'I will ascend to heaven; and set my throne above God's stars. I will preside on the mountain of the gods, far away in the north. I will climb to the highest heavens and be like the Most High."

So, the Lord cast Lucifer out of heaven and sent him to earth.

Isaiah 14:12, "How you are fallen from heaven, O shining star, son of the morning! You have been thrown down to the earth, you who destroyed the nations of the world."

Jesus says in Luke 10:18, "I saw Satan fall like lightning from heaven."

Lucifer took a third of the angels with him to form an evil army and then he became Satan or the devil. Now this may seem far-fetched but believe me it is not. *Satan is real and has a very real and tangible hold over the world.* He has a very real and evil agenda and would like nothing more than to destroy and mess up your life, and if you have any sort of faith, he will do whatever it takes to steal that as well. If God is love, then Satan is the opposite. And let me tell you something else, if Satan is real, *then so is hell.* Something else that seems unrealistic? Let me assure you, *it is a real place.*

Matthew 35:42, "Away with you, you cursed ones into the eternal fire prepared for the devil and his demons."

So why does Satan still exist?

John 10:10, "The thief's purpose is to steal and kill and destroy. My purpose is to give them a rich and satisfying life."

You see, until Jesus returns, Satan will attempt to take as many souls as he can with him to hell. He has been damned to an eternity in the fiery lake, and he will take whoever he can with him. He knows his future, he knows that he is doomed, but until Jesus comes back, he will try and drag you to hell with him.

Satan comes in many forms and has his evil hand in many areas of the earth, like some of the music industry, certain movies, pornography, sex trafficking, these are to name a few, and since the birth of the internet, well, he has tightened his grip even further. If you are married, Satan will try and destroy it. If you are a parent, he will try and steal your baby away into the darkness, drugs, alcohol, sex, you name it. If you are a man, Satan will entice you to cheat, lie and hurt women and the ones you love. If you are a woman, he will entice you to sleep around, choose unsuitable partners and encourage you to try things like Only Fans to 'liberate yourself.' Satan's plans are never ending, and often come in glittering packages. Do not be deceived my friends, *if you think that the devil is not real, then you are only deluding yourself.*

the good news

But there is good news in all this doom and gloom, and his name is **JESUS**.

God sent his only son Jesus to earth as a human, to live a life alongside other humans. He had a mortal mother, Mary, was raised as Joseph's son, but his immortal Father was God.

Mark 14:61, "Then the high priest asked him, "Are you the Messiah, the Son of the Blessed One?" Jesus said, "I am."

Even though Jesus was still God's son, He had to live a human life just like us. Jesus felt fear, pain, sorrow, and betrayal, just like us. God chose to do this so that we would have a Saviour who knew what it was like to be human, so we could relate to Him and know that whatever we suffered, that Jesus suffered it too.

Jesus was beaten, flogged, mocked, and jeered and made to carry His own cross. He was *ransomed for* **you** *and* **me**, He was *crucified* for **you** and **me.**

Matthew 20:28, "For even the Son of Man came not to be served but to serve others and give his life as a ransom for many."

After Jesus was crucified on the cross He died.

John 19:30, "..he said, "It is finished! Then he bowed his head and released his spirit."

But on the third day Jesus rose again, He defeated sin, death and Satan, what a victory!

You see, Satan might be still wreaking havoc on earth, but Jesus Christ has absolute power and authority over him and one day Jesus will return, and the devil will be destroyed forever.

Revelation 20:10, "Then the devil, who deceived them, was thrown into the fiery lake of burning sulfur... tormented day and night forever."

Many of you will know the story of Adam and Eve in the Garden of Eden.

Genesis 2:16-17, "But the Lord God warned him, "You may freely eat the fruit of every tree in the garden – except the tree of the knowledge of good and evil. If you eat its fruit, you are sure to die."

You will be familiar with how Satan then tempted Eve to eat the fruit from that tree.

Genesis 3:1, "The serpent was the shrewdest of all the wild animals the lord God had made. One day he asked the woman, "Did God really say you must not eat fruit from the trees in the garden?"

Genesis 3:2, "Of course we may eat fruit from the trees in the garden," the woman replied. "It is only the fruit from the tree in the middle of the garden that we are not allowed to eat. God said, "you must not eat it or even touch it; if you do, you will die."

God had given them strict instructions, however the serpent had other plans.

Genesis 3:4-5, "You won't die!" the serpent replied to the woman. "God knows that your eyes will be opened as soon as you eat it, and you will be like God, knowing both good and evil."

Even though God had forbidden it, Eve was tempted to eat the fruit.

Genesis 3:6, "The woman was convinced. She saw that the tree was beautiful, and its fruit looked delicious, and she wanted the wisdom it would give her. So, she took some of the fruit and ate it. Then she gave some to her husband, who was with her, and he ate it too."

It was at that moment that history was changed forever; Eve and Adam went against God and committed the world's first sin, The Fall. It was like they just could not resist, they wanted to do their own thing, they wanted to be wise and knowledgeable like God.

You may think it is just a story, well I am here to tell you that it is true, *it really did happen.* Adam and Eve's actions all those years ago cost humankind dearly, *and we have been living with the consequences of sin ever since.* We have never been able to make up for what Adam and Eve did, and we still cannot make up for what was lost in the Garden of Eden today; humankind can never make up for all the sin in the world, *there is no way that we humans can ever do enough good things to make up for all that sin.* But there is someone who can, Jesus, a perfect man who committed no sin, but was put to death on a cross to atone for all mankind's sin, *once and for all.* Because of Jesus, we can now be reunited back with God, which is where we are meant to be.

So, this is why God sent Jesus; it all makes sense, and it makes sense that we should believe in Jesus and give our lives to Him. We honour Him by declaring that He is our Saviour and that He died on a cross for all our sins, past, present, and future.

Wow that is huge, and it is such good news! We do not have to be controlled by the evil one, we can choose to give our hearts and lives to the one *who gave His life for us.*

And here is the other good news, you do not have to be perfect, nope, not at all. In fact, Jesus prefers sinners. Why?

Luke 5:32, "I have come to call not those who think they are righteous, but those who know they are sinners and need to repent."

Matthew 9:12, "When Jesus heard this, he said, "Healthy people don't need a doctor – sick people do.""

You see Jesus died for you and me, and do not be fooled, *everyone* is born a sinner, and *no one* deserves to go to heaven, not one of us does, it is a gift from God that we are saved, and we are only saved by His grace.

And you do not have to let your life be controlled by your sin, nope, Jesus forgives *all* sin. Look at me, I did some horrible things, but Jesus forgave each one of my sins.

I must tell you that honorable deeds will not get you to heaven either. That person you know who works endlessly and is the most wonderful person, nope not them. The person who is kind to everyone or works hard to love their family and friends, not them either. That person who donates their money or time to charities, well sorry but that person will not get to heaven, not unless they are saved. *There is only one way to heaven, and that is through Jesus.*

Romans 10:9, "If you openly declare that Jesus is Lord and believe in your heart that God raised him from the dead, you will be saved."

In John 14:6, "Jesus told him, "I am the way, the truth, and the life. No one can come to the Father except through me.""

John 3:5, "Jesus replied, "I assure you; no one can enter the Kingdom of God without being born of water and the spirit.""

So, there you have it. *It is the absolute truth*; I cannot express it any more clearly.

You may think this is a harsh way to end my story, well, it is, but you see, I care about each one of you my friends, **I care about where you end up.**

It is important that you *listen to the truth that I am speaking*; God created the heavens and the earth, and He created us to be in a relationship with Him. God became flesh and sent His son to earth, to teach us about love, forgiveness and how to repent for our sins. Jesus went to the cross willingly, He died for you and me so that we can follow Him and be with Him in heaven one day, for all eternity. I know that my future is safe with Jesus Christ, can you say the same about your future?

My dear friends, will you pray this prayer with me?

"Dear God. Thank you that you sent your son Jesus to die on a cross for me. I ask that you forgive me of my sins and wash me clean. I confess that Jesus is my Lord and Saviour, and today God, I choose to live for you. Help me follow you all the days of my life. In Jesus' name, Amen."

If you have prayed this prayer for the first time, congratulations you have been born again. Please reach out to a bible-based church near you or connect with me on Tik Tok, loved_saved_healed.

May God bless you abundantly.

www.ingramcontent.com/pod-product-compliance
Lightning Source LLC
Chambersburg PA
CBHW011154090426
42740CB00018B/3389